I0793015

IMAGES
of America

DETROIT'S HOLY CROSS CEMETERY

On the cover: Stanley Selwa arrived in the United States from his native Poland in 1890. He met and married Victoria Samojedna in Ohio, moving back and forth between Ohio and Illinois before finally settling, at retirement age, in Michigan. Stanley, Victoria, and two of their children are buried in section H. (Author's collection.)

IMAGES
of America

DETROIT'S HOLY CROSS CEMETERY

Elaine Walters Raymo

ARCADIA
PUBLISHING

ISBN 978-0-7385-7703-6

Published by Arcadia Publishing
Charleston SC, Chicago IL, Portsmouth NH, San Francisco CA

Printed in the United States of America

Library of Congress Control Number: 2009925644

For all general information contact Arcadia Publishing at:
Telephone 843-853-2070
Fax 843-853-0044
E-mail sales@arcadiapublishing.com
For customer service and orders:
Toll-Free 1-888-313-2665

Visit us on the Internet at www.arcadiapublishing.com

I dedicate this book to my father, Richard James Walters, who was part of the Greatest Generation and the first true hero in my life.

Contents

ACKNOWLEDGMENTS

Family is a quilt whose stitches hold the many pieces together by love. I want to thank my family; my children, Bryan and Jason, and Jason's wife, Sara, the parents of my beautiful grandchildren, Kevin and Ryan; and my brothers Richard and Michael for their undying support and love. They are my quilt.

I want to express the most grateful thanks to my mentor and friend Gail Hershenzon for her guidance, encouragement, and support. Special heartfelt thanks go to my old friend Steven Schonwald for his tireless words of encouragement.

This book would not be possible without the help from those who work at Holy Cross Cemetery, particularly Timothy Daniels, for his constant multifaceted assistance. Profound thanks also go to William Barry and cemetery manager Greg Kolasa.

Many thanks go to Heidi Christein at the Archdiocese of Detroit archives, Elizabeth Clemens at the Walter P. Reuther Library, Fr. Edward Hannah at SS. Peter and Paul Syrian Orthodox Church, Patricia Higo at the University of Detroit Archives, Monte G. Kniffen at the Archives Department of the Redemptorists, Bertha Miga and Helen Mamalakis at the Dearborn Historical Museum, Bloyce Brown at the Ecorse Public Library, John Solosy of Solosy Funeral Home, John Michalak of Czopek Funeral Home, Harry Schueren, Thomas Lynch, Kenneth Michalak, David Reckinger, and all the others who shared their family photographs and stories with me.

All images are from the author's collection unless otherwise noted.

INTRODUCTION

In 1834, a deadly cholera epidemic was spreading from Detroit along the river, working its way down to Toledo. At the same time, the Redemptorist fathers arrived in Michigan, having left Green Bay to begin their missionary work and build schools. Burying the cholera victims and tending to the ill delayed their work. On June 16, 1835, just two years after the Diocese of Detroit was established, Fr. Vincent Baden, a Redemptorist priest from Ste. Anne Church, blessed a mission in Dix Settlement that he named Holy Cross after Saint Croix in France. The purlieu, named after Jacob Dix, who owned a large expanse of land in the area, private claim 41, later to become part of Springwells, sat about six miles southwest of Detroit city center. A dirt road ran through the middle of his land allowing an easily accessible route into Detroit for neighboring farmers and being the only route with a bridge over Baubee Creek. Eventually the dirt road, Dix Road, became the southern border and location of the main entrance to the cemetery.

The little log cabin mission periodically held religious services and by 1838, if not earlier, performed burials adjacent to the structure; however, the little two-acre cemetery was not dedicated until 1840, making it one of the oldest, if not the oldest, still active Catholic cemeteries in Detroit. As a mission and consequently with no priest, the cemetery fell under care and jurisdiction of the Redemptorists from Ste. Anne and St. Mary Churches and eventually, as churches were built, to St. Alphonsus and Sacred Heart, both located in what is now Dearborn. Since no single repository held responsibility for the cemetery burials, the fate of the earliest records remains a mystery. The oldest stone found in the cemetery belongs to Matilda Rupley, whose death in 1849 preceded her father, John, by three years. John, a hotel owner and politician from Springwells, lies a few feet from Matilda. Headstone transcriptions from 1849 to 1866 provide the only record to the early burials, although many were buried without headstones.

In the early 1850s, a new frame structure replaced the old log mission and sat on the same site. It is unknown what happened to the old mission, whether it burned or became too small or simply inefficient. A standard form of recordkeeping for the cemetery began in 1867, for which there are two possible reasons. Funerary and mortuary practices changed dramatically after the Civil War. The deceased were taken home in droves to be buried. The sudden influx of deceased put a strain on churches and cemeteries to keep pace with the substantial number of waiting burials. That single event in the 19th century changed cemetery recordkeeping nation-wide, putting the onus on the cemetery and away from the church.

Secondly and most probably, in 1867, Bishop Peter Paul Lefevere received a directive to purchase land to expand church holdings. Through the bishop's advocacy, a Michigan law passed in 1867 making him the sole owner of church property in the diocese. The law allowed that land titles to the church's property be held in trust in his name and passed down to his successor at the time of his death. This law still governs church property today. With legal protection of its properties, the church in earnest began to purchase land to accommodate the sprawling population's need for churches and schools, including cemetery land. Also as part of Lefevere's massive organization, he insisted on better accountings from church properties. Since burials at the cemetery came from different churches, there was no central register of sales. This, along with the changes after the Civil War, led to the first official recording, a ledger whose first entry was in September 1867, of Holy Cross burials.

Augustine Laurain owned approximately 20 acres of land both north and south of Dix Road, adjacent to the old two-acre cemetery. It is unclear when he became the sexton of the old cemetery, but it is noted in 1911 board meeting minutes that he and his son Richard were the caretakers and in charge of the records and cemetery finances in the name of Bishop John Foley. Due to Augustine's age, it seems that he took over sexton duties at the time of the 1867 ledger and that the entries are in his handwriting. Also noted is that the records were kept in a primitive manner. Augustine died in 1905, and Richard, in ill health and feeling that he was close to dying, asked for a written statement from the cemetery releasing him from any inaccuracies or insufficiencies relating to the manner by which he and his father maintained the records and collected monies. In 1904, when the Laurains turned over the books and receipts to the newly formed cemetery committee, the secretary-treasurer audited the books and was satisfied that a true accounting was made.

At the dawn of the 20th century, the church recognized a need for a Catholic cemetery to serve the residents on Detroit's west side. They chose to expand the old cemetery due to its picturesque setting, the right soil composition, the ease of access from Detroit and its surrounding communities, and the opportunity to acquire surrounding land for expansion. Organizers began the task of establishing a committee, and by the fall of 1904, the new committee asked the Laurains for the books and monies so that they would have full supervision of burials and control of receipts. The committee's first purchase of land came in 1905, buying just over 17 acres from Martin and Gertrude Schneider. The Schneider property ran in an even line along the eastern edge of the old cemetery from Dix Road extending north to the Michigan Central Railroad tracks; the west side ran in a straight line along Laurain property also from Dix Road to the railroad tracks. The new land purchase surrounded the old cemetery on the north and west sides. The next land purchase came in 1911 with 10 acres from Richard Laurain, followed in 1914 with two purchases, 20 acres belonging Catherine Hackett and Mary Schneider to the west of the Laurain property, and 21 acres from Gottleiben Reiden to the west of that.

On March 23, 1906, the cemetery officially incorporated under the name of the New Holy Cross Cemetery. Bishop Foley held the major shares of stock in the name of the Church, and the remaining stock was divided among 11 working directors who made the all decisions regarding the cemetery. Plans were laid out, contractors hired, and construction began to make Holy Cross Cemetery the "largest and most beautiful Catholic cemetery in the nation" as stated in board meeting minutes. Although that wish did not happen, the cemetery remains a beautiful resting place for many of Detroit's west side Catholics. Their stories create the essence of who built Detroit, of who worked in the factories or tilled the land, and of the immigrants who brought with them the customs and traditions of their native land.

One

The Nascent Years

The newly elected board of directors eagerly accepted the challenge to create a lovely garden-style cemetery and with a capital of $25,000, promised a modern cemetery with wide drives of crushed stones and lawns sporting up-to-date landscaping. They hired engineer Mason L. Brown to lay out the grounds. The main roads were excavated on various grades, and different sections were built up to resemble rolling hills. Drainage sewers were installed, emptying into Baubee Creek located south of Dix Road and 20 feet below the level of the cemetery. On Decoration Day, May 30, 1907, the revamped cemetery was thrown open to the public. Visitors could easily take the Baker and Sherman streetcar to Livernois Street, catch a connecting car dropping them off at Springwells Avenue, and walk a quarter mile down Dix Road to the cemetery. Visitors with lunch baskets were directed to unimproved areas of the cemetery to enjoy their lunch.

To suit the new landscaping design, the directors elected in 1906 to move the chapel located in the old section of the cemetery to make room for more burials, which it was, 30 feet south toward Dix Road. Many houses and barns still stood on undeveloped cemetery property, most of them still occupied and used. A questionable early-morning fire in a barn rented by Charles Stevens, located close to the chapel, destroyed the barn and incinerated a horse, lamb, and four dogs before lighting the chapel roof afire. By the time the fire department had been summoned, the chapel had been reduced to ashes. Nothing remained except for a few charred oak beams. Cemetery workers raked through the ashes, but nothing remained of the altar, its furnishings, or the priceless paintings, statues, and relics.

For many years after incorporation, the trustees developed a spectacular cemetery, expanding its boundaries and creating a lush garden of green, planting countless trees and shrubbery-lined pathways. These efforts created a beautiful necropolis for visitors to remember their deceased.

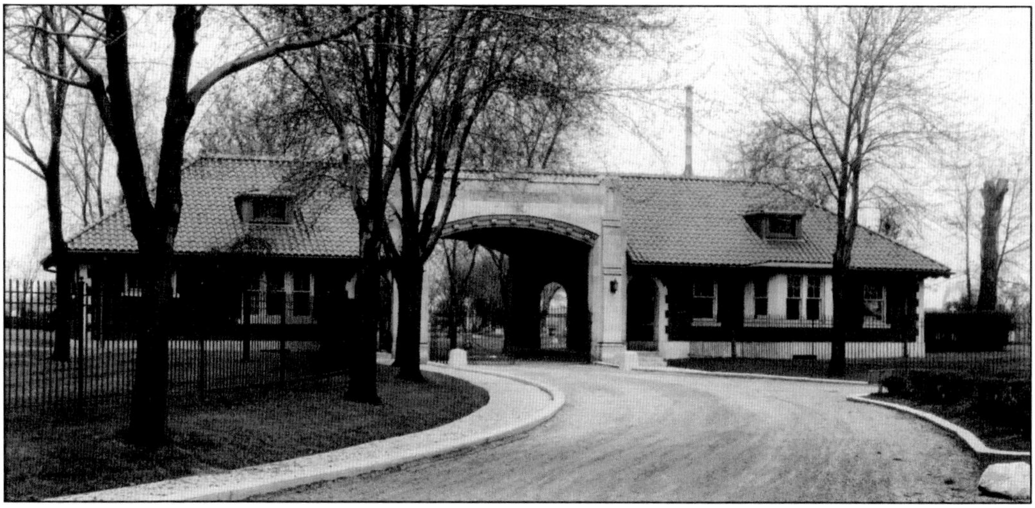

On All Souls' Day, November 2, 1922, Detroit's Bishop Michael Gallagher, with assistance of Fr. Peter Esper of St. Gabriel Church, celebrated mass in the new cemetery office to honor its completion. Anticipating sizeable attendance, cemetery directors erected a large tent outside, and in spite of inclement weather, the crowd overflowed onto Dix Road. This 1923 photograph was taken one year after construction of the office (right) and comfort station (left). Prior to its completion different houses, including at one time the old, unused chapel, accommodated makeshift offices. In 1923, Anchor Post Iron Works erected the wrought-iron fence that extends along the front of the cemetery. (Holy Cross Cemetery.)

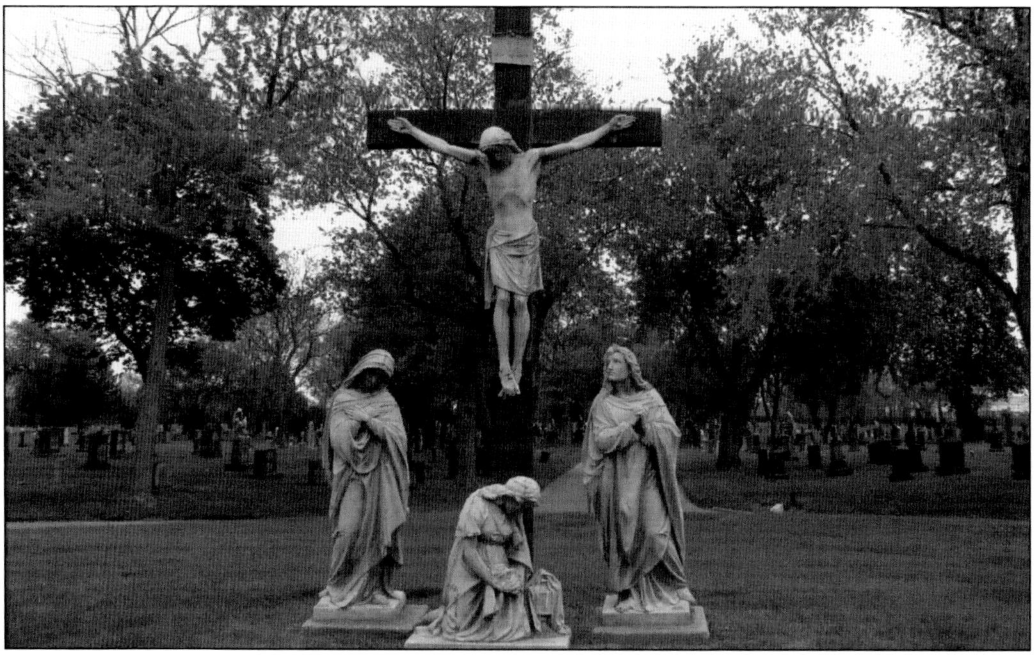

This central, iconic, crucifixion group greets visitors as they pass through the front entrance. The group originally stood in section J on the Hewelt lot. In 1952, the Hewelt family and the cemetery association struck a deal that moved the grouping to the more stately and impressive site in section E. As part of the agreement, the cemetery association paid for a new monument for the Hewelt family.

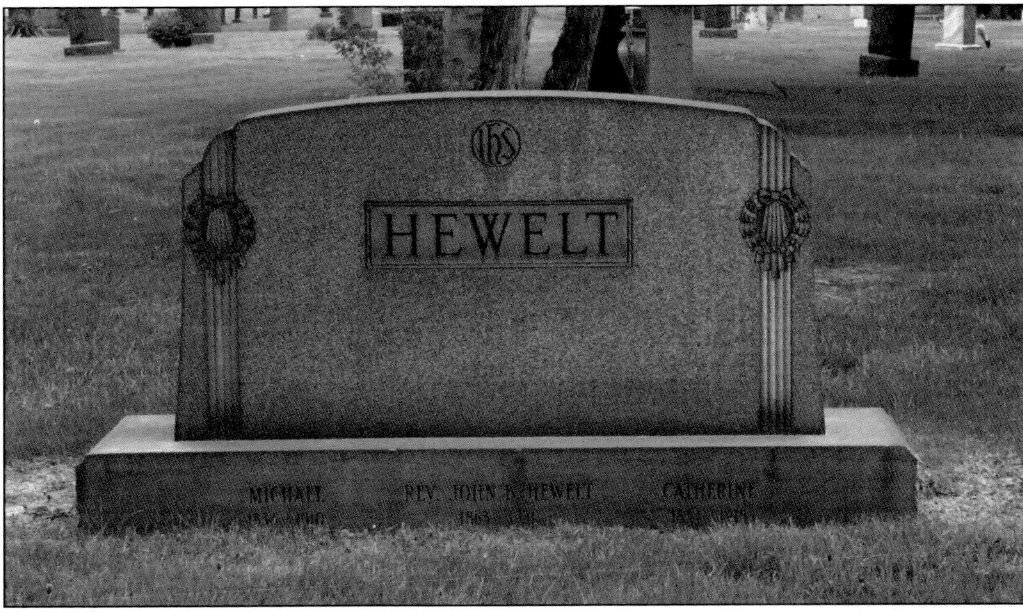

Rev. John B. Hewelt earned his education in his native county of Prussia and continued it in France, England, and Ireland before coming to the United States in 1880. He spent several years of his pastorate at St. Mary's Church in Branch County, Michigan, where his assiduous efforts succeeded in building a school for the parish in 1900. The cemetery association erected this monument to replace the crucifixion group.

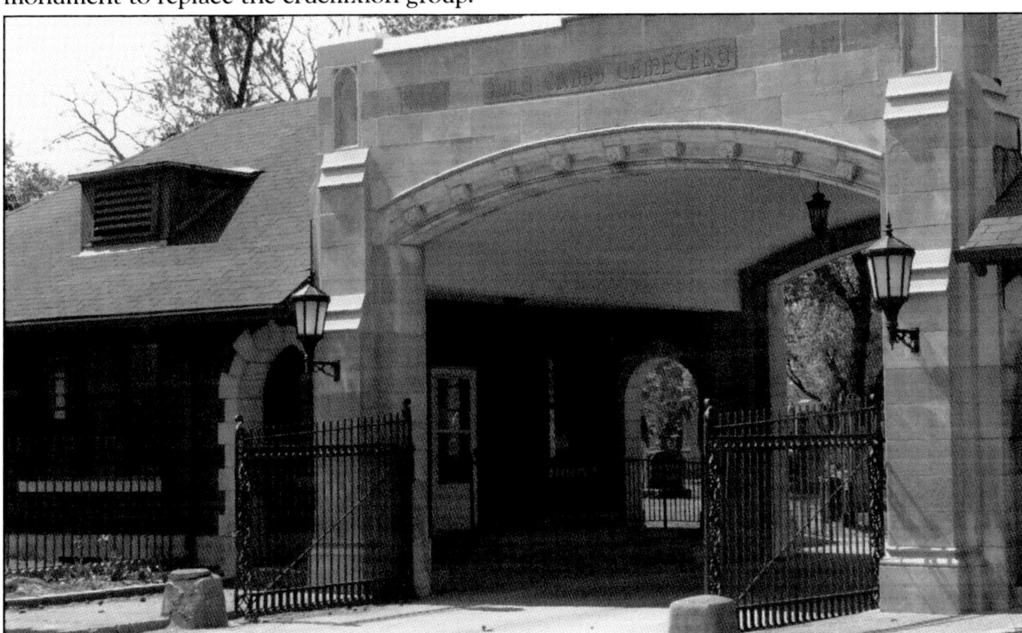

This archway entrance to the cemetery looks much the same today as when built in 1922. The building left of the archway, shown here, dubbed the comfort station and waiting room, contains the ladies' and men's lavatories and a large lobby designed to give visitors a brief respite from cold, windy, or rainy days when visiting their loved ones or waiting for impending burials. The basement, now empty, was used for storage.

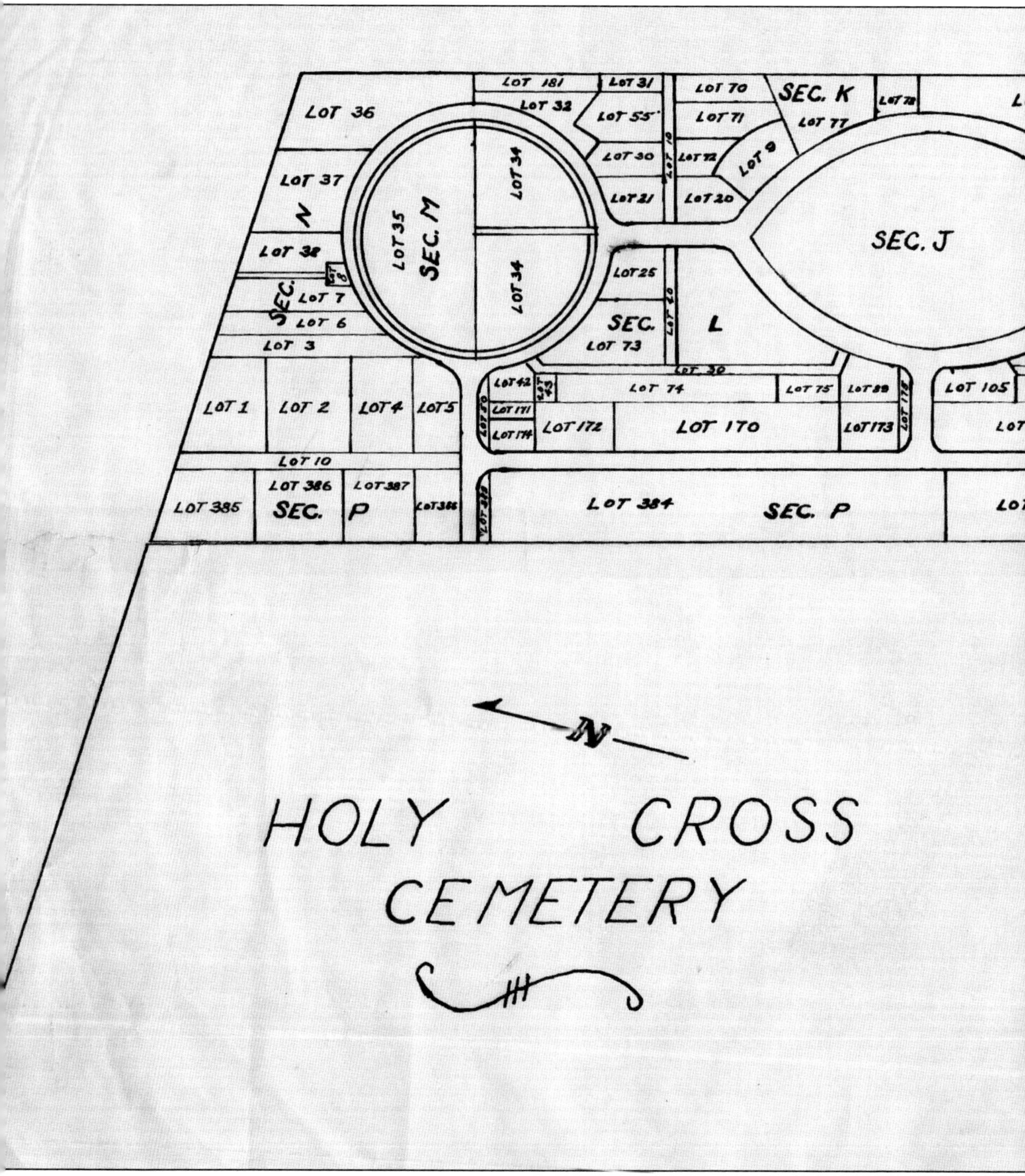

This map shows the cemetery at its current 65-acre size. The southern side of the cemetery, where the main entrance is located, is along Dix Road. The northern border butts against the Michigan Central Railroad tracks. Levy Gravel Company borders the east and west sides. Section B contains the oldest part of the cemetery and is where the original 1835 mission sat. The office/comfort station building flanks the main road in sections B and Y. The other structure in section Y shows where the supervisor's house once stood. The garage and chapel sit in section X. At one

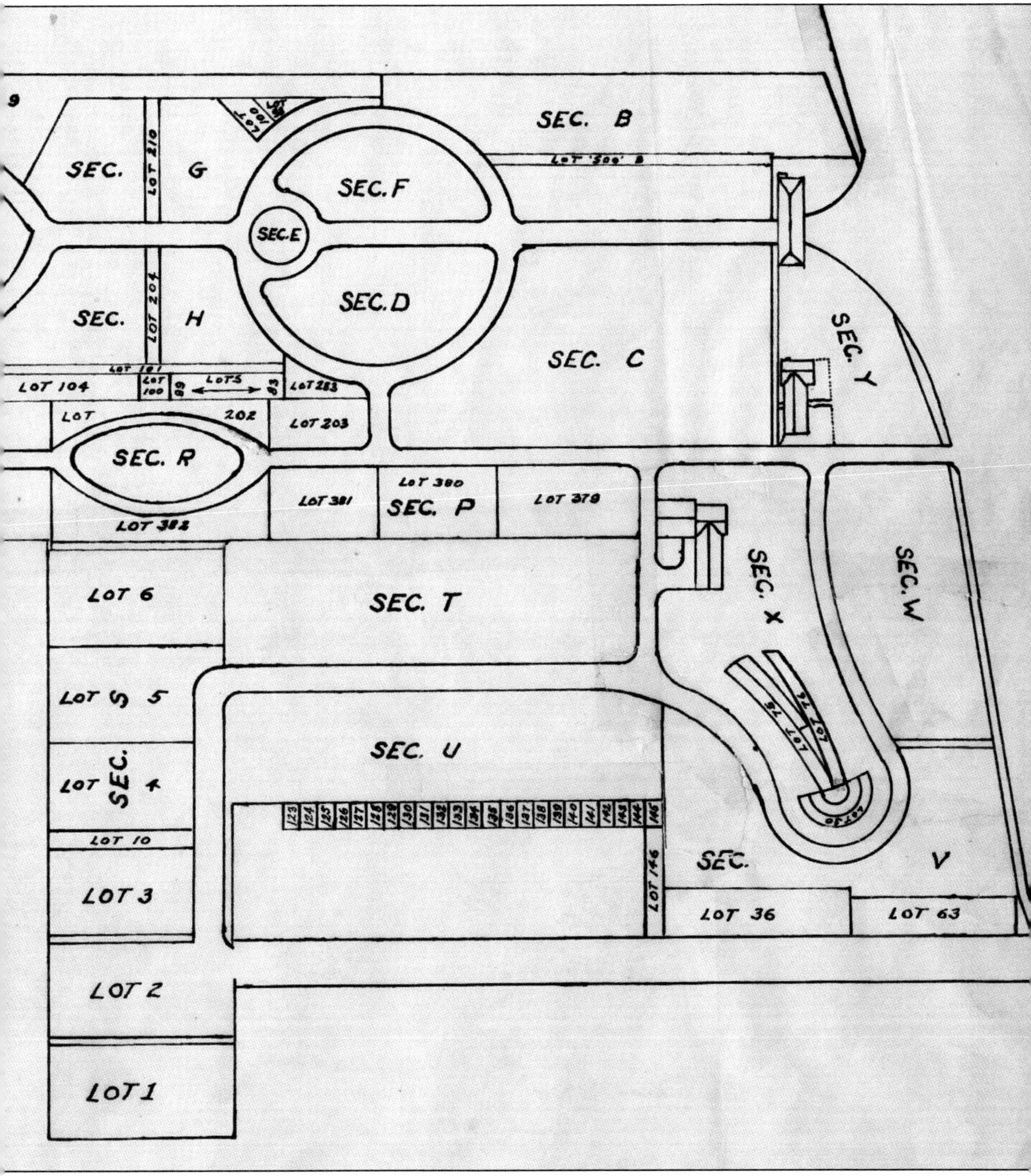

time, numerous farms, houses, barns, outbuildings, and greenhouses lined along Dix Road in sections B, Y, W and V, while actually sitting on cemetery property. Martin Schneider sold his land to the cemetery that became part of section B, Augustine Laurain and his son Richard sold 10 acres of land to the cemetery as part of section C, and John Kramer's general store was razed to develop more plots in section W.

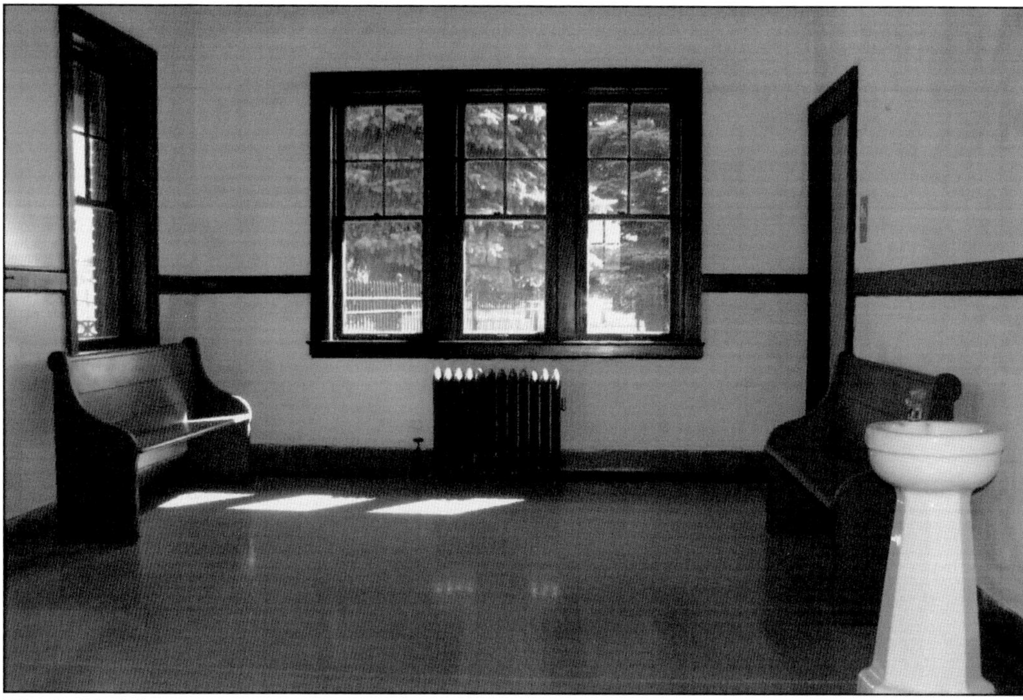

The half of the waiting room pictured here looks south toward Dix Road. The door to the ladies' room is at the right; the entry to the men's room is in the other half of the comfort station and not shown in this photograph. The terrazzo floor, benches, and drinking fountain are all original to the construction of the building.

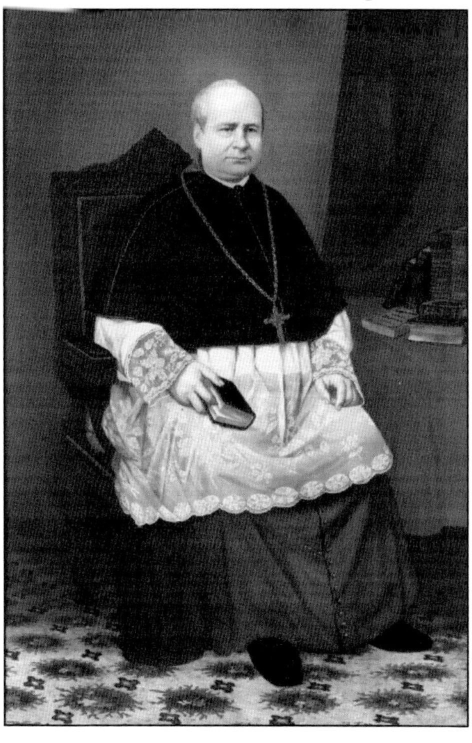

During his tenure as bishop of the Detroit diocese, Bishop Peter Paul Lefevere systematically obtained land for the church. In 1867, he successfully fought for sole ownership of church property, ceded to his successors upon his death. This legislation governs church property today. Sections of private claim 40, where the cemetery now stands, were conveyed to him as early as 1849 in an effort to annex the old mission and cemetery "for the use and benefit of the Roman Catholic Church of Ste. Croix at Holy Cross," as stated in the land deed. (Archdiocese of Detroit Archives.)

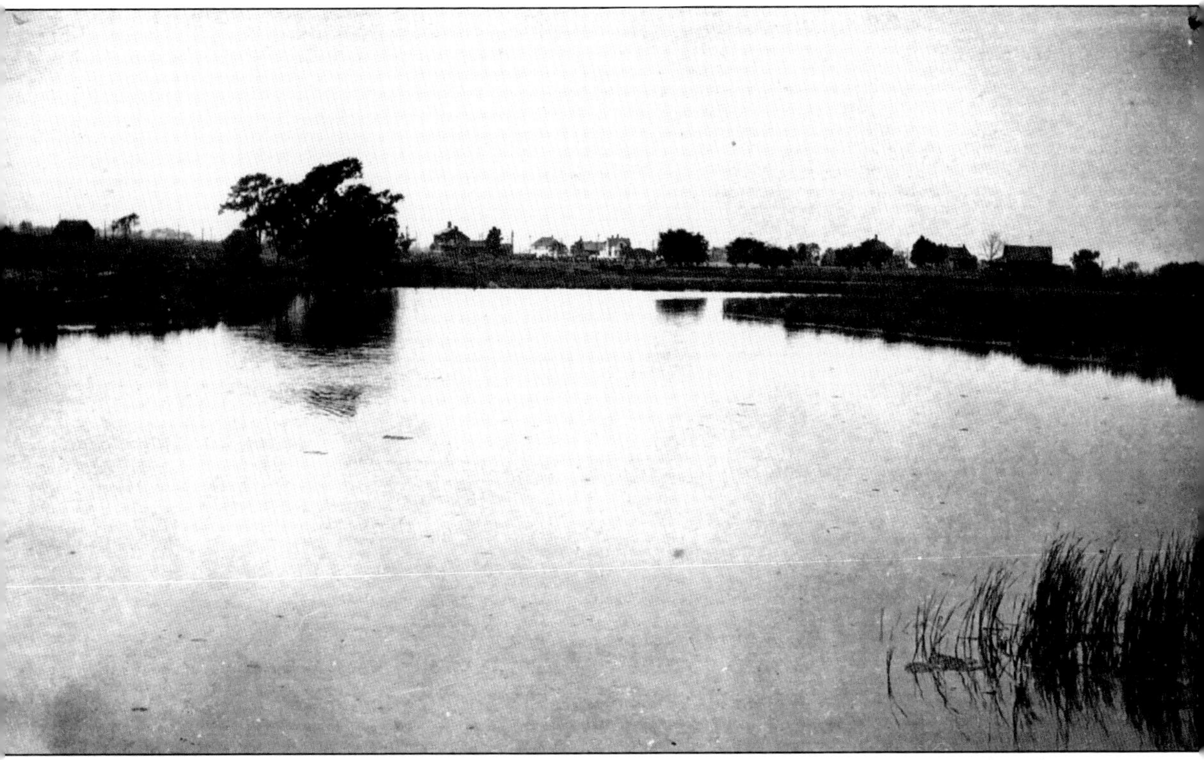

Martin Schneider owned farmland both north and south of Dix Road adjacent and to the east of the original two-acre cemetery, and in 1905, his land north of Dix Road, a 17-acre farm, became the first purchase of the newly conceived cemetery association at a cost of $15,453. Martin's son Frederick became the owner of the three-acre farm south of Dix Road that ran from the road south to Baubee Creek. The cemetery purchased this land as well and used the buildings remaining on the property after the Schneider family moved their houses, the barn, and outbuildings for equipment storage. Although Baubee Creek at one time formed the southern border of Holy Cross Cemetery and the northern border of Woodmere Cemetery, the creek no longer remains. This photograph of Baubee Creek, taken from Woodmere Cemetery, is one of the few known photographs of the creek. (Gail Hershenzon.)

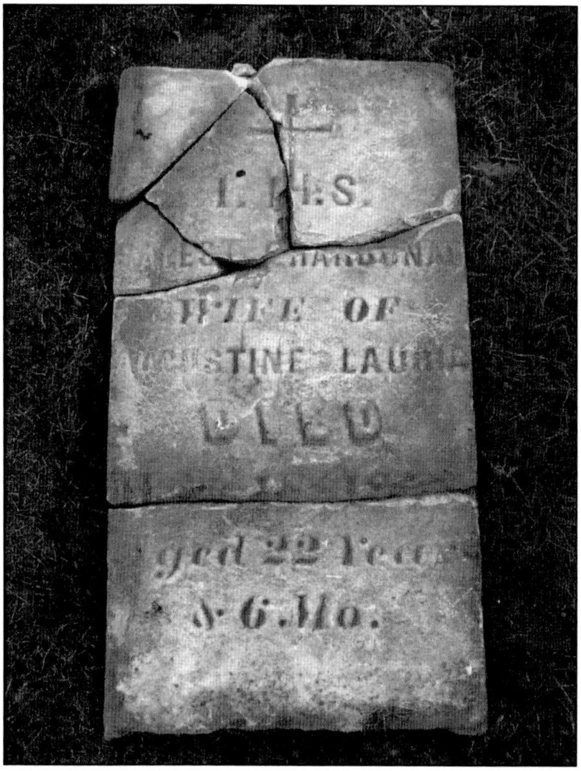

Joseph Charboneau educated Celeste, engraved on the stone as Salest, Charboneau, born Beaucles, and at the age of 16, she married Augustine Laurain on July 14, 1846. Celeste died in 1852 at age 22 years and 6 months. Augustine owned a large parcel of land extending north and south of Dix Road that he passed on to his son Richard. Eventually Richard sold the land north of Dix Road to the cemetery. Celeste is buried in section B.

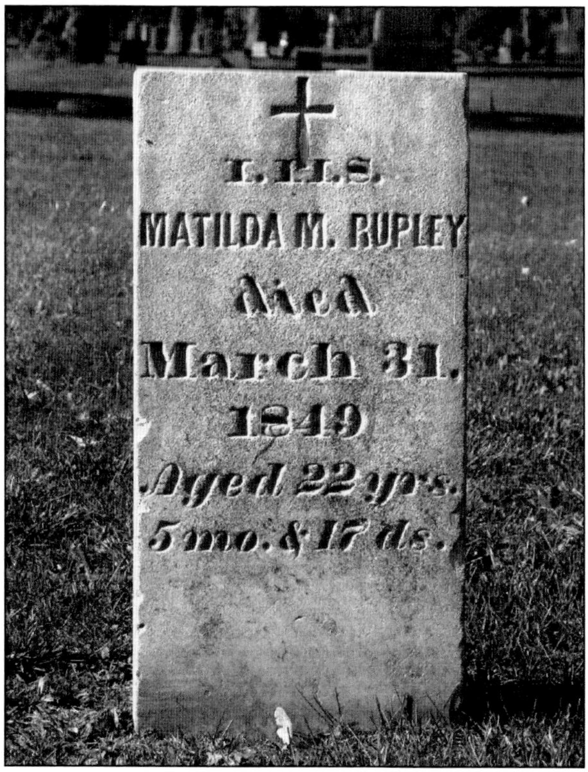

The oldest stone in the cemetery belongs to Matilda Rupley, the daughter of John Rupley and Margaret Dumay. Matilda died on March 31, 1849, at 22 years, 5 months, and 17 days. She is buried in the oldest section of the cemetery, for which there are no written records. Her grave lies a few feet from her parents.

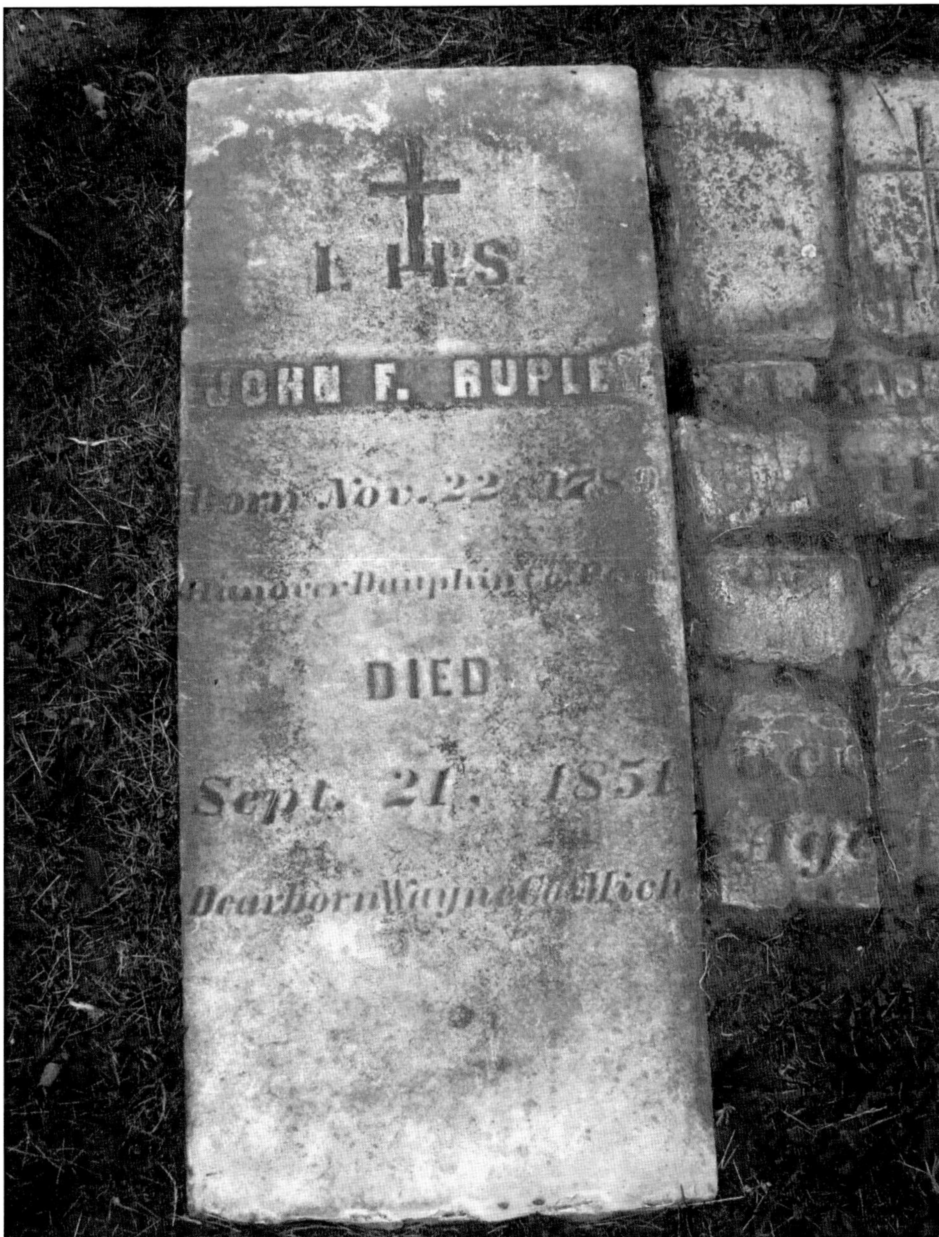

Aside from owning a hotel, Matilda's father, John, held several elected positions in Pekin, Bucklin, and Dearborn townships, among them overseer of the poor, pound master, and commissioner of highways. As pound master in 1838, he proposed that stallions over the age of two years old are not allowed to run at large under penalty of a fine of $10 and that boars over the age of six months are not allowed to run at large under the penalty of $10 for each offense. Both proposals passed. John earned $9 for his year as commissioner of highways in 1839. He served with many prominent names in the Dearborn area, such as Gulley, Howard, Nowlin, and Ten Eyck; many streets and schools bear their names. John's stone reads that he was born in Hanover, Dauphin County, Pennsylvania, in 1798, and that he died in Dearborn in 1851. He is buried next to his wife, Margaret.

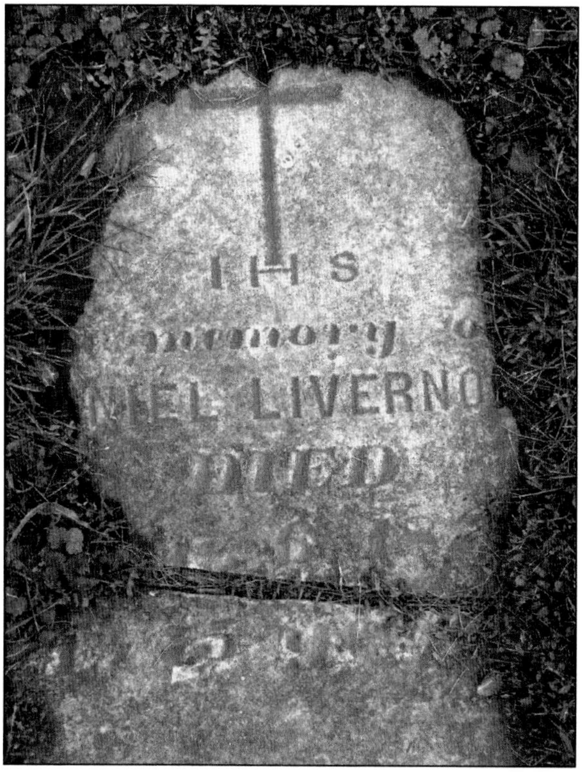

As a descendant of the early Livernois settlers, Daniel lived and farmed on land in Springwells, not far from the major Detroit street that bears his family name. Daniel was born in 1799 to Joseph Livernois and Marie Theresa Meloche. Daniel's brother Stephen, who died in 1852, lies close to Daniel and Daniel's daughter Josephine. They, along with dozens of other members of the Livernois family, are buried without markers in section B.

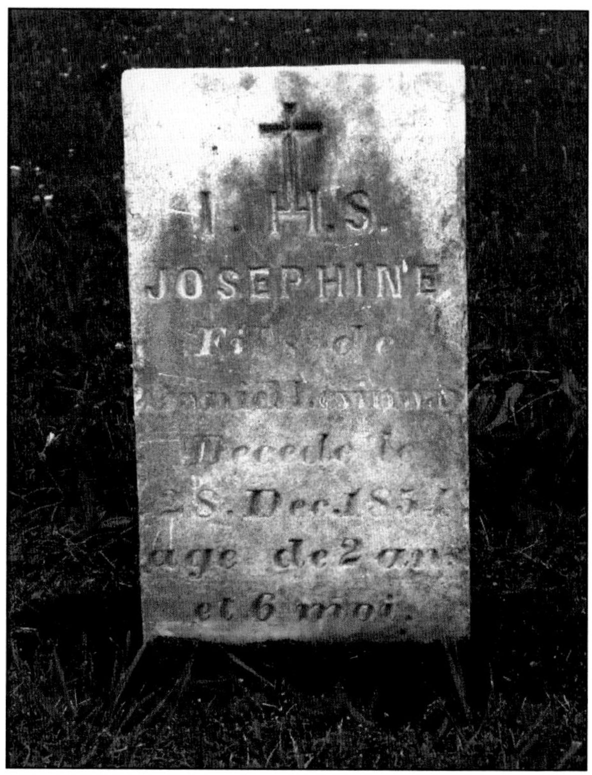

The stone reads, "Josephine, Fil de Daniel Levinway, Decede de 28 Dec. 1851, age de 2 ans 6 moi." Translated, it says "Josephine, daughter of Daniel Levinway, died December 28, 1851, age 2 years and 6 months." She was the young daughter of Daniel. Levinway is an alternate spelling of Livernois. Josephine's stone is the second oldest found in the cemetery.

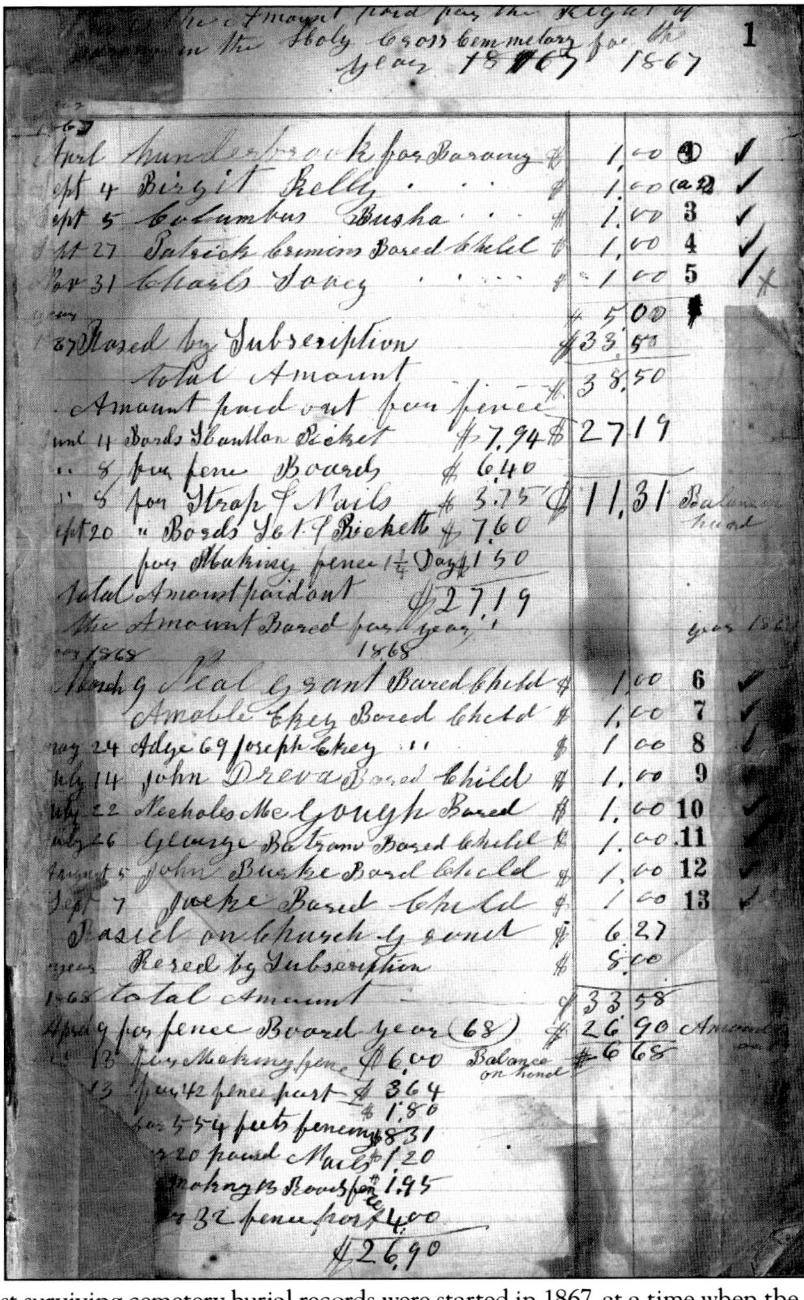

1

the Amount paid for the Right of burying in the Holy Cross Cemmetary for the year 1867 1867

April	Hunderbrook for Barny	$ 1.00	1
Sept 4	Birgit Kelly	$ 1.00	2
Sept 5	Columbus Busha	$ 1.00	3
Sept 27	Patrick Cremins Bored Child	$ 1.00	4
Nov 31	Charls Sovey	$ 1.00	5
		$ 5.00	
	Rased by Subscription	$ 33.50	
	total Amount	$ 38.50	
	Amount paid out for fence	$ 27.19	
		$ 11.31	Balance on hand

total Amount paidout $27.19

1868

March 9	Neal Grant Bored Child	$ 1.00	6
	Amable Ebey Bored Child	$ 1.00	7
May 24	Joseph Ebey	$ 1.00	8
July 14	John Dreva Bored Child	$ 1.00	9
July 22	Nicholes McGough Bored	$ 1.00	10
July 26	George Bertram Bored Child	$ 1.00	11
August 5	John Burke Bored Child	$ 1.00	12
Sept 7	Burke Bored Child	$ 1.00	13
	Rased by Subscription	$ 8.00	
	total Amount	$ 33.58	
	for fence Board year (68)	$ 26.90	
	Balance on hand	$ 6.68	

$26.90

The earliest surviving cemetery burial records were started in 1867, at a time when the church was actively expanding its holdings and requiring more complete recordkeeping. The diocese employed Augustine Laurain as the sexton and caretaker of the cemetery. Holy Cross Cemetery's records from 1838 to 1866 are lost, but it is believed that hundreds are buried in the original two-acre mission cemetery. The first page of the 1867 ledger records an unnamed stillborn child of Barney Hunderbrook as burial number one. Bridget Kelly, burial number two, was buried on September 4, 1867, at a cost of $1, the same as the Hunderbrook infant. The numbering system began in 1867 ended in 1906 when the cemetery incorporated. In 1906, the numbering system began over, creating two sets of identical burial numbers. (Holy Cross Cemetery.)

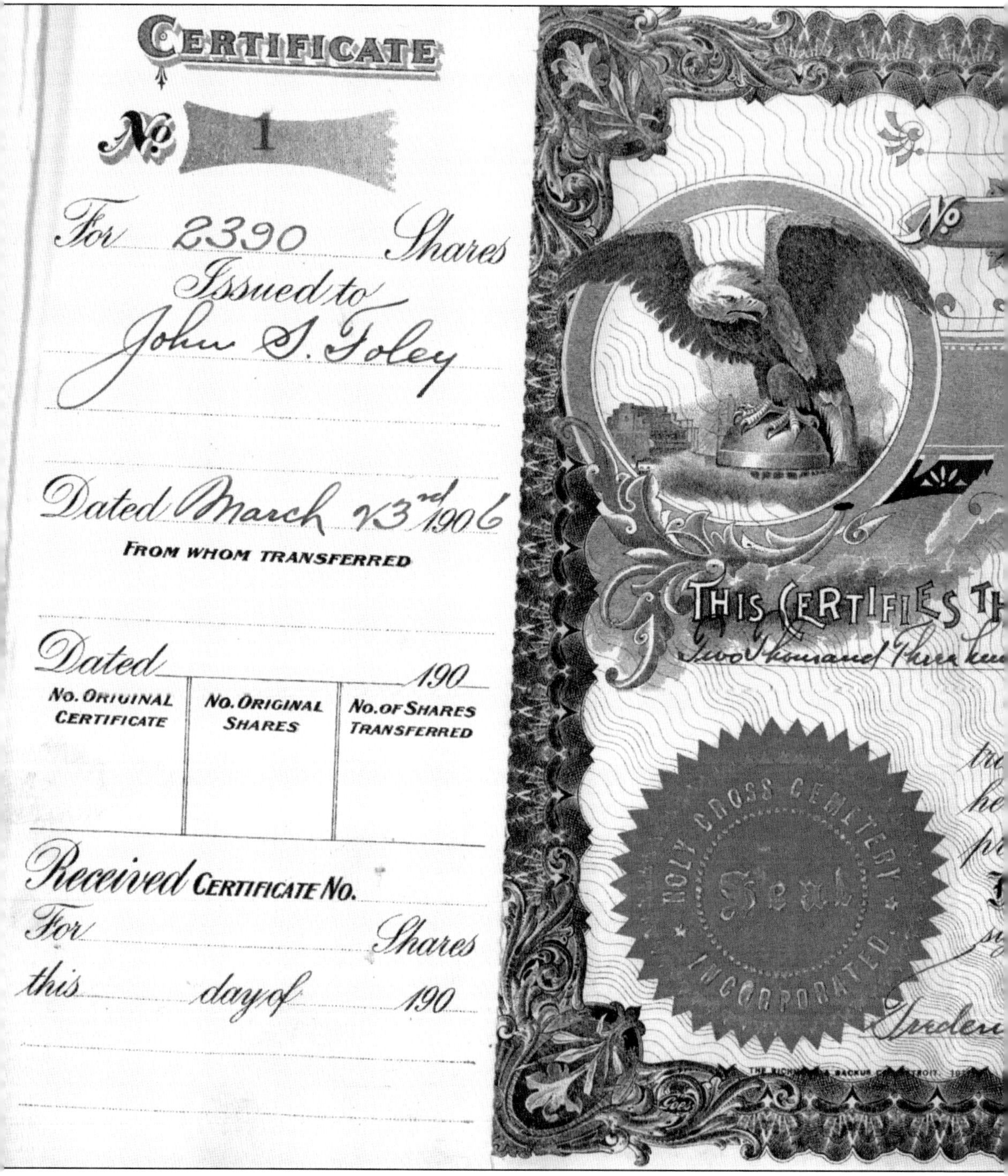

CERTIFICATE

No. 1

For 2390 Shares

Issued to

John S. Foley

Dated March 23rd 1906

FROM WHOM TRANSFERRED

Dated 190

No. Original Certificate	No. Original Shares	No. of Shares Transferred

Received Certificate No.

For Shares

this day of 190

THIS CERTIFIES TH

Two Thousand Three hun

HOLY CROSS CEMETERY Seal INCORPORATED

On the day of incorporation, March 23, 1906, the newly appointed board of directors received stock certificates. Bishop Foley, as representative of the church and the owner of the cemetery, acquired 2,390 shares in certificate number one, as shown here in the original book of certificates. Each of the 11 directors received 10 shares, at a value of $10 per share, to equal 2,500 shares. Bishop Foley gave secretary-treasurer Frederick Sevald power of attorney over all administration

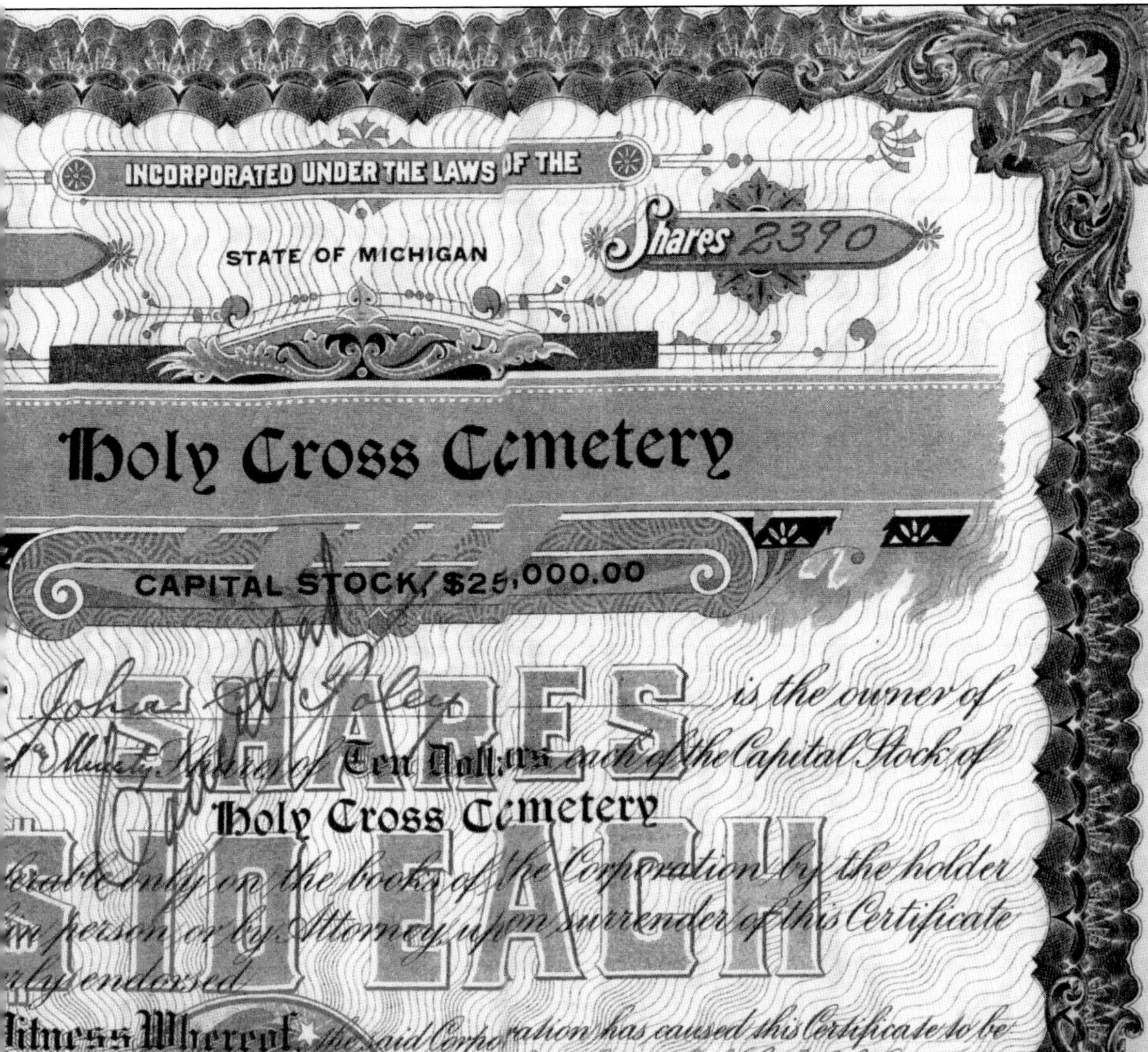
INCORPORATED UNDER THE LAWS OF THE
STATE OF MICHIGAN
Shares 2390
Holy Cross Cemetery
CAPITAL STOCK, $25,000.00
John … Foley is the owner of
… Ninety Shares of Ten Dollars each of the Capital Stock of
Holy Cross Cemetery
…erable only on the books of the Corporation by the holder
in person or by Attorney upon surrender of this Certificate
…ly endorsed
…itness Whereof, the said Corporation has caused this Certificate to be
… by its duly authorized officers and to be sealed with the Seal of the Corporation
this … day of March A.D. 1906
SECRETARY
PRESIDENT
…RES $10.00 EACH

matters concerning cemetery management. The 11 trustees became responsible for the direction, expansion, and daily running of the cemetery. Upon death, each stockholder's certificate was relinquished to the cemetery and handed down to his successor, and Bishop Foley's shares acceded to Bishop Gallagher. (Holy Cross Cemetery.)

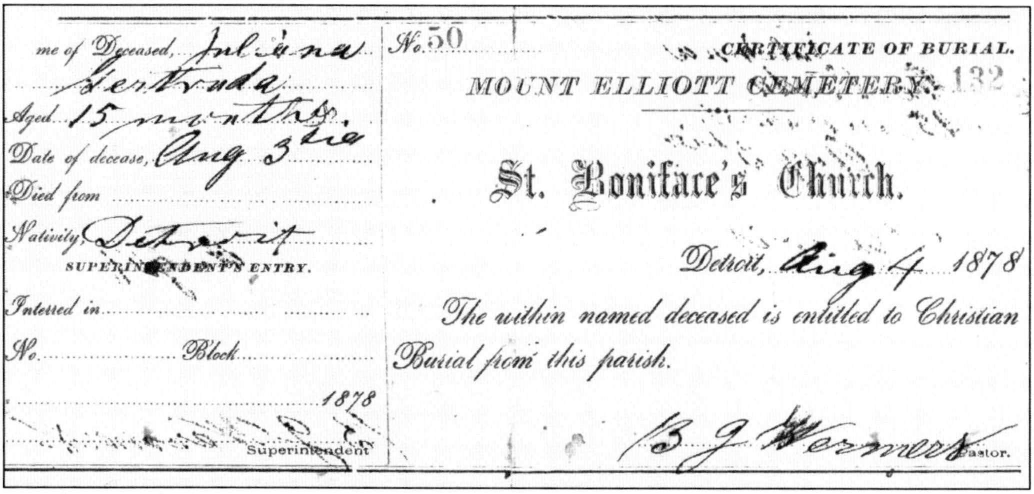
Name of Deceased, Juliana Gertruda
Aged 15 months
Date of decease, Aug 3rd
Died from
Nativity, Detroit
SUPERINTENDENT'S ENTRY.
Interred in
No. Block
1878
Superintendent

No. 50
CERTIFICATE OF BURIAL.
MOUNT ELLIOTT CEMETERY. 132
St. Boniface's Church.
Detroit, Aug 4 1878
The within named deceased is entitled to Christian Burial from this parish.
B. J. Wermers Pastor.

Burial in a Catholic cemetery required that a parish priest provide permission for the deceased to be buried on consecrated ground. Since Holy Cross Cemetery had no affiliation with a specific church and was without funds for its own burial permits, they came from other cemeteries and several churches. This permit for 15-month-old Juliana Gertruda, signed by Fr. Bernard Wermers of St. Boniface Church, is on a permission slip from Mount Elliot Cemetery and the oldest one in cemetery files. (Holy Cross Cemetery.)

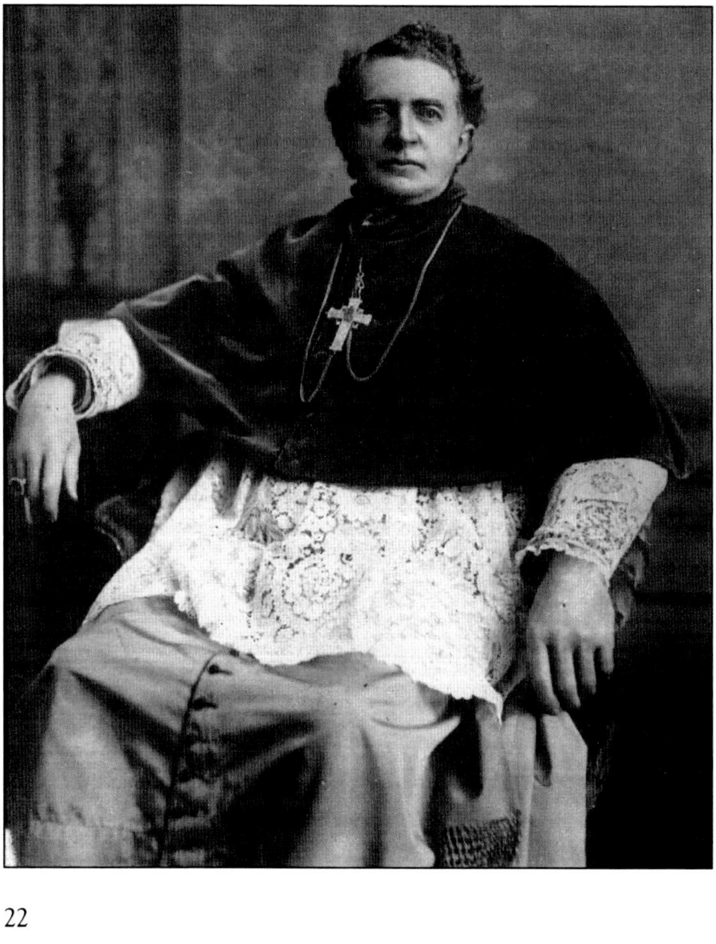

In keeping with the policy established by his predecessor Bishop Lefevere, Bishop Foley continued to purchase land in his name for the church. In 1906, he sold the old churchyard cemetery conveyed to him from Caspar Borgess in 1888 to Frederick Sevald, secretary-treasurer of the newly formed cemetery association for $1. Bishop Foley purchased the 17-acre Schneider tract and sold it to Sevald for $15,000, and Sevald, in turn, sold it to the cemetery association for $1. The cemetery association paid on the note to the church in monthly installments. (Archdiocese of Detroit Archives.)

The trustees commemorated the cemetery incorporation and the role of the directors involved by hiring the McCoy Bronze Company to construct this memorial tablet that is affixed to the exterior brick of the office building. The plaque cost $76 when commissioned in November 1922. (Holy Cross Cemetery.)

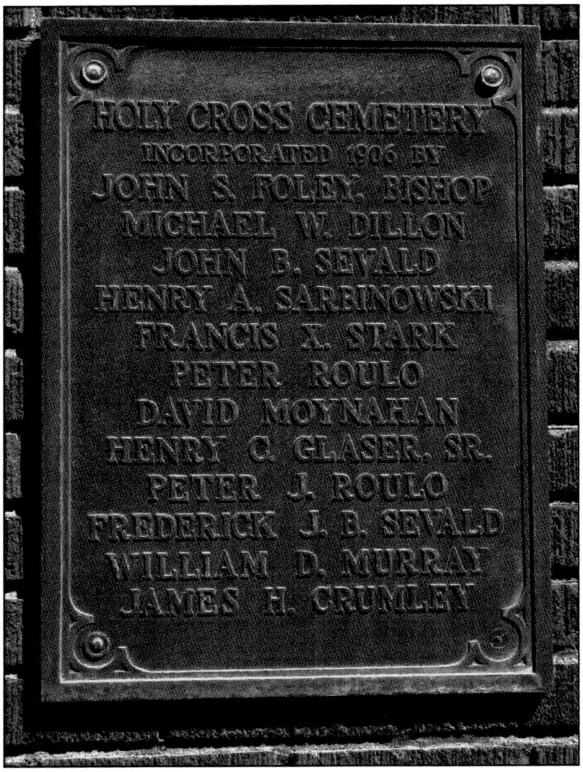

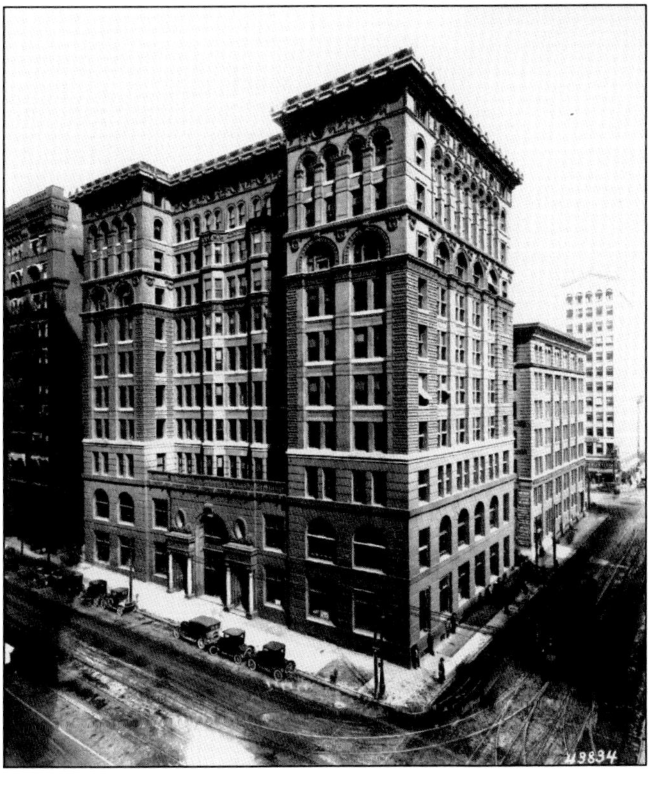

The trustees rented an office at the Union Trust building in Detroit. Rent included lights and janitorial service, use of a typewriter, and minor typewriter supplies, amounting to $10 a month. As secretary-treasurer, Frederick Sevald received a salary of $100 a month. Other expenses included telephone at $22 a month, the cemetery name in the telephone book for $1 per month, and stenographer's salary of $3 per month. (Walter P. Reuther Library.)

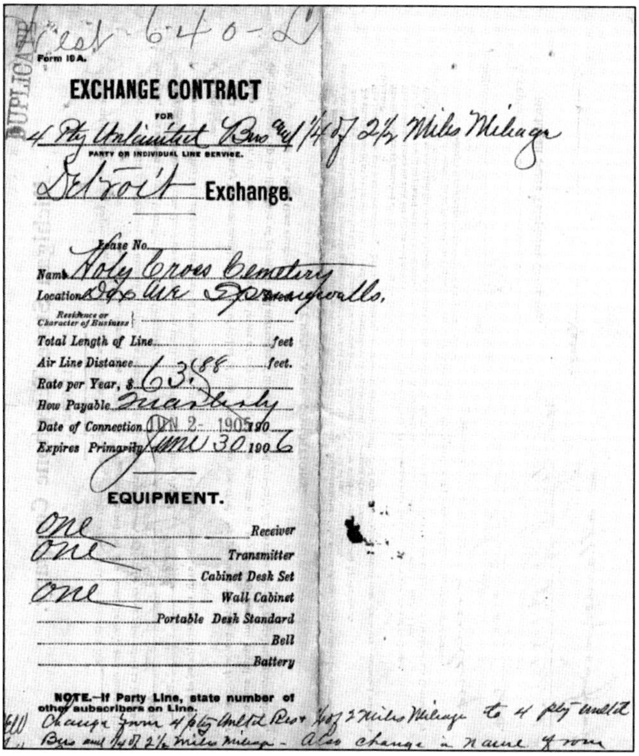
Form 19A.

EXCHANGE CONTRACT

FOR

4 Pty Unlimited Bus w/ 1/4 of 2½ Miles Mileage

PARTY OR INDIVIDUAL LINE SERVICE.

Detroit Exchange.

Lease No.

Name Holy Cross Cemetery

Location

Residence or Character of Business

Total Length of Line .... feet

Air Line Distance .... feet.

Rate per Year, $ 63.88

How Payable Quarterly

Date of Connection JUN 2 1905

Expires Primarily June 30 1906

EQUIPMENT.

One .... Receiver

One .... Transmitter

.... Cabinet Desk Set

One .... Wall Cabinet

.... Portable Desk Standard

.... Bell

.... Battery

NOTE.—If Party Line, state number of other subscribers on Line.

During the years prior to incorporation, the cemetery established a foothold on cemetery grounds using Richard Laurain's house and telephone to conduct on-site business. In 1905, it transferred Laurain's four-party unlimited residential telephone service to four-party unlimited business service. This first telephone bill for the cemetery is for $63.88, which included one quarter of the two-and-a-half-mile line charge. (Holy Cross Cemetery.)

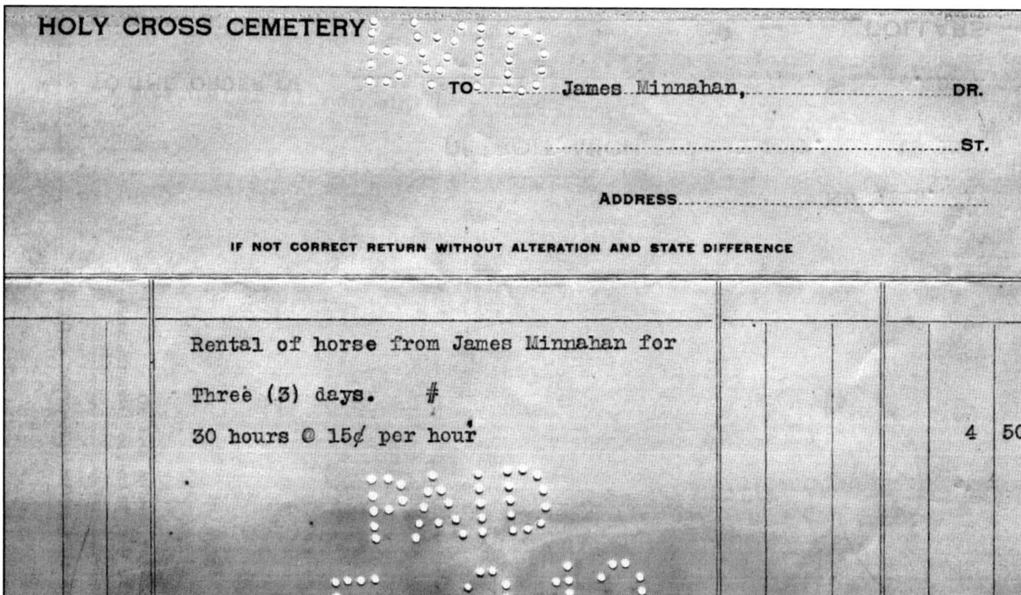
HOLY CROSS CEMETERY

TO James Minnahan, DR.

ST.

ADDRESS

IF NOT CORRECT RETURN WITHOUT ALTERATION AND STATE DIFFERENCE

Rental of horse from James Minnahan for

Three (3) days.

30 hours @ 15¢ per hour 4 50

PAID

As the cemetery grew, the need for additional labor increased. Supervisor Peter Roulo's horse worked for the cemetery; Roulo was paid "15 cents per hour for the use of his horse upon the grounds of Holy Cross Cemetery for the time which said horse actually works for Holy Cross Cemetery," according to a 1910 report. This voucher shows that James Minnahan, a livery stable owner on Junction Avenue, received $4.50 for the use of his horse in April 1912. (Holy Cross Cemetery.)

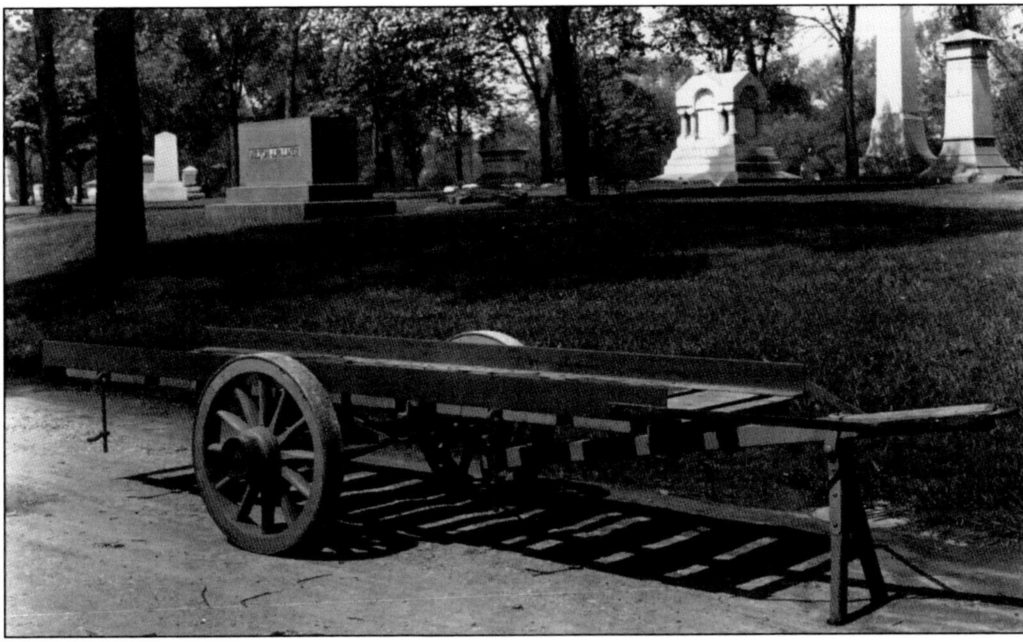

Holy Cross Cemetery purchased this slab cart from Peter Schuttler Company of Chicago. Schuttler began making wagons, buggies, stagecoaches, horse-drawn sleighs, and other farm wagons in 1843. By the time of this 1921 photograph, the company had expanded to include cemetery vehicles. With the advent of automobiles the Schuttler wagon works closed in the mid-1920s. This wagon could hold 2,000 pounds. (Holy Cross Cemetery.)

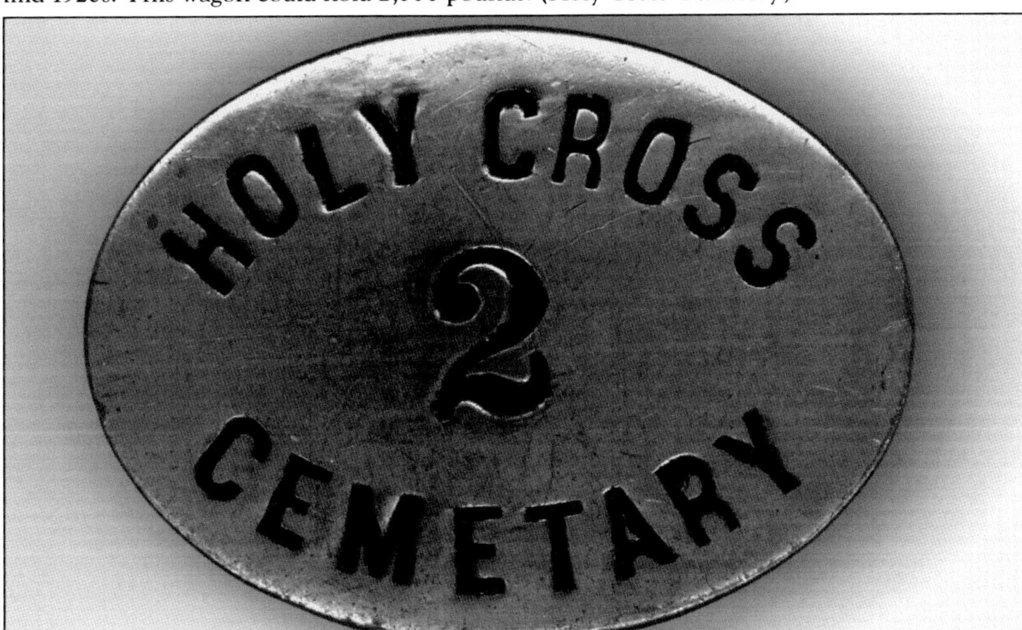

Phonetic spelling and vernaculars abound in the old cemetery records. People were "bared" in a grave, a father was paid for "bareing" a child, a junior was the son of "cenor," and cemetery became "cemetary." This worker's badge is from the early days of the cemetery after incorporation. (Holy Cross Cemetery.)

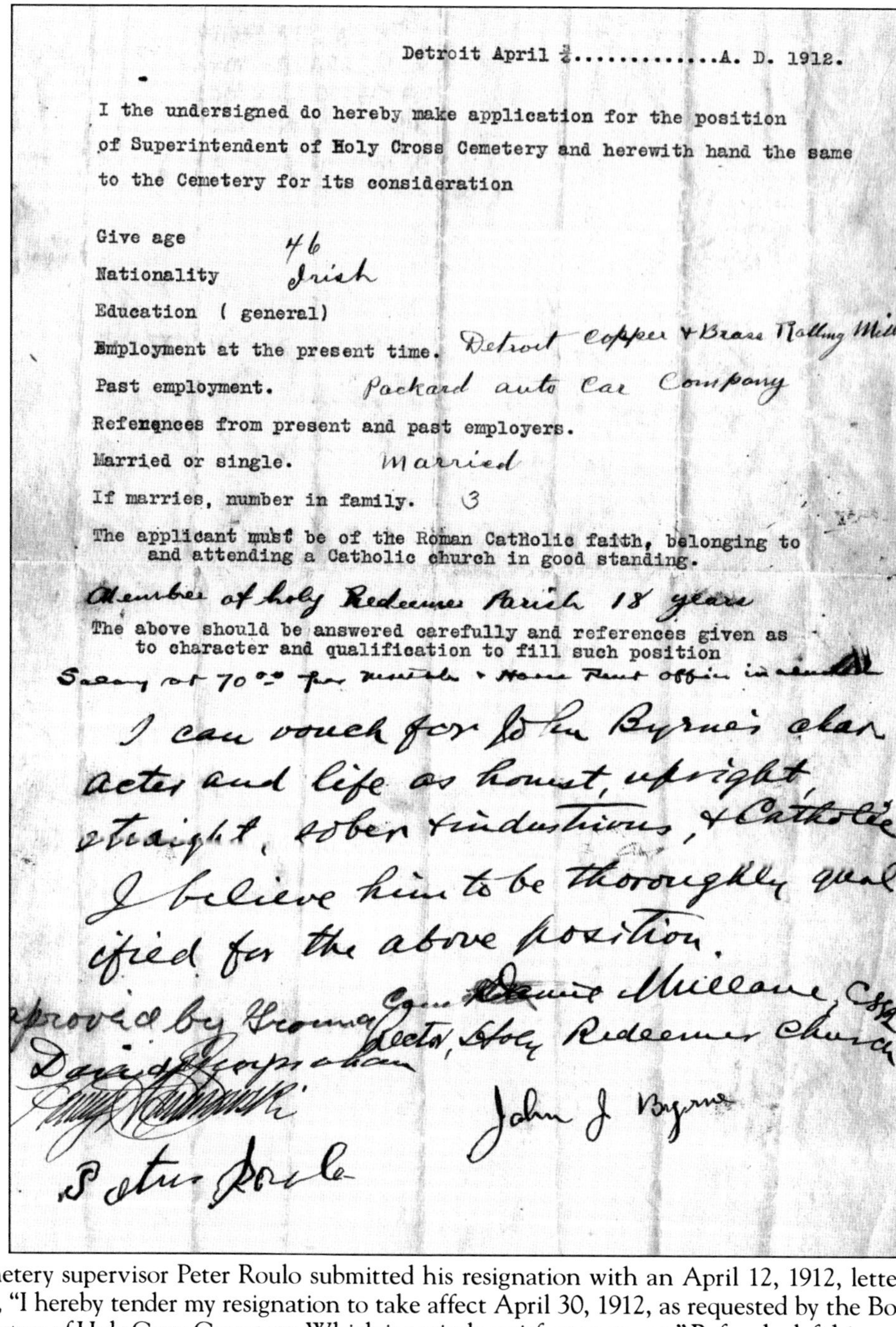

Detroit April 1 .... A. D. 1912.

I the undersigned do hereby make application for the position of Superintendent of Holy Cross Cemetery and herewith hand the same to the Cemetery for its consideration

Give age 46

Nationality Irish

Education (general)

Employment at the present time. Detroit Copper & Brass Rolling Mills

Past employment. Packard auto Car Company

Refenences from present and past employers.

Married or single. Married

If marries, number in family. 3

The applicant must be of the Roman Catholic faith, belonging to and attending a Catholic church in good standing.

Member of holy Redeemer Parish 18 years

The above should be answered carefully and references given as to character and qualification to fill such position

Salary at 70.00 per month + House Rent office included

I can vouch for John Byrne's character and life as honest, upright, straight, sober & industrious, & Catholic. I believe him to be thoroughly qualified for the above position.

Dennis Mullane, C.S.S.R.
Rector, Holy Redeemer Church

Approved by Geo. [illegible]

David [illegible]

[illegible]

John J Byrne

Peter Roulo

Cemetery supervisor Peter Roulo submitted his resignation with an April 12, 1912, letter that read, "I hereby tender my resignation to take affect April 30, 1912, as requested by the Board of Directors of Holy Cross Cemetery. Which is entirely satisfactory to me." Before he left his position, Roulo accepted John Byrne's application for the job. Fr. Dennis Mullane of Holy Redeemer Church vouched for Byrne's good character, citing him to be an honest, upright, straight, sober, industrious Catholic. Byrne earned $70 per month, house rent and office included. He lived on cemetery grounds in the farmhouse formerly belonging to Richard Laurain. The Laurain house became the supervisor's residence after 1911 replacing the old Schneider home used as the office after the 1907 chapel fire. (Holy Cross Cemetery.)

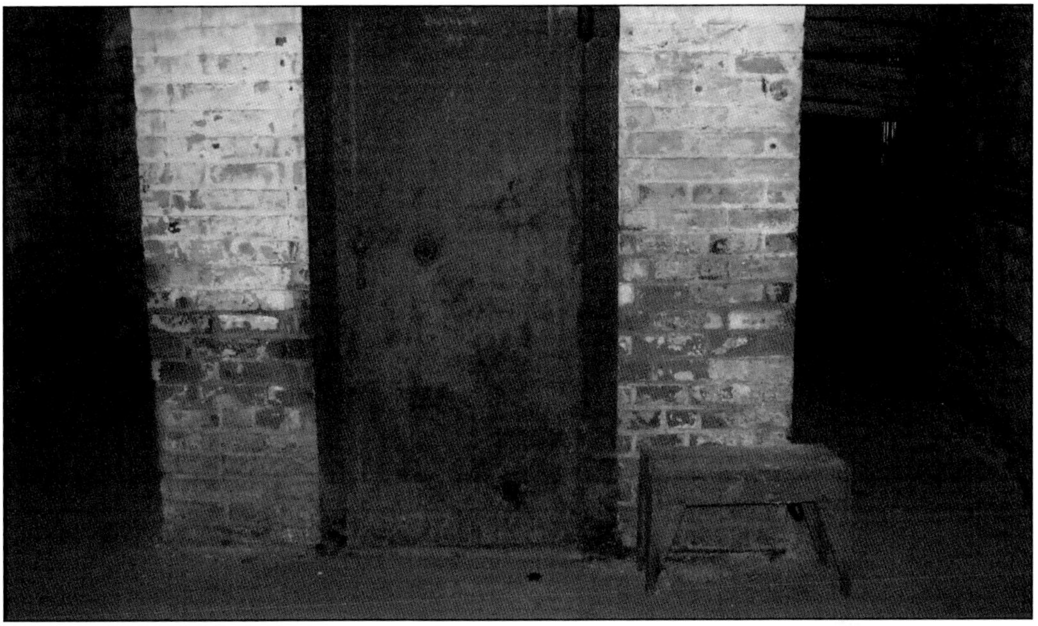

Since the late 19th century, the chapel held an office safe. After a fire in 1907 that destroyed the chapel, the safe was removed to the Laurain house, which was used as the supervisor's house and office. In 1912, the directors purchased a new safe to replace the fire-damaged one no longer of sufficient capacity or ability to close properly. During the 1922 construction of the office, workers installed a safe (above) in the basement below the office. Unfortunately, recurrent flooding made the basement safe impractical.

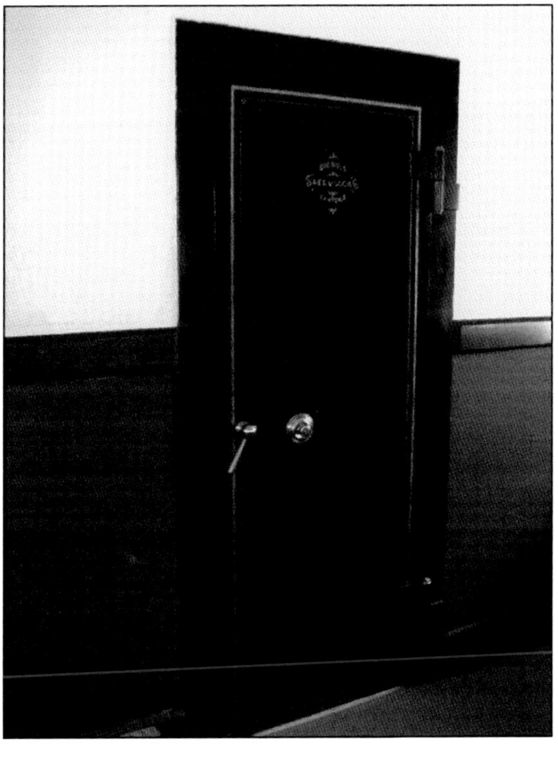

In 1927, Northwood Building Company installed a first-floor safe (right) in the office. To do this, the majority of the walls around the vault had to be removed, the concrete floor was replaced as well as the ceiling, the lavatory was repositioned to part of the director's room, the terrazzo floor was removed from the lavatory to make room for the safe, the electrical outlets were recentered, and the thermostat was moved. The new and current safe sits on a six-inch concrete slab that sits upon a nine-inch I-beam. The ceiling of the safe holds a five-inch concrete slab.

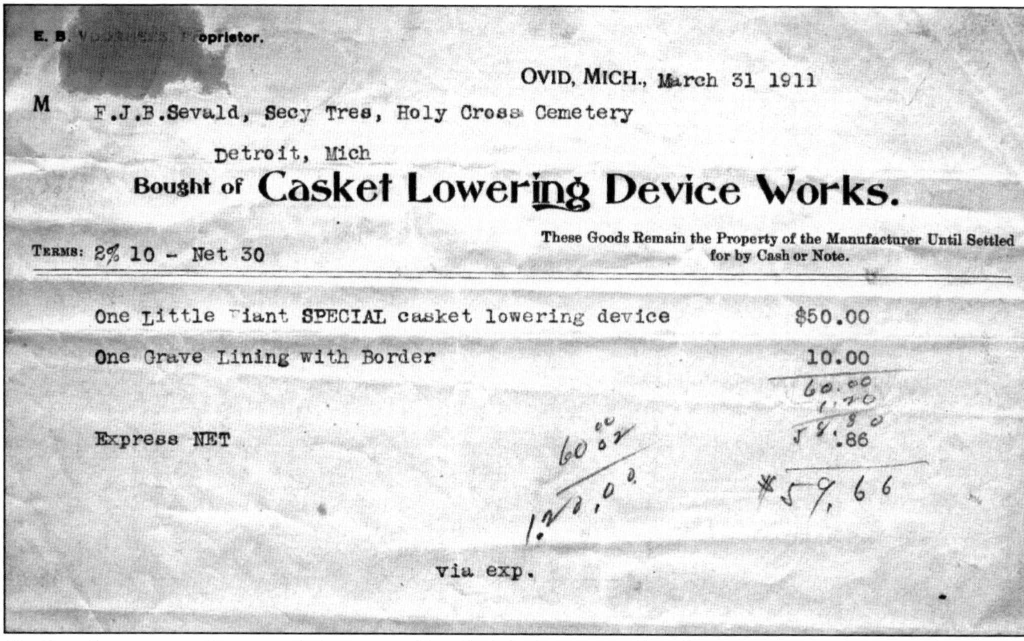

E. B. V[illegible] Proprietor.

OVID, MICH., March 31 1911

M F.J.B.Sevald, Secy Tres, Holy Cross Cemetery

Detroit, Mich

Bought of **Casket Lowering Device Works.**

TERMS: 2% 10 - Net 30

These Goods Remain the Property of the Manufacturer Until Settled for by Cash or Note.

One Little Giant SPECIAL casket lowering device	$50.00
One Grave Lining with Border	10.00
	60.00
	1.20
	58.80
Express NET	.86
	$59.66

60.00
1.20

via exp.

Casket Lowering Device Works at Ovid, Michigan, sold the cemetery this Little Giant casket-lowering device, an essential purchase for the expanding cemetery. The grave lining covered the rough edges of grave, creating a more agreeable appearance for the mourners. Minus a 2 percent discount and adding 86¢ for express shipping, the bill came to $59.66. (Holy Cross Cemetery.)

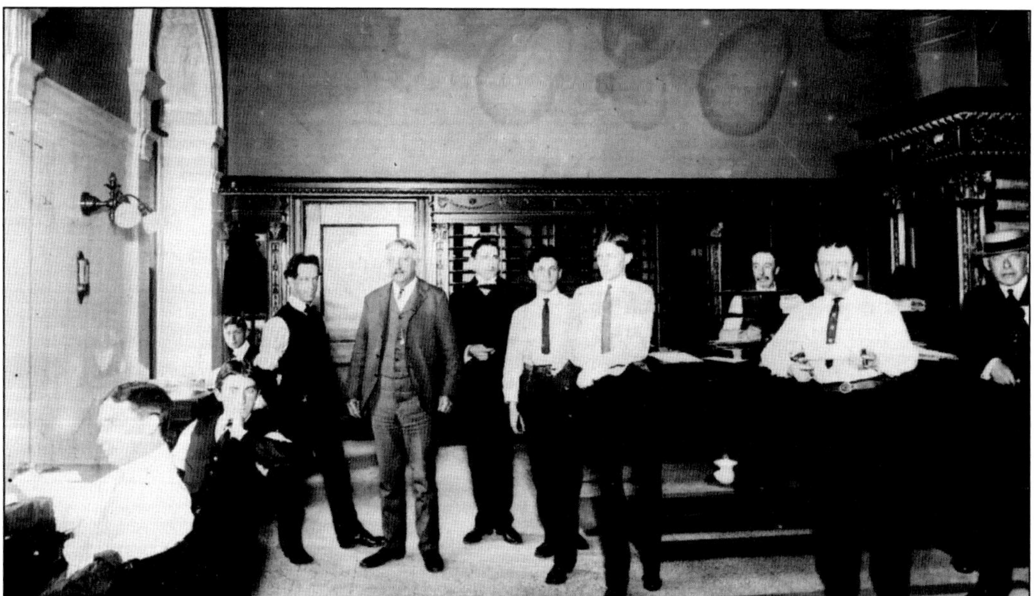

Frederick Sevald, an employee of Clarence Burton in land abstracts, is standing (third from left) in the register of deeds office at the county building. As a lawyer, he purchased land for the cemetery in the name of Bishop Foley and acted as the bishop's attorney for several years. Frederick held the position of secretary-treasurer for the cemetery association. (Walter P. Reuther Library.)

Born in Posen, Germany, in 1869, Henry Sarbinowski's commitment to the cemetery's incorporation in 1906 earned him the position of vice president, a title he held until 1933. In addition to owning a dry goods business, Henry invested in real estate, becoming instrumental in the development of Michigan Avenue while consecutively serving as president of the West Side Improvement Association.

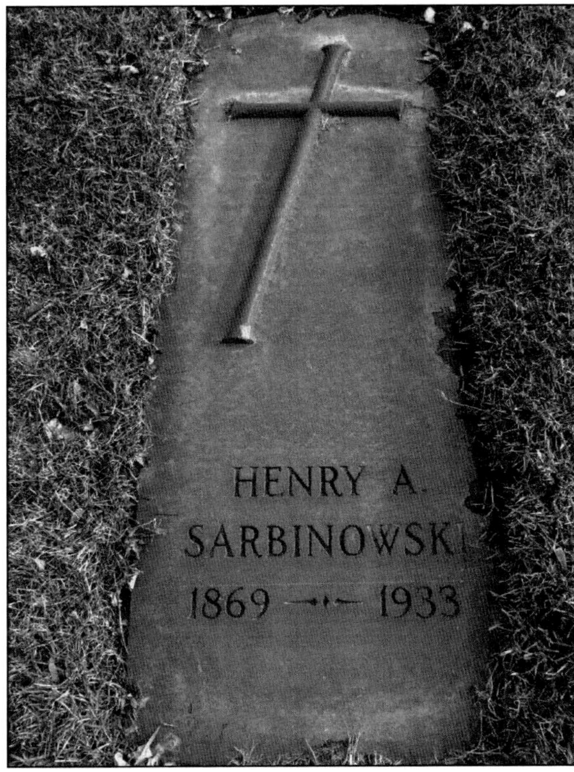

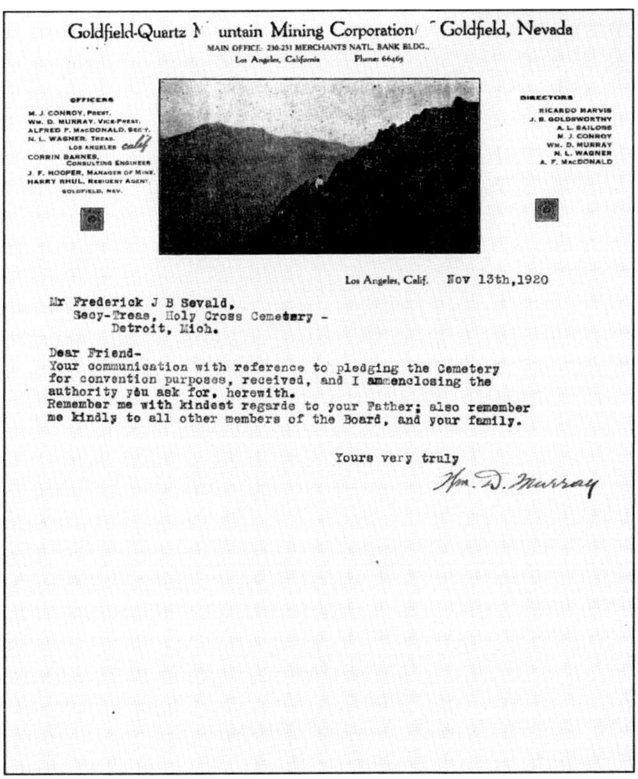

Goldfield-Quartz M untain Mining Corporation, Goldfield, Nevada
MAIN OFFICE: 230-231 MERCHANTS NATL. BANK BLDG.,
Los Angeles, California Phone: 66465

OFFICERS
M. J. CONROY, PREST.
WM. D. MURRAY, VICE-PREST.
ALFRED F. MACDONALD, SEC'Y.
N. L. WAGNER, TREAS.
LOS ANGELES calif
CORRIN BARNES, CONSULTING ENGINEER
J. F. HOOPER, MANAGER OF MINE.
HARRY RHUL, RESIDENT AGENT.
GOLDFIELD, NEV.

DIRECTORS
RICARDO MARVIS
J. B. GOLDSWORTHY
A. L. SAILORS
M. J. CONROY
WM. D. MURRAY
N. L. WAGNER
A. F. MACDONALD

Los Angeles, Calif. Nov 13th,1920

Mr Frederick J B Sevald,
Secy-Treas, Holy Cross Cemetery -
Detroit, Mich.

Dear Friend-
Your communication with reference to pledging the Cemetery for convention purposes, received, and I am enclosing the authority you ask for, herewith.
Remember me with kindest regards to your Father; also remember me kindly to all other members of the Board, and your family.

Yours very truly
Wm. D. Murray

William D. Murray served on the board of directors in the finance committee. A capitalist by trade, he had interests in several ventures. When Murray retired, he and his wife left on a world tour to such places as China, Hong Kong, Saipan, Java, India, Germany, Egypt, Palestine, Italy, France, Hungary, Greece, Holland, and New South Wales. This letter written to trustee Frederick Sevald discusses the possible use of the cemetery as a convention site. (Holy Cross Cemetery.)

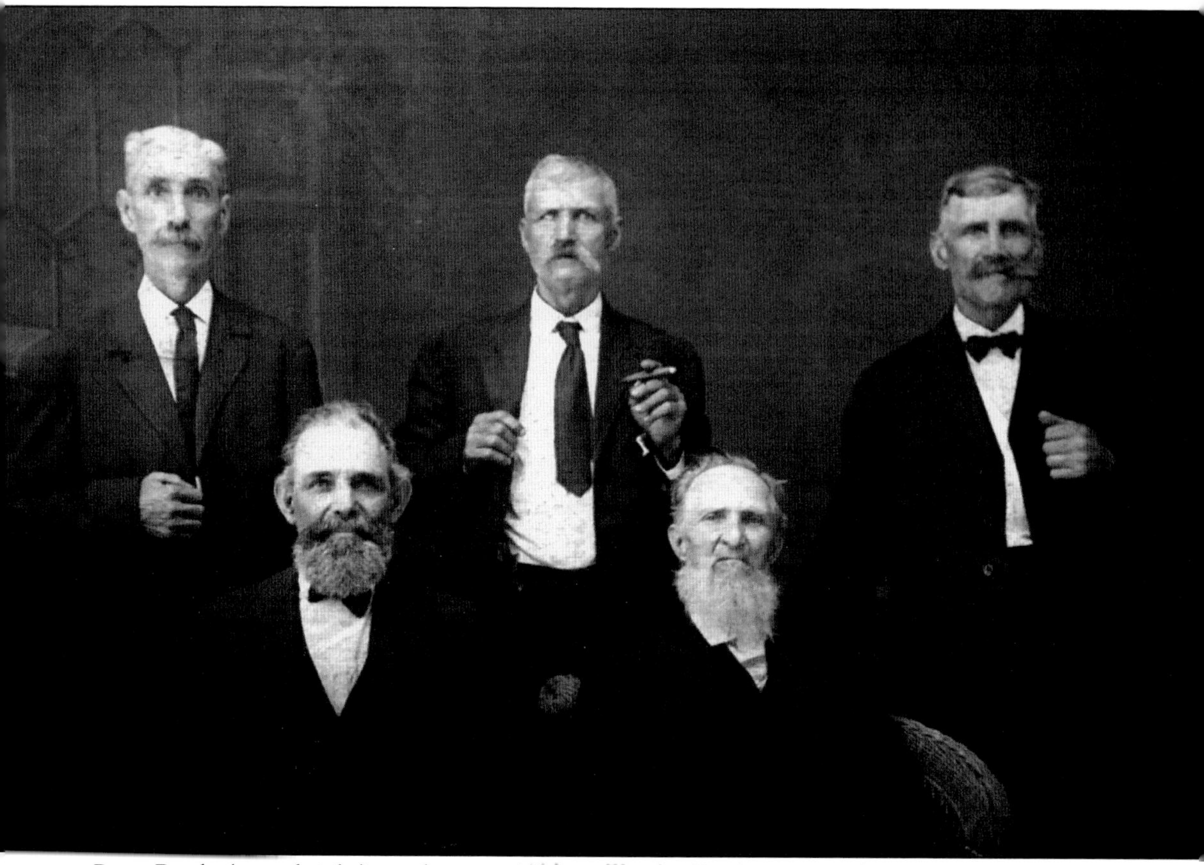

Peter Roulo (seated right) was born in 1820 to Charles Rouleau, one of Detroit's early pioneers and original strip farmland owner; he also owned a gristmill on the Rouge River. Roulo remained on his father's land, and his wife, Margaret (née Cicotte), gave birth to four sons in their small log cabin. They are Peter Francis (seated left), and, standing left to right, Edward, Charles, and Joseph. The four boys played with Native American children during their youth and at times of upheavals their father hid them in the swamps until danger passed. Peter Francis served as one of the original trustees of the cemetery. Bygone Roulo Creek that emptied into the Rouge River, a two-room schoolhouse-turned-church that burned in 1972, and a Dearborn street were all named for the pioneer family. All four sons and their wives are buried at Holy Cross Cemetery. (Dearborn Historical Museum.)

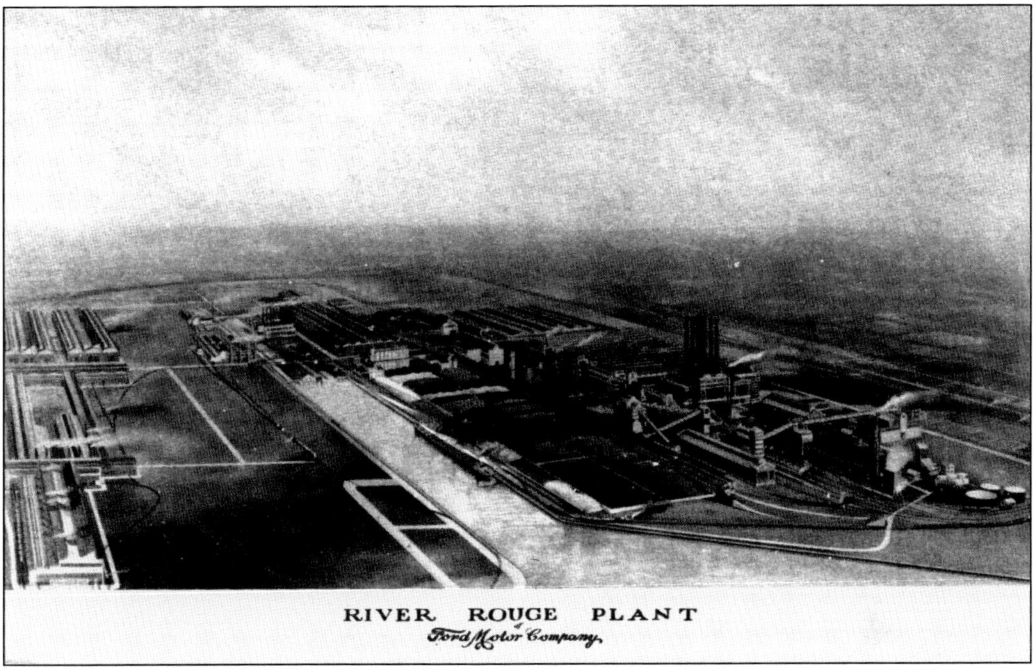

Three sons of Peter Roulo, Charles, Edward, and Joseph, inherited a fraction their father's land through a decree of partition granting them ownership in 1879. They sold this fraction of land to Henry Ford on August 30, 1915, to become part of the Ford Rouge Plant. The home sat where the famous Battle of the Overpass took place between labor leader Walter Reuther, Richard Frankenstein, and Ford's Harry Bennett's security men.

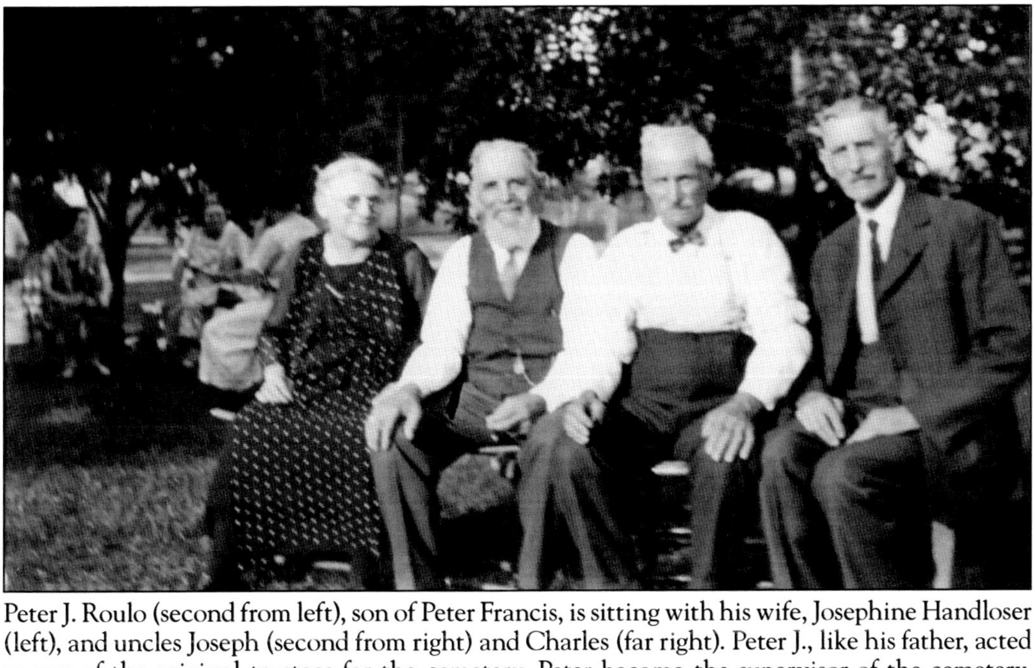

Peter J. Roulo (second from left), son of Peter Francis, is sitting with his wife, Josephine Handloser (left), and uncles Joseph (second from right) and Charles (far right). Peter J., like his father, acted as one of the original trustees for the cemetery. Peter became the supervisor of the cemetery, lived on the grounds, and handled all on-site responsibilities. (Dearborn Historical Museum.)

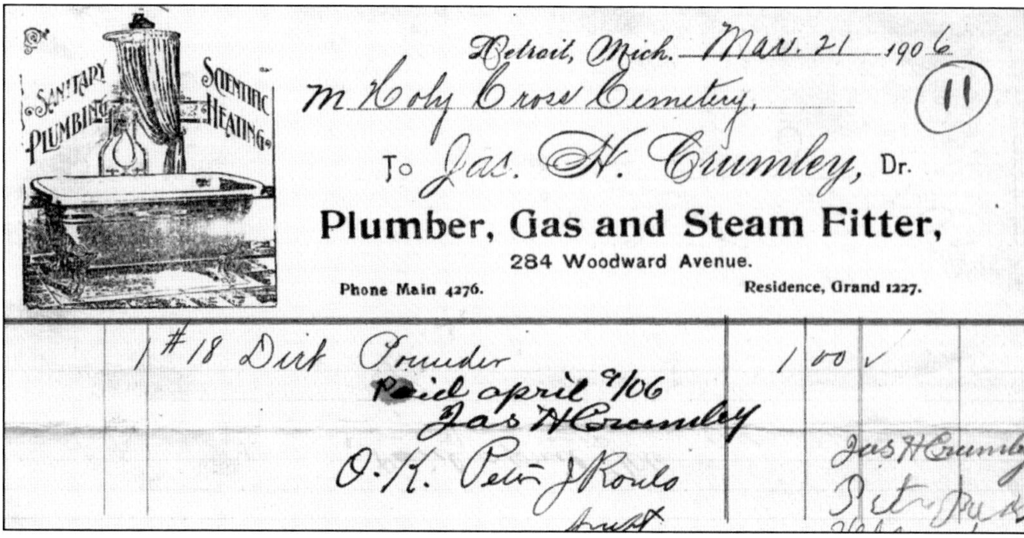
Sanitary Plumbing

Scientific Heating

Detroit, Mich. Mar. 21 1906

M Holy Cross Cemetery

(11)

To Jas. H. Crumley, Dr.

Plumber, Gas and Steam Fitter,

284 Woodward Avenue.

Phone Main 4276. Residence, Grand 1227.

1	#18 Dirt Powder	1	00

Paid april 9/06
Jas H Crumley

O.K. Peter J Rouls

The cemetery incorporators elected James Crumley to the original board of directors. Crumley, as proprietor of his own plumbing business, provided the cemetery with his services at the time of incorporation and for several years thereafter. The cemetery paid this bill for $20.10 on April 9, 1906. (Holy Cross Cemetery.)

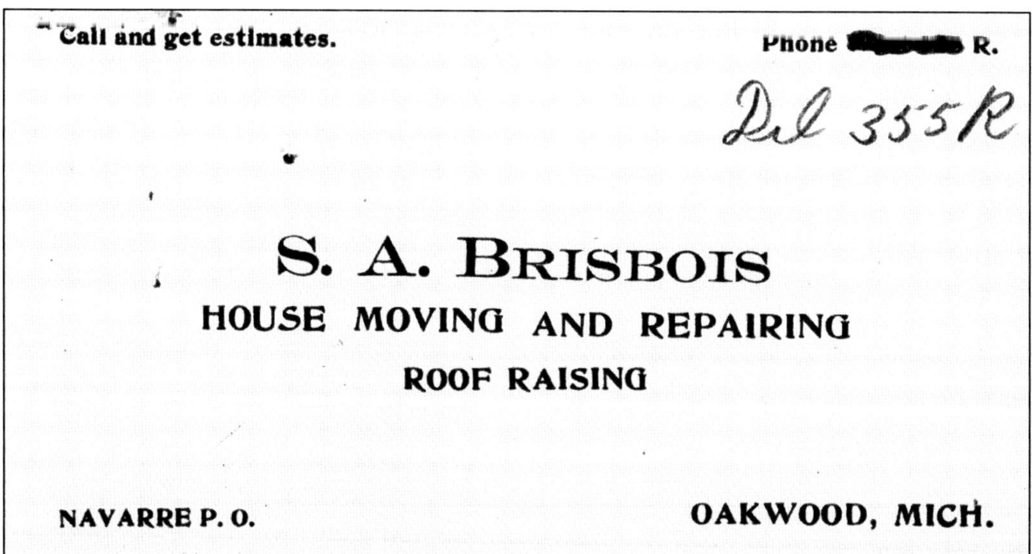
Call and get estimates.

Phone [illegible] R.

Del 355R

S. A. BRISBOIS

HOUSE MOVING AND REPAIRING

ROOF RAISING

NAVARRE P. O. **OAKWOOD, MICH.**

Sylvester Brisbois was 34 years old in 1906 when the cemetery hired him to move the 50-year-old chapel 300 feet from its current location at the center of the old two-acre cemetery to the western edge of the original cemetery and 41 feet north of Dix Road, a more optimal location. The cemetery directors employed the Oakwood House Moving Company, owned by Brisbois, as part of their massive landscaping plan. (Holy Cross Cemetery.)

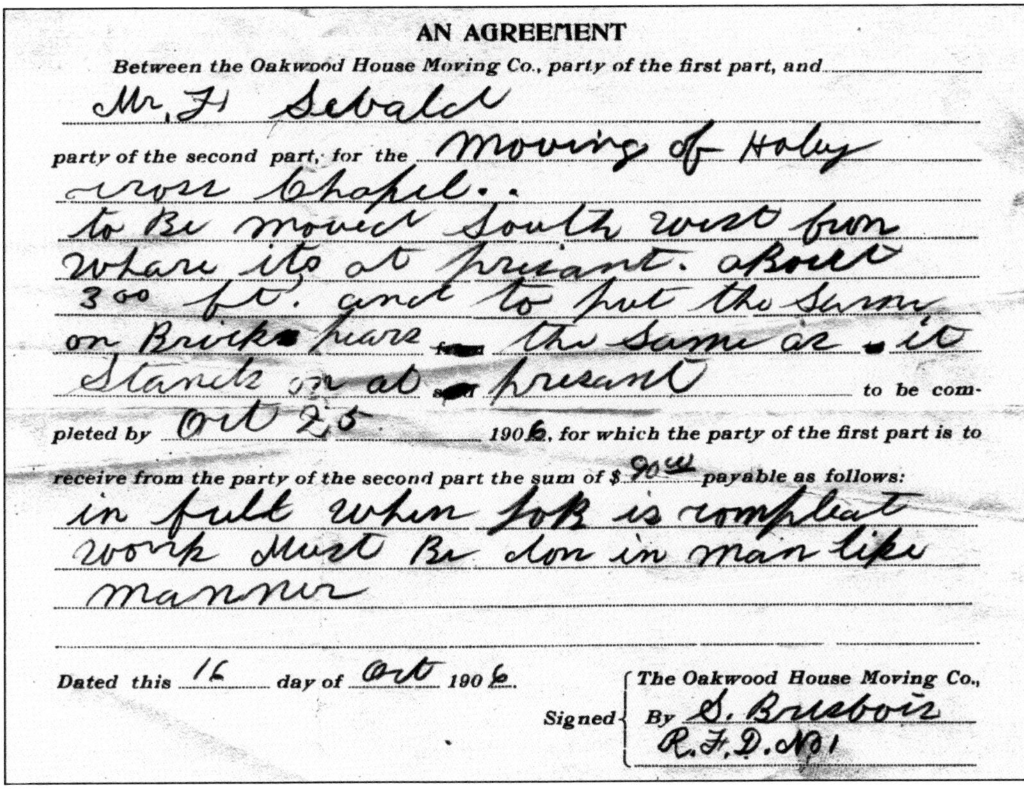

AN AGREEMENT

Between the Oakwood House Moving Co., party of the first part, and Mr. F. Sebald

party of the second part, for the moving of Holy cross Chapel.. to Be moved South west from where its at preasant. about 300 ft. and to put the Same on Brick peare the Same as it Stands on at preasant *to be completed by* Oct 25 *190*6*, for which the party of the first part is to receive from the party of the second part the sum of $* 90.00 *payable as follows:* in full when Job is compleat work Must Be don in man like manner

Dated this 16 *day of* Oct *190*6.

Signed The Oakwood House Moving Co., By S. Brisbois R.F.D. No 1

Brisbois submitted this $90 bid for the job claiming that he would perform the task in a "man like manner." The contract called for him to excavate the new site to a depth below the frost line to set the piers, to reuse the old brick piers and supports if feasible, and to ensure that the chapel sills sit at least two-and-a-half feet above grade level. (Holy Cross Cemetery.)

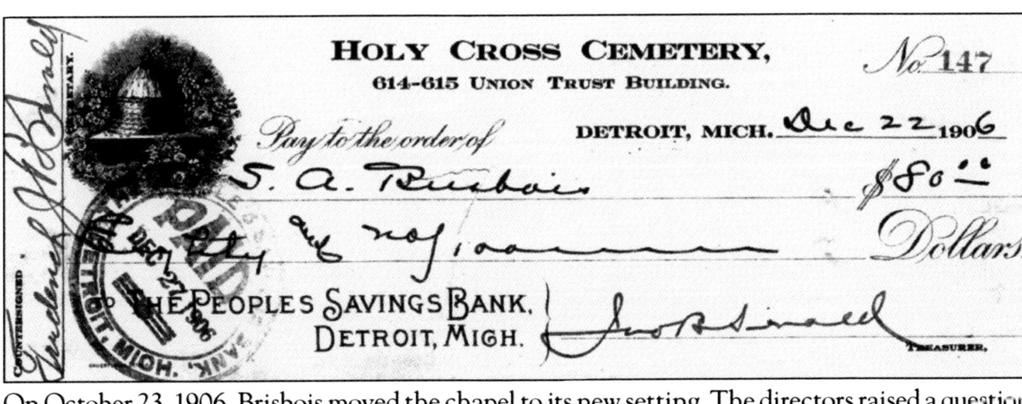

HOLY CROSS CEMETERY, No. 147

614-615 UNION TRUST BUILDING.

DETROIT, MICH. Dec 22 1906

Pay to the order of S. A. Brisbois $80.00

Eighty & no/100 Dollars

To THE PEOPLES SAVINGS BANK, DETROIT, MICH.

TREASURER.

COUNTERSIGNED SECRETARY.

On October 23, 1906, Brisbois moved the chapel to its new setting. The directors raised a question of aesthetics, feeling reuse of the old brick piers impressionably unsuitable. To compromise, Brisbois admitted that the piers "don't look so neat and fancy as they might be" and reduced his bill by $10. (Holy Cross Cemetery.)

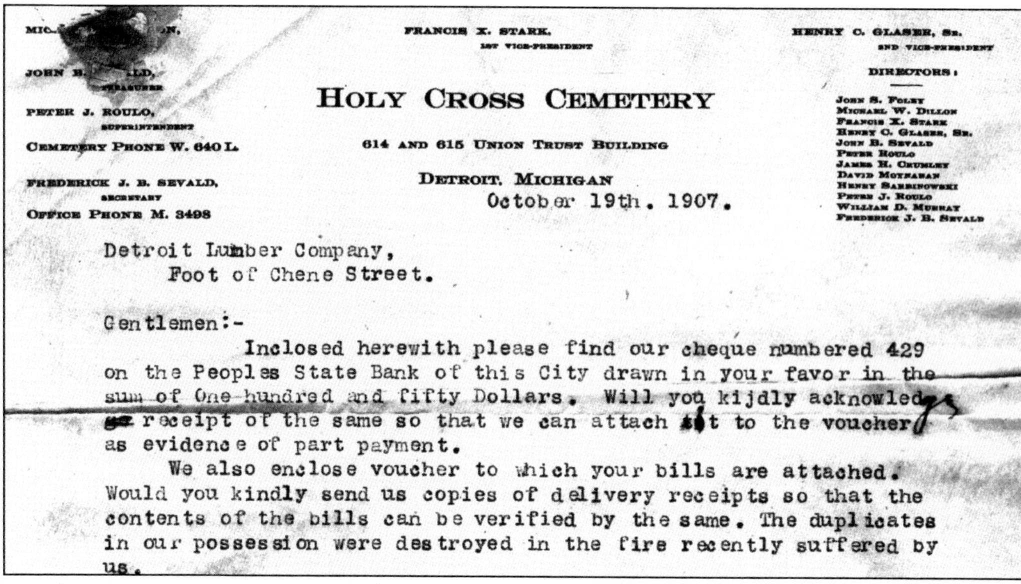

FRANCIS X. STARK, 1ST VICE-PRESIDENT

HENRY C. GLASER, SR., 2ND VICE-PRESIDENT

JOHN B. [illegible]LD, TREASURER

PETER J. ROULO, SUPERINTENDENT

CEMETERY PHONE W. 640 L.

FREDERICK J. B. SEVALD, SECRETARY

OFFICE PHONE M. 3498

HOLY CROSS CEMETERY

614 AND 615 UNION TRUST BUILDING

DETROIT, MICHIGAN

DIRECTORS:

John S. Foley
Michael W. Dillon
Francis X. Stark
Henry C. Glaser, Sr.
John B. Sevald
Peter Roulo
James H. Crumley
David Moynahan
Henry Sarbinowski
Peter J. Roulo
William D. Murray
Frederick J. B. Sevald

October 19th. 1907.

Detroit Lumber Company,
Foot of Chene Street.

Gentlemen:-

Inclosed herewith please find our cheque numbered 429 on the Peoples State Bank of this City drawn in your favor in the sum of One-hundred and fifty Dollars. Will you kijdly acknowledge receipt of the same so that we can attach it to the voucher as evidence of part payment.

We also enclose voucher to which your bills are attached. Would you kindly send us copies of delivery receipts so that the contents of the bills can be verified by the same. The duplicates in our possession were destroyed in the fire recently suffered by us.

Just shy of the chapel move, sparks from a nearby burning barn lit the chapel roof afire, reducing it to ashes in the early-morning hours on October 6, 1907. Many business papers burned, leaving the need for replacement of the wood used to make pine boxes that was stored there to cemetery supervisor Peter J. Roulo. In a voucher used to pay for the replacement wood, Roulo asks Detroit Lumber for copies of previous receipts to replace those lost in the fire. (Holy Cross Cemetery.)

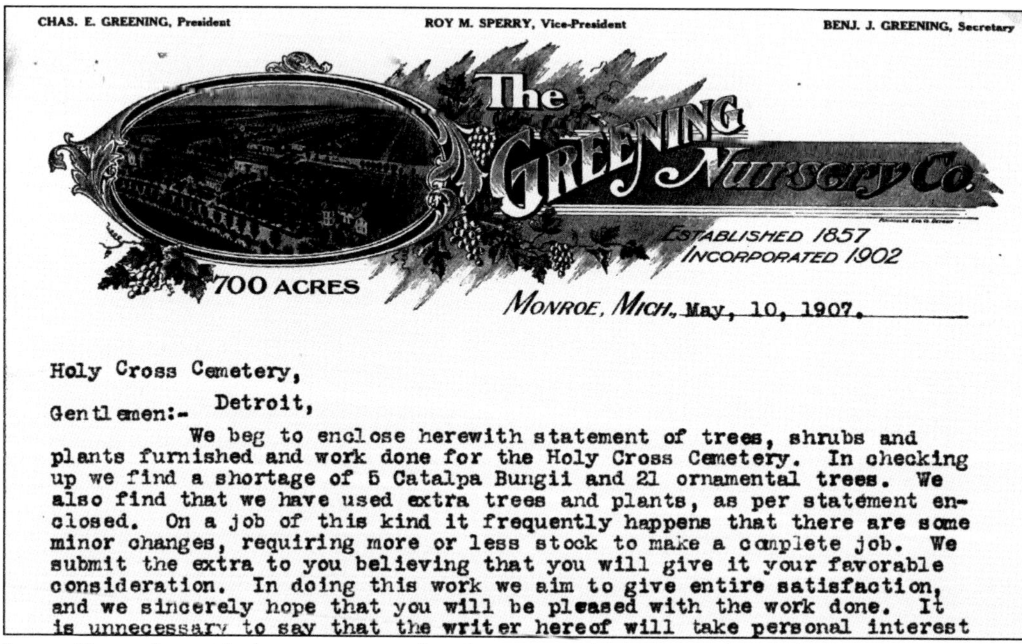

CHAS. E. GREENING, President

ROY M. SPERRY, Vice-President

BENJ. J. GREENING, Secretary

The Greening Nursery Co.

700 ACRES

ESTABLISHED 1857
INCORPORATED 1902

MONROE, MICH., May, 10, 1907.

Holy Cross Cemetery,
Detroit,

Gentlemen:-

We beg to enclose herewith statement of trees, shrubs and plants furnished and work done for the Holy Cross Cemetery. In checking up we find a shortage of 5 Catalpa Bungii and 21 ornamental trees. We also find that we have used extra trees and plants, as per statement enclosed. On a job of this kind it frequently happens that there are some minor changes, requiring more or less stock to make a complete job. We submit the extra to you believing that you will give it your favorable consideration. In doing this work we aim to give entire satisfaction, and we sincerely hope that you will be pleased with the work done. It is unnecessary to say that the writer hereof will take personal interest

In an effort to beautify the cemetery and with a personal recommendation from Bishop Foley, the directors hired the Greening Nursery Company at Monroe to landscape the grounds. Blueprints were drawn, varieties were selected, and planting began in 1907. The nursery sent the trees and plants by train, arriving later with workers to unload and haul by dray to the cemetery. (Holy Cross Cemetery.)

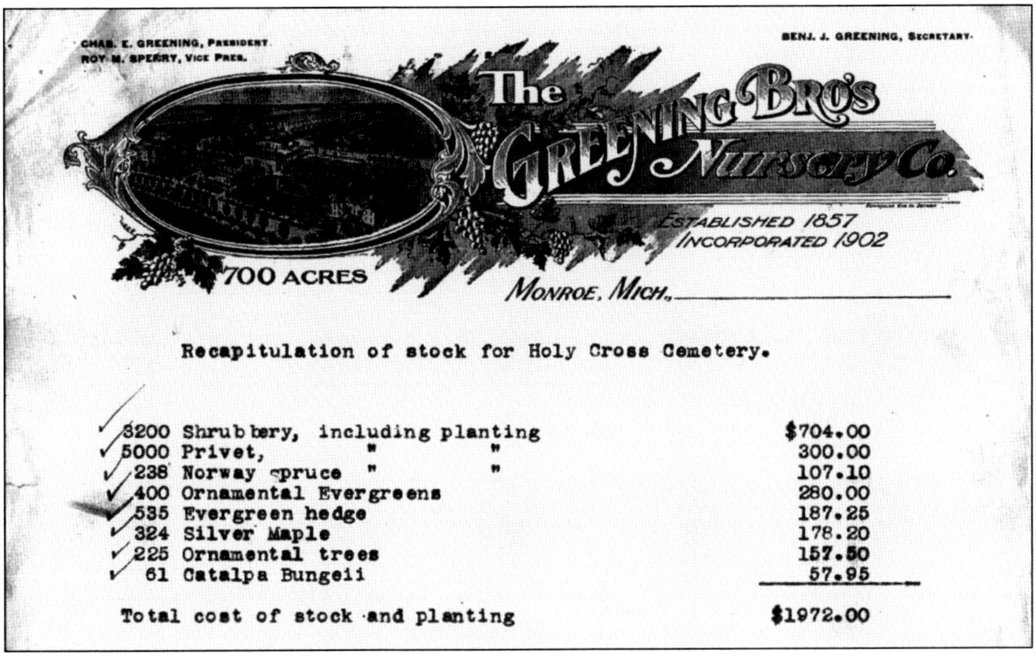

CHAS. E. GREENING, PRESIDENT
ROY M. SPEERY, VICE PRES.

BENJ. J. GREENING, SECRETARY.

The Greening Bro's Nursery Co.

Established 1857
Incorporated 1902

700 ACRES

Monroe, Mich.,

Recapitulation of stock for Holy Cross Cemetery.

3200	Shrubbery, including planting	$704.00
5000	Privet, " "	300.00
238	Norway spruce " "	107.10
400	Ornamental Evergreens	280.00
535	Evergreen hedge	187.25
324	Silver Maple	178.20
225	Ornamental trees	157.50
61	Catalpa Bungeii	57.95
	Total cost of stock and planting	$1972.00

The nursery planted 1,300 trees and hundreds of shrubs and plants in the 19-acre cemetery during the summer of 1907 at a cost of $1,972, including labor. During the cemetery's growth years, the expense of maintaining foliage was a large part of the budget. Each spring, the cemetery supervisor noted the trees and plants that died during the winter, and under obligation, the nursery planted replacements. (Holy Cross Cemetery.)

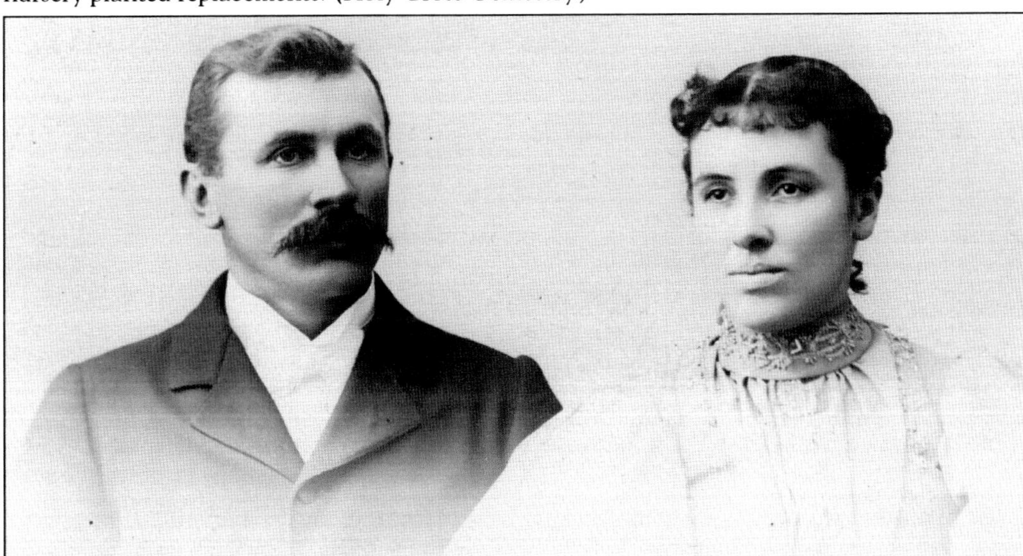

Charles Greening learned the nursery business from his father and formed a partnership in 1893 with his brother George under the name Greening Brothers. He became a premier nurseryman, publishing several books on horticulture and landscaping and earning a lifetime membership in the Michigan State Horticultural Society and the Isaak Walton League of America. Charles loved the water and as second commodore of the Monroe Yacht Club helped organize the indigenously popular Muskrat Carnival in 1906. (Monroe County Historical Museum Archives.)

THE MONROE MUSKRAT

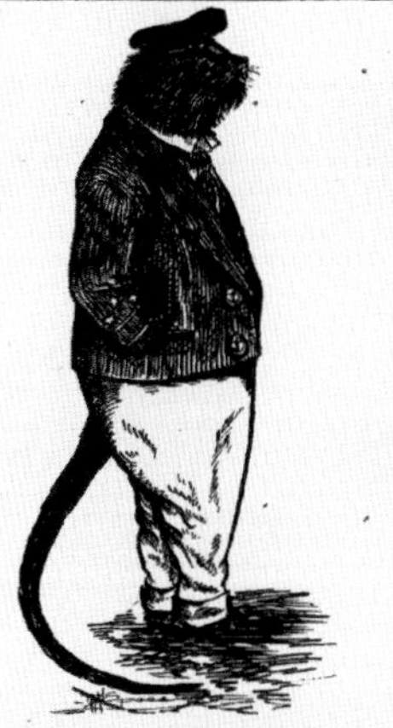

HONORARY MEMBER OF THE MONROE YACHT CLUB.

Fourth Annual Muskrat Carnival of the Monroe Yacht Club, at the Armory, Friday Evening, December 28th, 1906 The World's Greatest Feast of Delicious Rats and Carnival of Mirth and Merriment. Tickets $1. Apply to Geo. L. Little, Secretary, Monroe, Mich.

Monroe, Mich., Dec. 19, 1906.

Board of Directors of the Holy Cross Cemetery,
Detroit, Mich.
Fred J. B. Sevald, Sec.

I take great pleasure in sending you herewith a formal invitation to attend the big Muskrat Carnival to be held Friday, Dec. 28th at Monroe. I hope to see each and everyone of you present, and also would ask you to bring along as many of your friends as desire to come. Arrangements have been made so that you can return the same night. The event will be one of the greatest that has ever been held of its kind, and the entertainment and speaking will be one of the great features of this Carnival. The Carnival this year is of a general character and no formal invitations will be sent out, as last year. Everyone is invited and welcome.

Hoping to have the pleasure of meeting you here and awaiting your reply, I remain

Yours very truly,

Charles E. Greening

Muskrat Committee for 1906.
COMMODORE EDWARD S. WILDER
COMMODORE CHARLES E. GREENING
COMMODORE WILLIAM C. STERLING, SR.

Festivalgoers declared a bully good time at the 1906 Monroe Muskrat Carnival, devouring nearly 2,000 rat dinners. Attendees came from across the United States, some from as far as Seattle. J. Gellermann of Bismarck, North Dakota, timed his visit to Detroit to coincide with the festival. He took an oath with friends that if game laws permitted, he would ship a consignment of muskrats back home, complete with cooking instructions. Partiers chanted, "Muskrat town, muskrat town—Detroit is all right to see, but Monroe is the place for me. Roast 'em brown, roast 'em brown, gravy, gravy, gravy—choke 'em down!" Area breweries created special brews, leading many locals to stay home, fearing it would become a beer bash with drunken sailor songs sung all night long. Giant lifelike muskrats graced the banquet hall, symbolizing the popular regionalized tradition. Early French settlers at Monroe thought the muskrat a fish since it lived and swam in the water and thereby a suitable meal on Holy Days. In 1987, the archbishop of Detroit and Department of Agriculture got wind of the practice, nearly ending the centuries-old custom. The archbishop gave special compensation allowing Holy Day dinners to include the muskrat. Not quite as popular today as they were 300 years ago, muskrat dinners are still on the menu in Monroe. (Holy Cross Cemetery.)

Two

Prime Years of Growth

By 1919, the cemetery had purchased its first motor vehicle, a brand-new three-quarter-ton REO stake truck for $1,440, and insured it through the United States Fire Insurance Company of New York. Henry Ford had purchased thousands of acres directly west of the cemetery and was contemplating building Eagle Boats to aid the war cause. Walker and Frank Brick Company had taken over adjacent property to the east, and the cemetery had grown by 70 acres. Farms and homes still stood along Dix Road.

During the next 20 years, a subdivision had developed in the Peter Reiden land tract, the lots located on Western and Sharon Avenues, just west of the cemetery. In 1946, the cemetery purchased most of the lots on both sides of Sharon Avenue and the west side of Western Avenue. The city removed gas lines and fire hydrants, and homeowners were given the option of moving their houses and garages; many of them did. What homeowners did not take was sold to others or demolished, and the road was bulldozed to make room for what is now sections U, X, and V. Homes still stand on Western Avenue, but Sharon Avenue no longer exists next to the cemetery.

In 1947, Gertrude Moore sold her property to the cemetery. Walker and Company, as it was called then, paid rent to Moore for the privilege of maintaining an advertising sign on her property. After the cemetery acquired the property, Walker and Company continued the $25 per year payments, but to the cemetery.

Industrialization had firmly set foot in southwest Detroit, and its downriver communities were teeming with immigrants. Malodorous factories polluted the clean air. The Rouge Plant was operating three miles to the west, drawing workers from all nationalities. Businesses flourished, but the plans for a large, west-side Catholic cemetery vanished. As more and more immigrants sought the lure of industrial Detroit, the city limits expanded, immuring the once bucolic and peaceful cemetery.

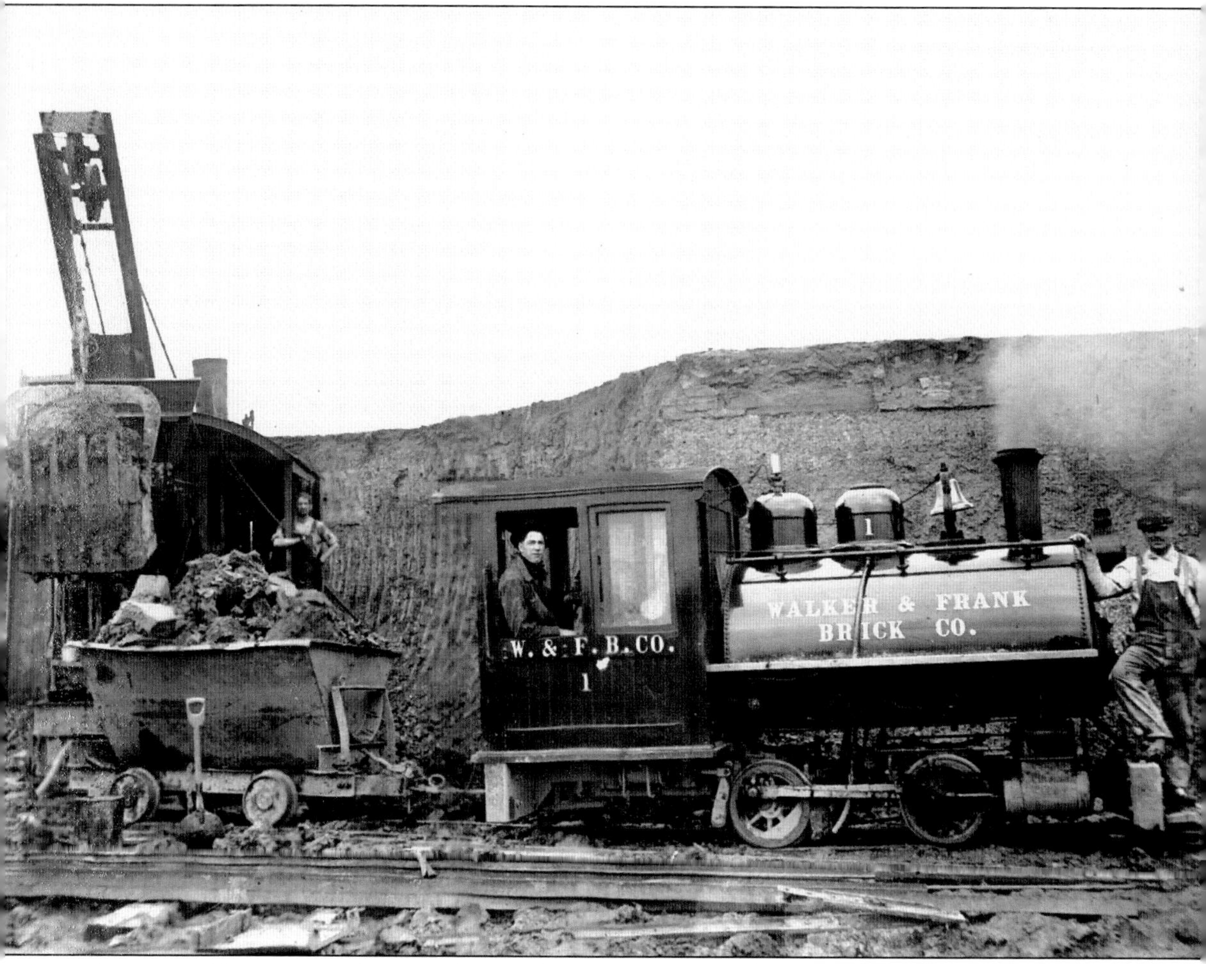

Since the 19th century, brickyards dotted the area around the cemetery, taking advantage of the rich clay soil. Walker and Frank Brick Company flanked the cemetery's east side. This c. 1914 photograph shows the brick company mining on land at the back part of the cemetery. In 1913, the cemetery granted Walker and Frank a right-of-way for a sidetrack across the northeast corner of the cemetery grounds, asking them to fill the mined area with ashes from their 100-ton-per-week coal usage. The man in the cab is Timothy Burns, who later became a Detroit city policeman. Burns is buried elsewhere, but many of his family are at Holy Cross Cemetery, including his cousin, another Timothy Burns who was crushed to death between two Michigan Central Railroad cars in Chicago. The railroad paid to have Timothy buried at Holy Cross Cemetery and erected a tall, obelisk-shaped monument engraved with several Burns family names. (John Graf.)

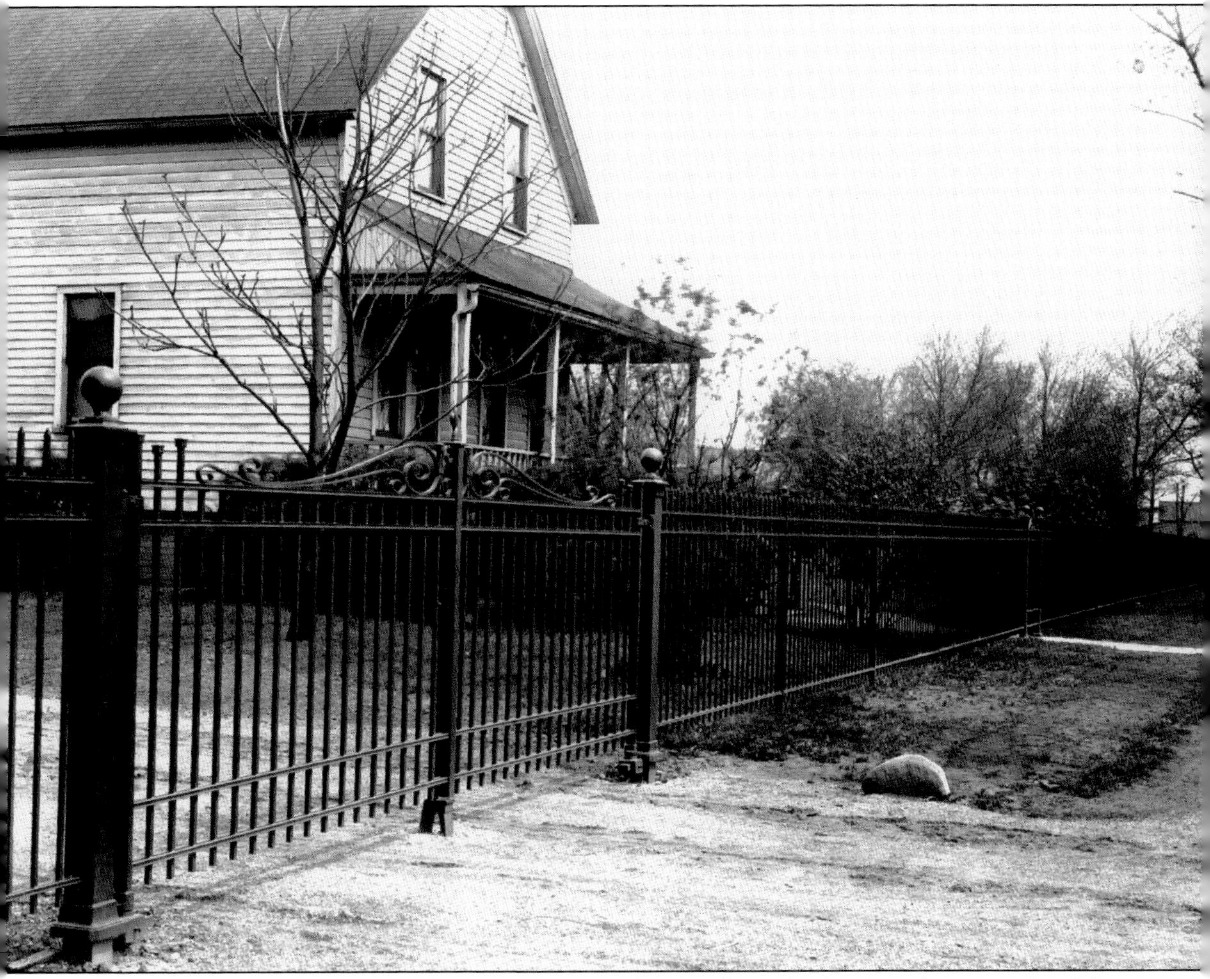

In 1911, Walker and Frank Brick Company wanted to purchase the land on the west side of the cemetery, a farm of 10 acres belonging to Richard Laurain. Richard, a good Catholic, wanted to sell his property to the cemetery for some time, but the two parties could not settle on a fair price. Once word leaked out that the brickyard was considering purchasing the land, the board of directors, realizing that the cemetery might be surrounded by brickyards, jumped to buy the land first, as indicated in board meeting minutes, so as not to "destroy the aesthetic beauty and peace of the cemetery." The $6,500 land transaction permitted Richard and his wife, Mary, to maintain ownership of the house but allowed the cemetery to rent the two front rooms for office space. Several years later, the cemetery purchased the house for $700. It sat in section Y near Dix Road and the comfort station. (Holy Cross Cemetery.)

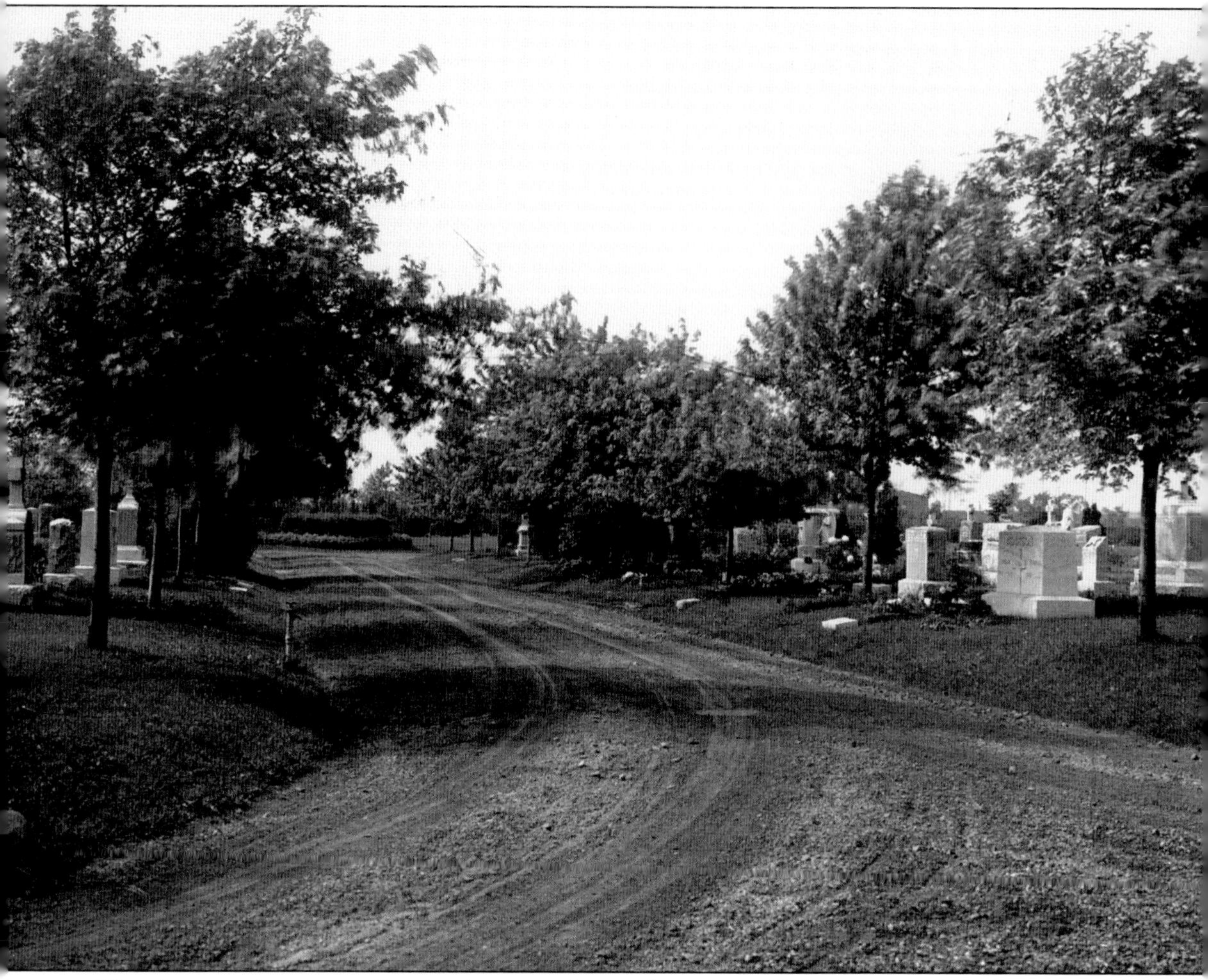

The photographer is standing in the central, circular section E, looking north past section H on the left and section G on the right, straight down to the undeveloped section J, where the road seems to end. According to burials noted, this photograph was taken around 1919. A brick pathway halfway down section G on the right runs through the section, and a wrought-iron bench sits along the pathway. The pathways, long gone, have given way to single burials. Not clearly seen in the same section is an iron gate with seasonal flowers surrounding a family lot. Families were encouraged to plant flowers and shrubs to give the cemetery a gardenlike appearance. Another bench sits in the section on the left close to an American flag honoring a fallen soldier. (Holy Cross Cemetery.)

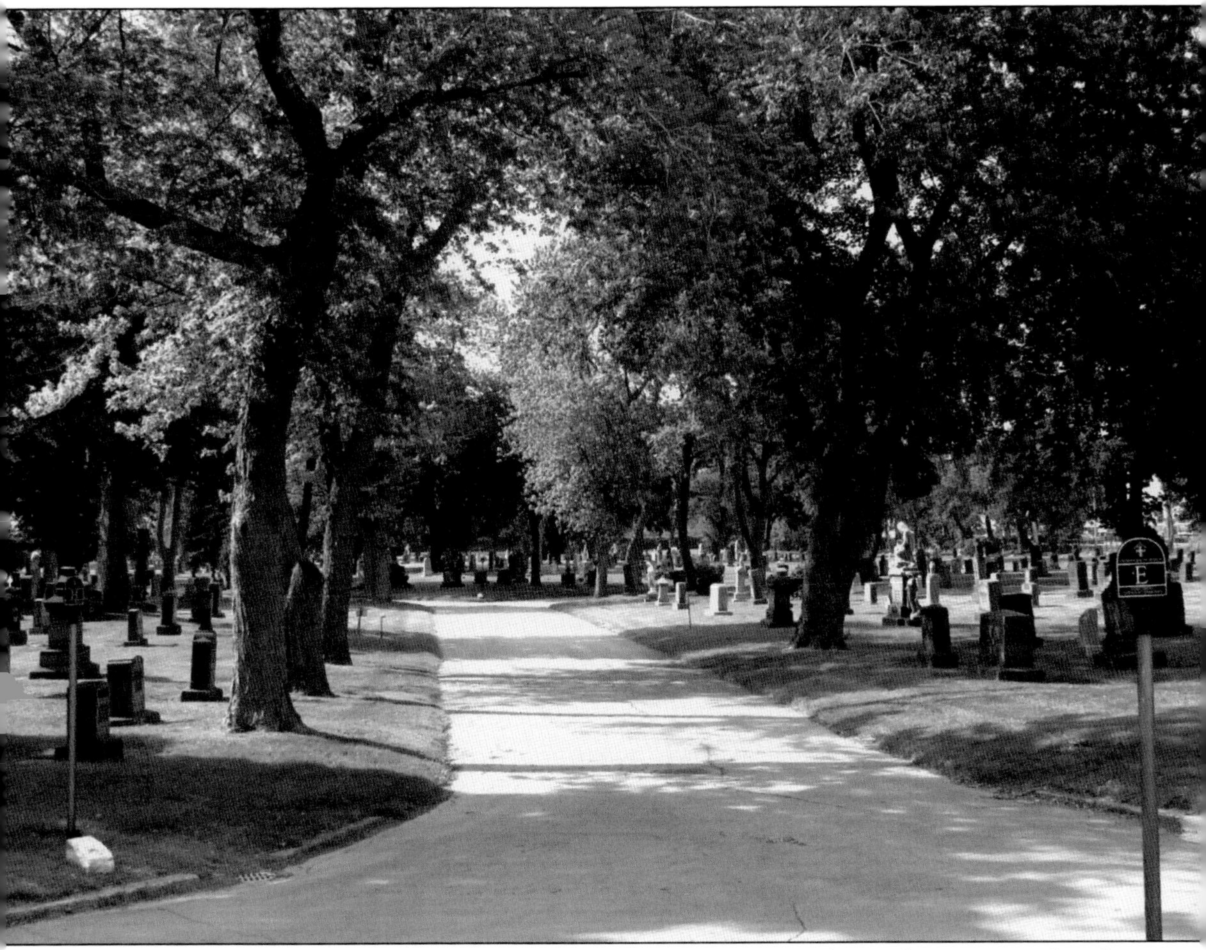

Standing in the same spot, today's view is significantly different. The road is now paved with proper drainage and sewer work finished. Few of the trees lining the road remain, and the monuments have turned gray with age and pollution from neighboring industries. The pathways are gone; the carefully planted flowers are gone, as are the iron benches, all to make room for additional burials. Very few lots are available in the long-ago-developed section J. One family purchased an eight-burial lot there for a family member, a contrary old curmudgeon disliked by family and friends. They buried him in the center of the lot, declaring that no other burials would take place close to him. He was obnoxiously distant and solitary in life and they wish him to be the same in death. (Holy Cross Cemetery.)

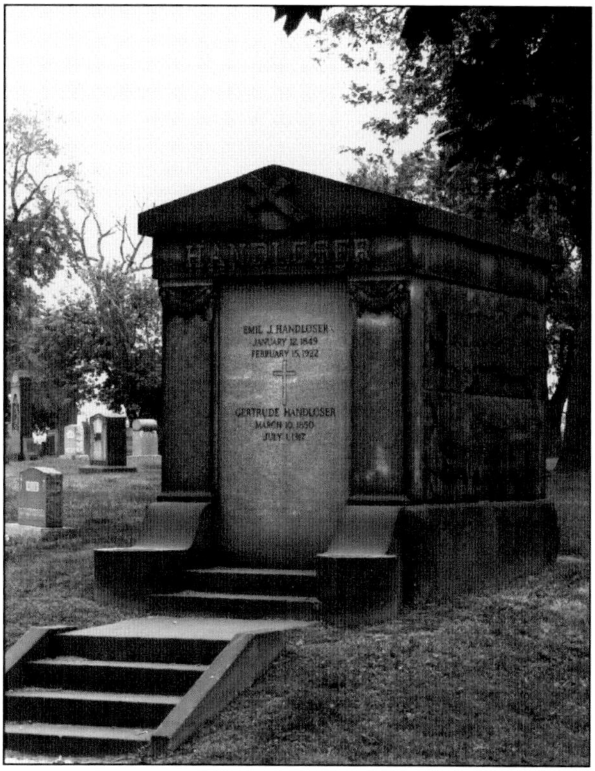

Born in Randegg, Baden, near the Black Forest, Emil Handloser immigrated to Michigan in 1853, leaving behind his family's 80-acre farm. His business, Handloser Hotel and Opera House, located on River Road in Delray, sported the longest bar in Michigan. It was known also as Handloser Hall, and heavyweight boxing champion Noah Brusso held several matches there. Brusso changed his name to Tommy Burns after a fight that nearly killed boxer Ben O'Grady. Emil married Gertrude Kaier in 1873. Their crypt is located in section F.

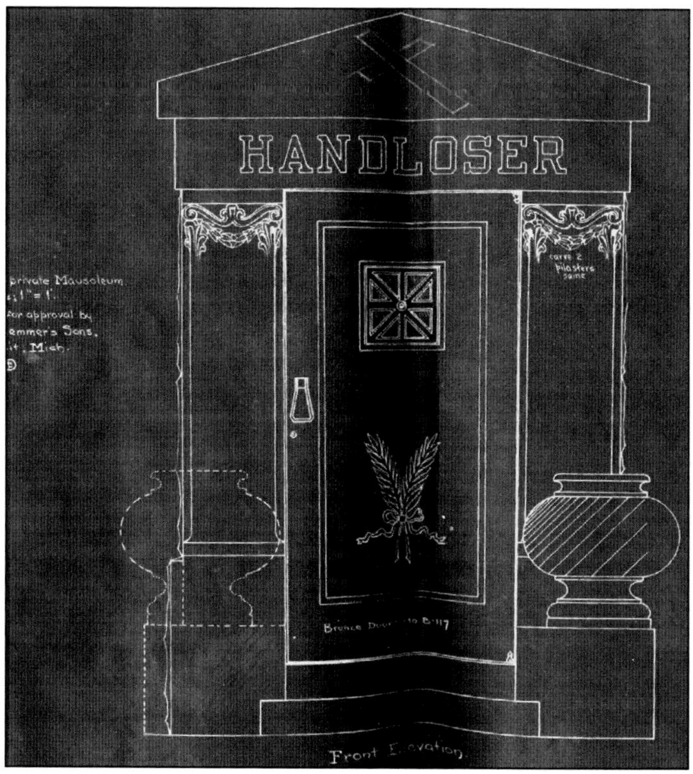

Henry Lemmer's sons constructed the Handloser mausoleum, the only mausoleum on cemetery grounds. With cemetery approval of the blueprints, construction began in September, two months after Gertrude's death on July 1, 1917. The foundation is six feet deep, the exterior is light Barre granite, and the interior walls are highly polished light Riverside marble. The roof is a solid piece of granite. A single marble door encloses two slate crypts at the rear of the vestibule. Eliminating the front door window is the only change from blueprints to final construction. One year later, on July 14, 1918, after resting in Woodmere Cemetery's vault, Gertrude was interred at Holy Cross. (Holy Cross Cemetery.)

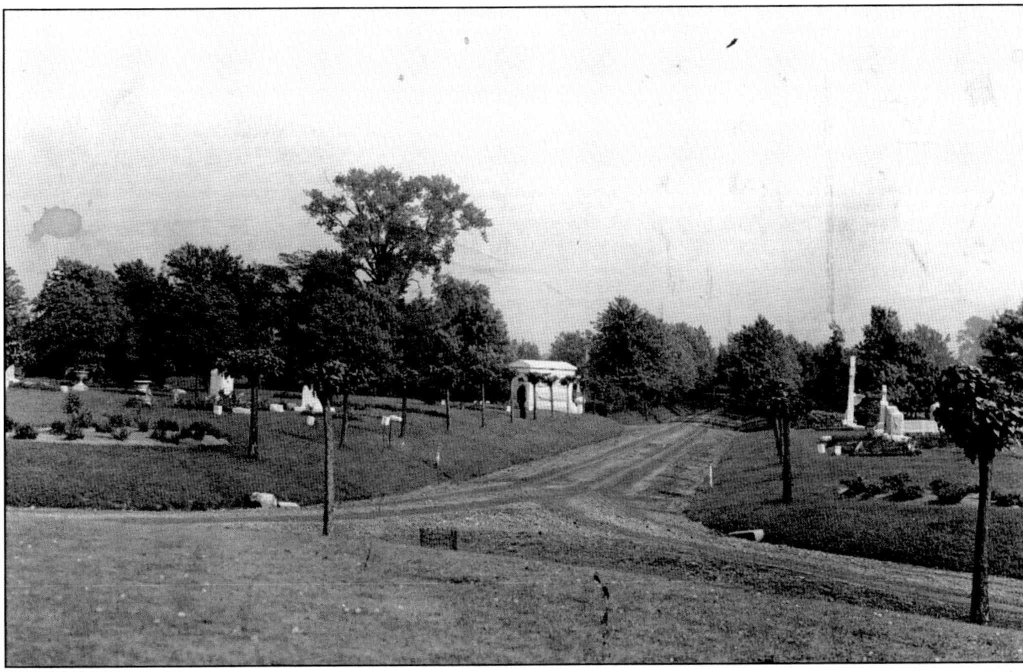

This 1919 photograph shows the Handloser mausoleum two years after its completion. The photographer stood in section E shooting toward the front entrance. Section E later became developed and nicknamed Incorporation Circle, the place that the 1906 cemetery's directors chose for themselves and their families. There are just 125 burials in section E. (Holy Cross Cemetery.)

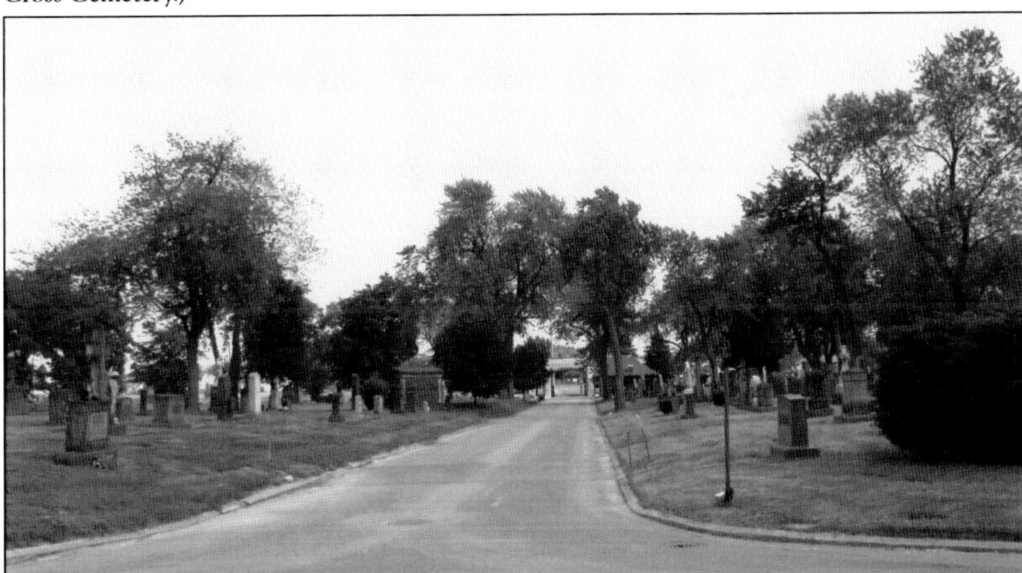

This current view, taken from the same spot as the 1919 photograph, shows the difference 100 years makes. The office with archway to the comfort station replaces the plain front gate at Dix Road. Fallen, diseased, and overgrown trees are gone; broken urns are removed, as well as visitors benches; and areas of shrubbery and extensive grave plantings have given their space for subsequent burials.

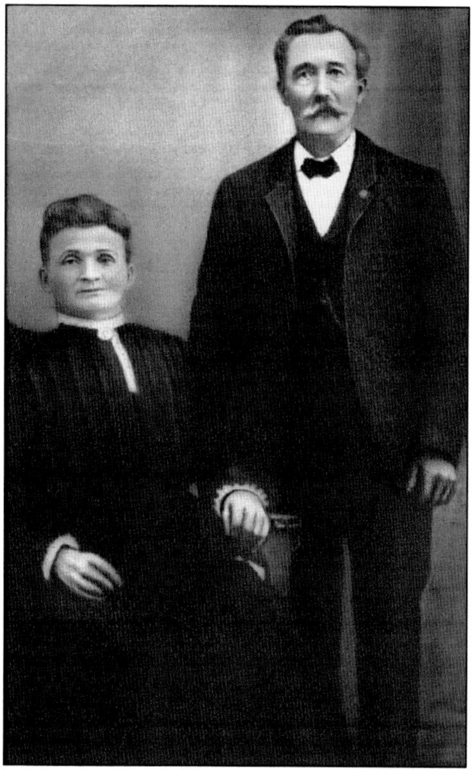

Leopold Handloser and his wife, Hedwiga, followed Leopold's brother, Emil, to Delray where he resumed his profession as a carpenter. Leopold came with few things, including his toolbox that held tools he made himself, a Bible, and a clock. Leopold's son, Gerhardt, gave the clock to his bride-to-be, Pauline, in lieu of a wedding ring. The toolbox has been passed down to Leopold's great-grandson. Leopold and Hedwiga lie in section E. (Joan Handloser.)

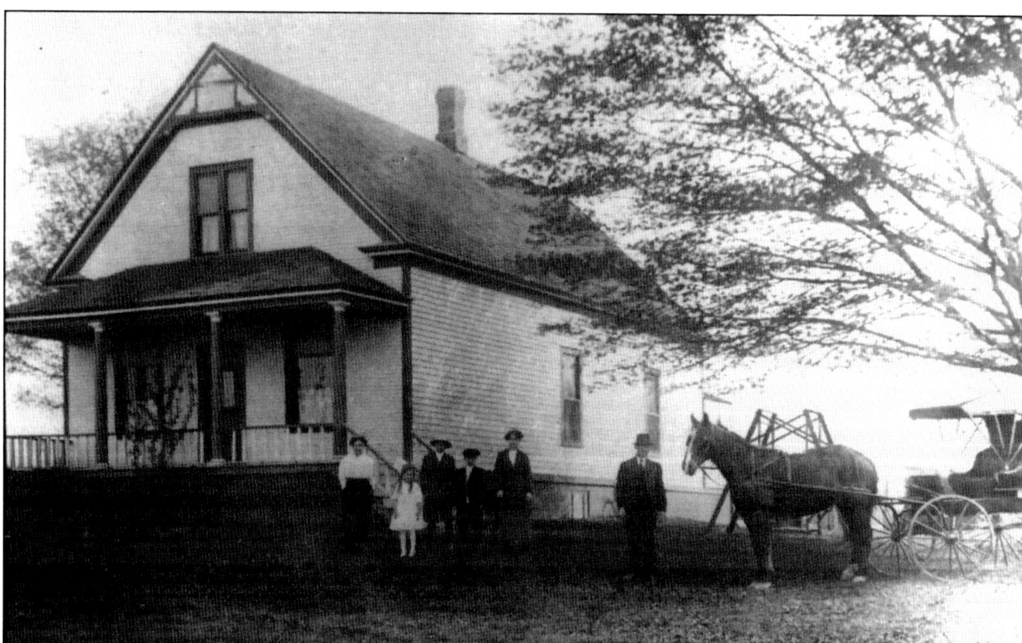

As an excellent carpenter, Leopold built this house on Fort Street for his daughter Anna, who married Albert Kaier. Leopold is standing next to the horse and buggy, and his daughter Anna is standing at the far left. Anna's children stand between their mother and grandfather. Leopold owned the land, a 20-acre farm, on which the house sits. (Joan Handloser.)

Katarzyna Pelc left her hometown of Budy Przeworskie, Poland, with her cousin, Mary Sliwa Nykiel, arriving in the United States in 1912. Shortly thereafter, in 1915, she married John Mazurek at St. Hedwig Church. Together they ran a small store at the corner of Ogden and Kirkwood Streets in Detroit. Pelc died in 1936. (Kamila Polanczyk.)

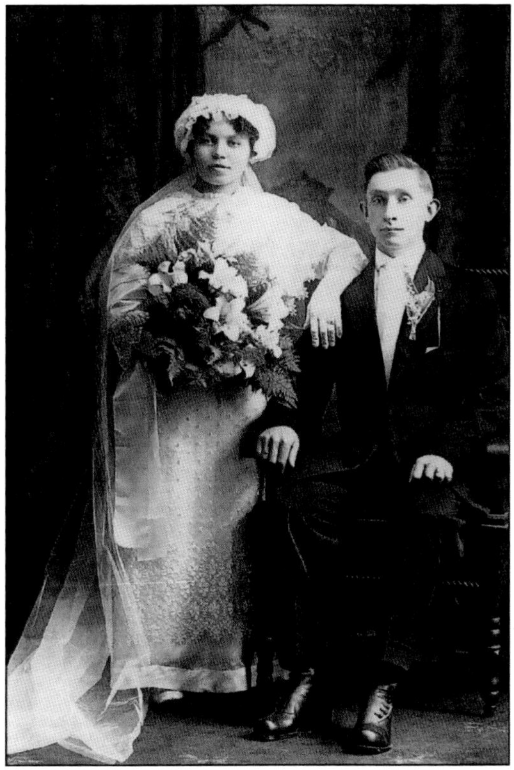

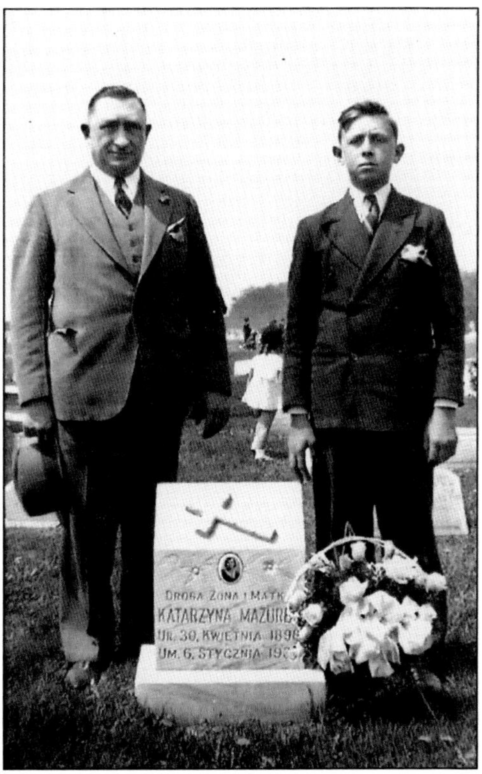

Katarzyna's husband, John, and their son, Stephen, are standing at Katarzyna's grave in section M, about 1940. When World War II broke out, Stephen enlisted and was sent to Europe. Seriously wounded at the Battle of the Bulge, he fell into a coma lasting six months, his gallantry earning him the Purple Heart. After the war ended, Stephen returned to Detroit to help in the family store. (Kamila Polanczyk.)

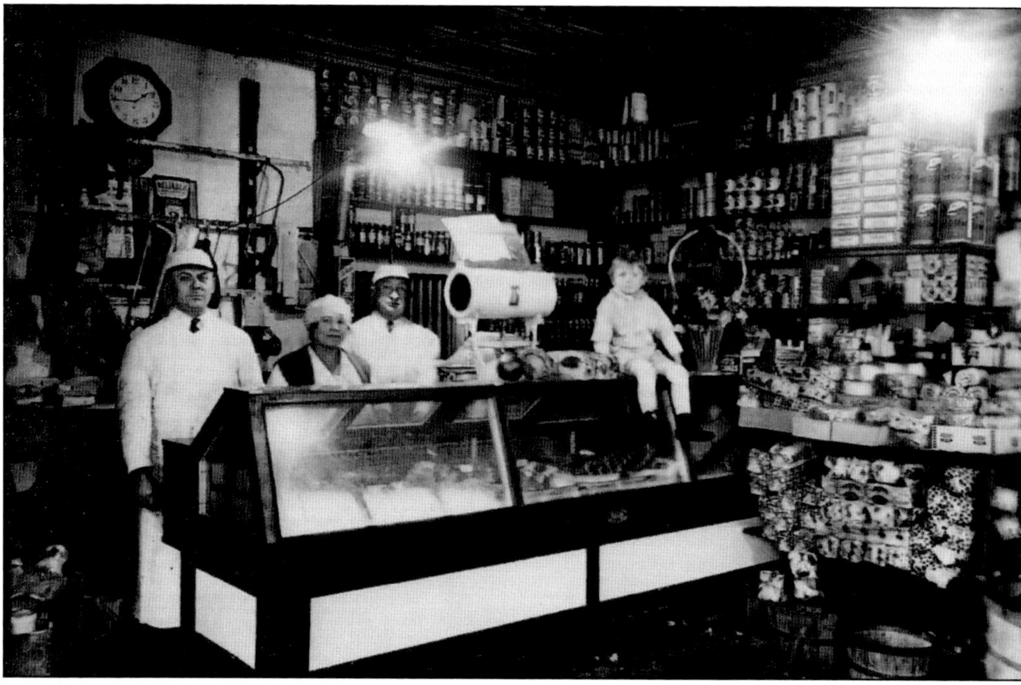

Standing in their Ogden Street store are, from left to right, Jan Pelc (Katarzyna's brother), Katarzyna and John Mazurek, and their five-year-old son Stephen Mazurek. John died in 1947, leaving the store to Stephen, who, not wishing to keep it, sold it to Peter and Anna Ziomek. Stephen fell in love with their daughter Irene, and the two were married in 1948. (Kamila Polanczyk.)

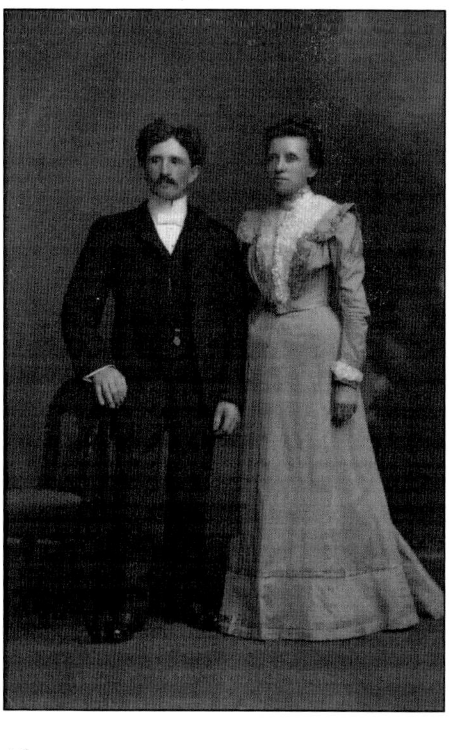

Although Herman Kolbe and his wife, Anna Pacek, lived near Detroit's Packard plant, Herman and his brothers Paul and Berthold ran a bakery on Grand River appropriately named Kolbe Brothers. A few years later, Herman and Anna opened their own store, H. A. Kolbe general store. They are buried in section S. (Michelle Kolbe.)

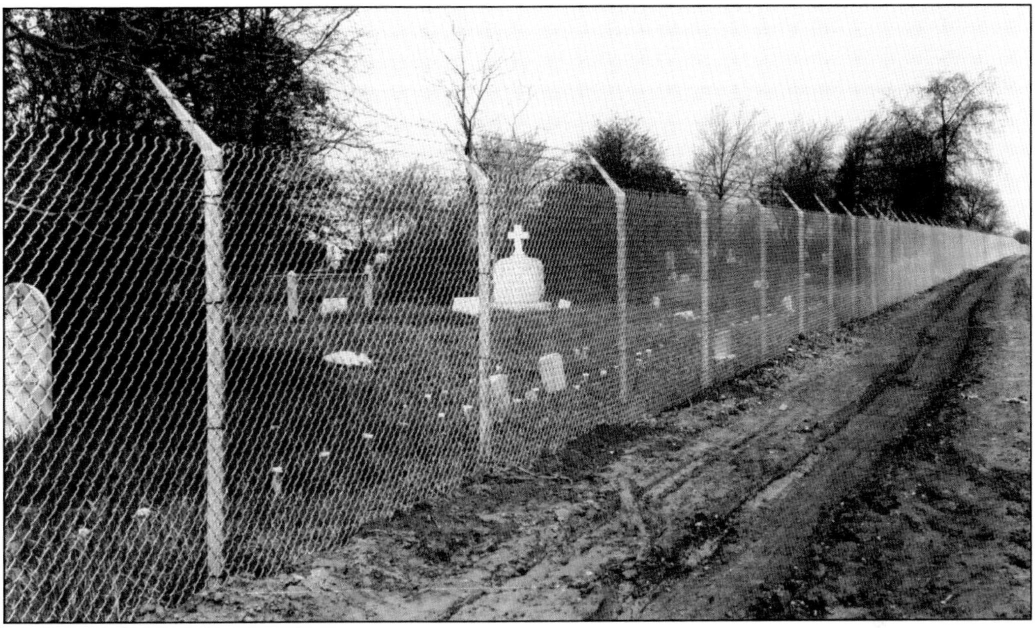

In 1924, the cemetery association replaced the old white-painted cedar fence built in 1906 that enclosed the cemetery on three sides. The Anchor Post Fence Company won the bid and installed the galvanized cyclone fabric, replacing the old cedar one along the north, east, and west sides of the cemetery, a length of one mile of fence netting. These photographs show the completed fencing along the east side at section B. The dirt road belonged to Walker Frank Brick Company, now paved and used by Levy Gravel Company. On September 10, 1924, a slightly tipsy employee of the brickyard ran into the fence, destroying 20 feet and damaging two posts. Frank fired the employee, froze his paycheck, and subtracted the cost of repair, $23, from his wages. In 1936, another employee, this time from Levy Company, the owners of the Walker Frank property, damaged the same section of fencing, causing a $26 repair bill. (Holy Cross Cemetery.)

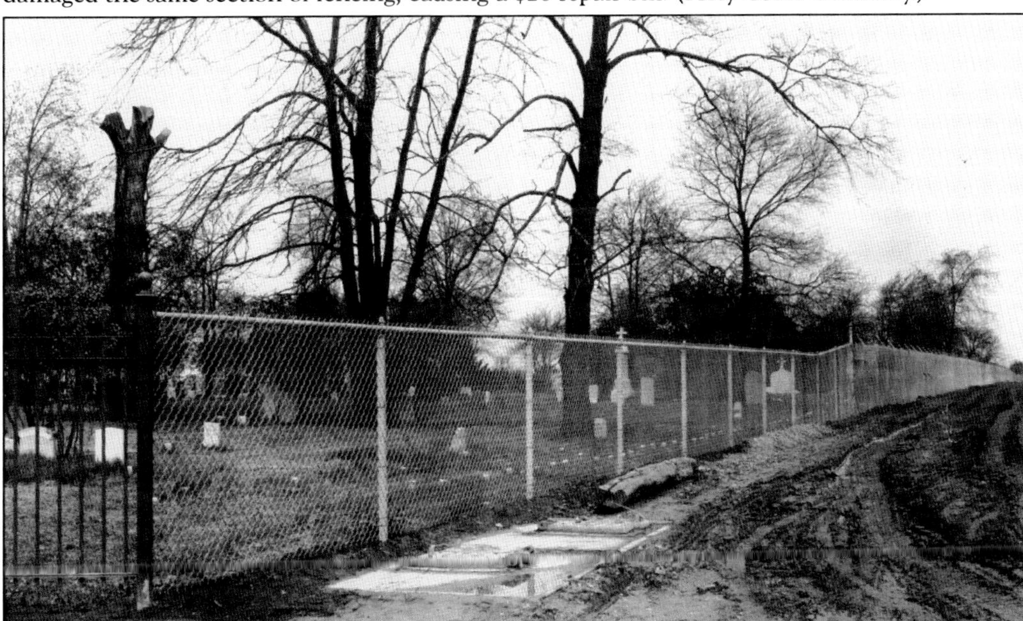

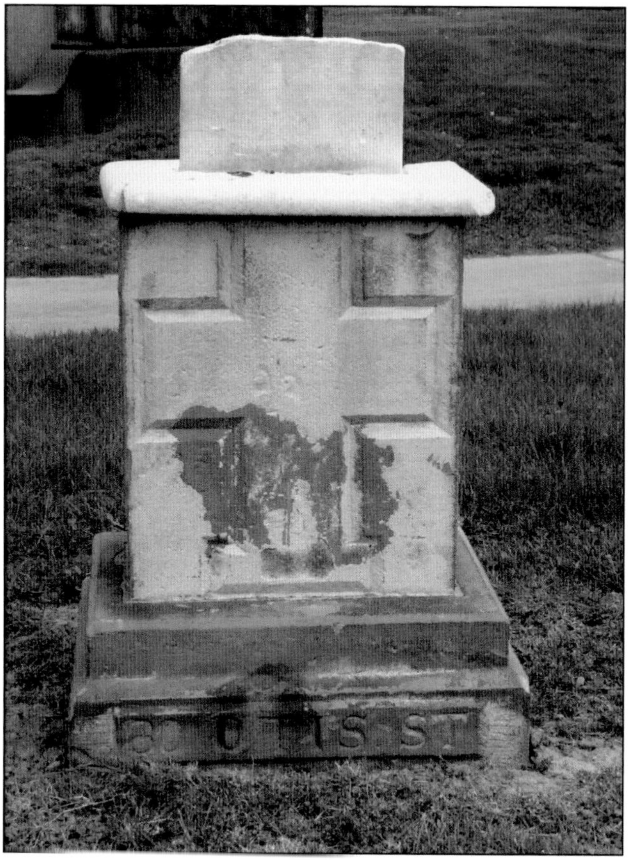

Two of the oddest stones in the cemetery belong to Maria Szembara and Ceslaus Strugala, both located in section B. Szembara's stone has "30 Otis St" engraved on the bottom, while Strugala's stone reads "Otis St 30." Szembara and Strugala never lived at 30 Otis Street, a boardinghouse, nor did any of their family. Szembara, an immigrant from Budapest, Hungary, died on September 12, 1903, at 18 years of age; Strugala, a native of Poland, died on June 22, 1905, at 37 years old. The Szembara and Strugala families shared no lineage, and most likely did not know each other. The answer to this riddle lies in that construction on 30 Otis Street began in 1899, and was purchased on July 13, 1900, at the time of completion. The 30 Otis Street stones marked the location of the house on lot 63 before construction and were repurposed as headstone bases when no longer needed on the construction site.

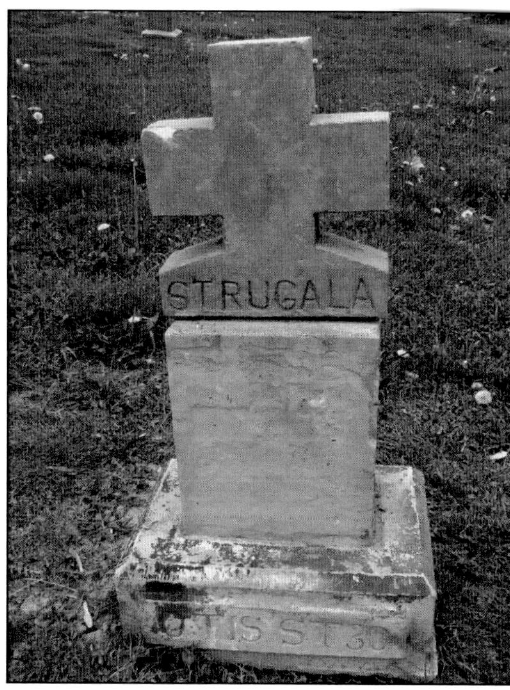

In 1869, at the remarkable age of 14, Dennis Mullane immigrated to the United States alone, leaving the rest of his family behind, to make a new life for himself in a new land. He met and married a Canadian Irish woman named Hannah Sullivan and settled in Detroit. Dennis found employment with the Detroit, Grand Haven and Milwaukee Railway Company.

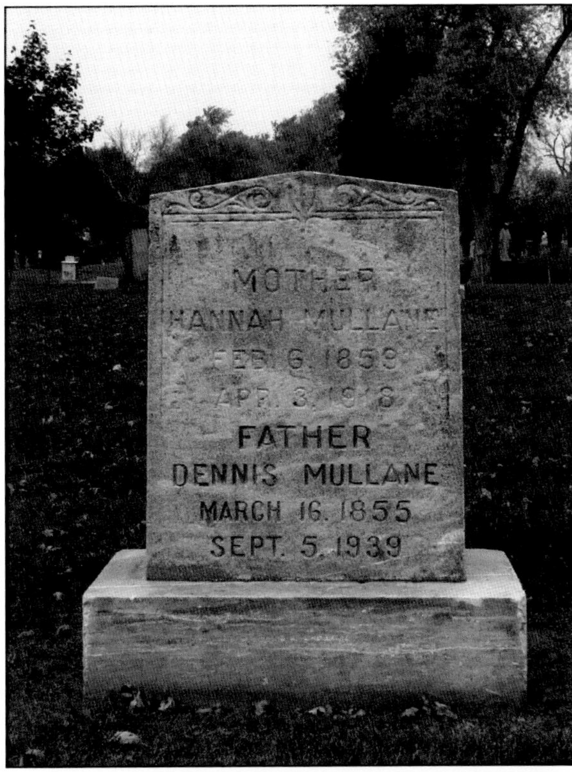

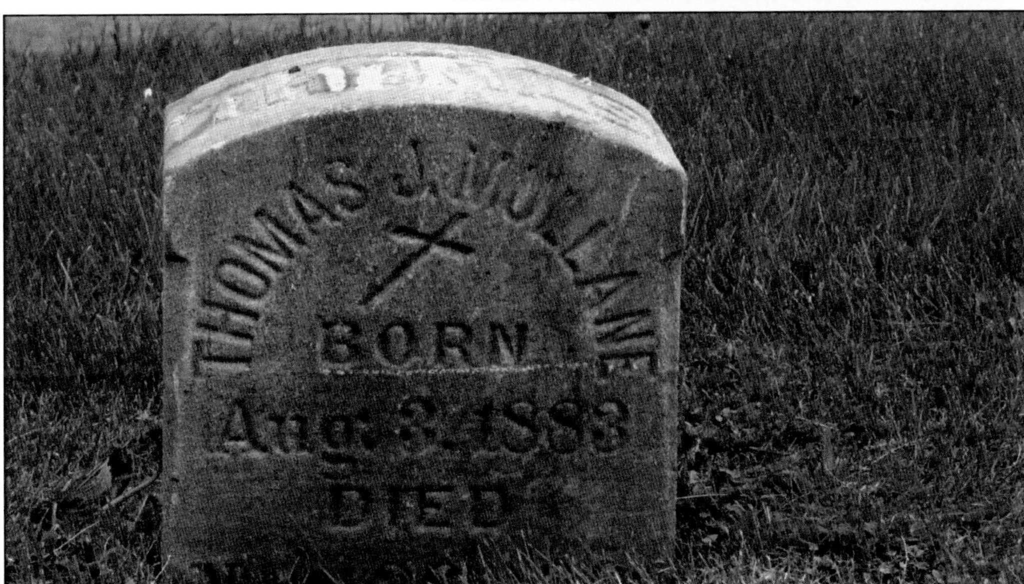

Thomas Mullane, the eldest child of Dennis and Hannah, worked at Penberthy Injector Works at the corner of Abbott Street and Brooklyn Avenue. At 9:30 a.m. on November 26, 1901, a massive boiler explosion obliterated the building killing 30 men. City employees and 200 volunteers worked late into the night removing charred bodies and wreckage, but it was not until the next day that Thomas's parents were able to identify their son. He is buried in section B near his parents.

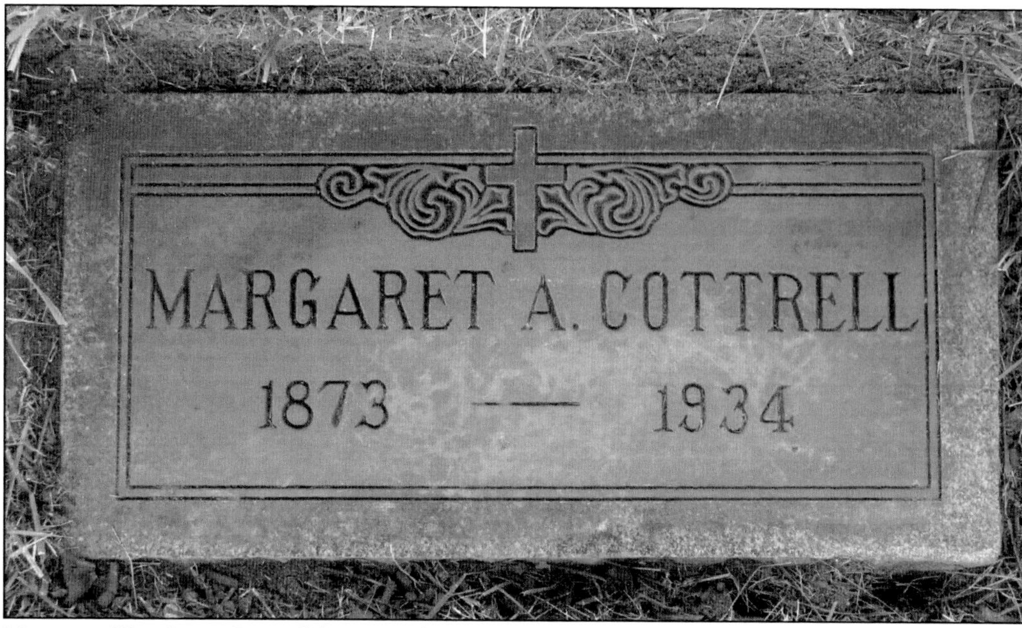

Margaret Kleinhaus Cottrell became the first sacristan at Holy Redeemer Church, tending to the altar linens and coordinating the women volunteers. Because of that duty, she was the first woman married inside the altar rail at the church. On October 7, 1934, a patrol car on its way to another accident struck and killed Cottrell as she was crossing Junction Avenue on her way to church. She is buried in section B. (William McAskin.)

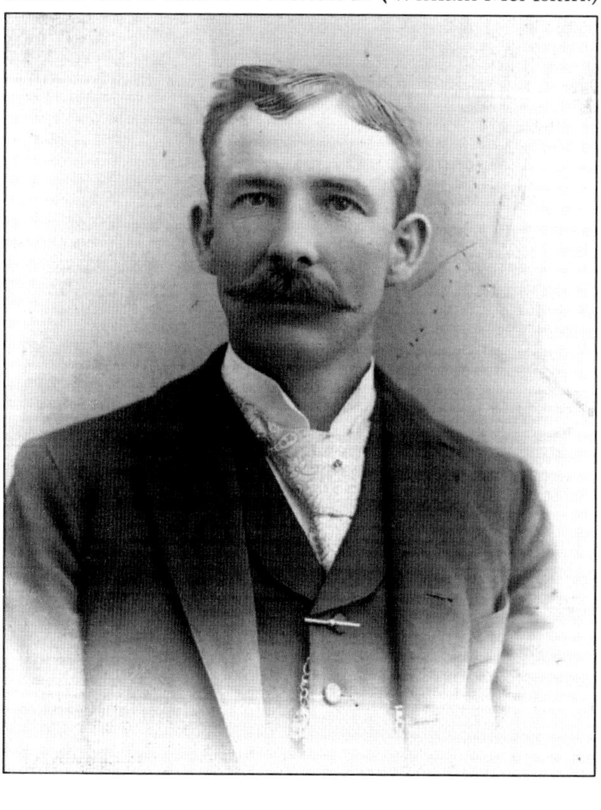

After the death of his wife, Margaret, William Cottrell moved into the home of his son, Wilson. Every school day in 1934, William walked his granddaughter home from kindergarten at Guest School to keep the WPA men working on nearby Calfonte Street from stopping work to lean on their picks and shovels and watch her walk past. William died on February 13, 1938, and is buried near his wife. (William McAskin.)

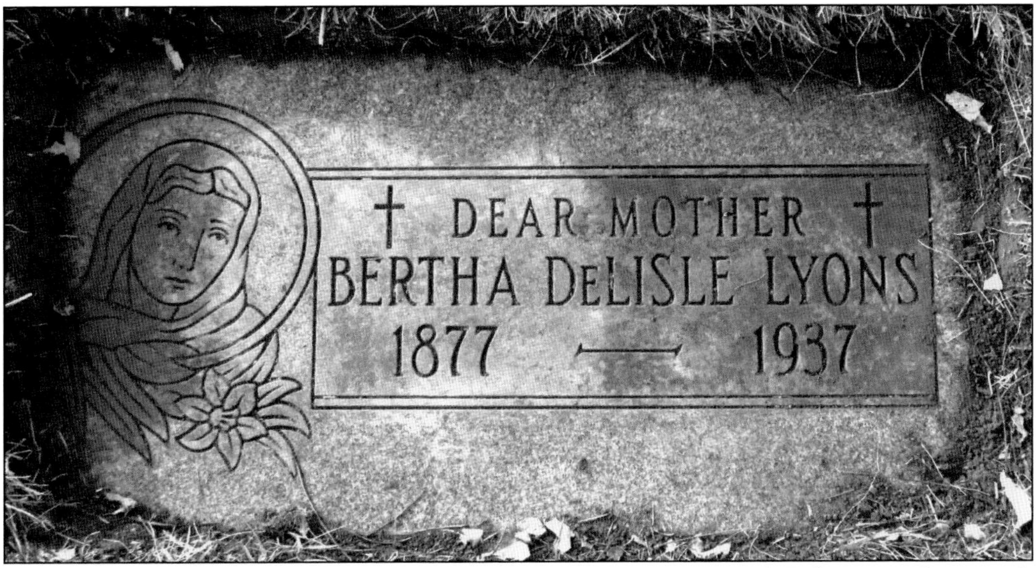

Nicknamed the "Belle of Delray," Bertha DeLisle Lyons captivated Delray's residents with her beauty and enchanting soprano singing. Her endearing qualities led her to win many beauty contests. Bertha met her husband, Michael Lyons, at All Saints' Church where both were members of the choir. Against her parents' wishes, they married at the same church on Thanksgiving Day, 1900. Michael died tragically in 1930, the result of a streetcar accident. They are buried in section H.

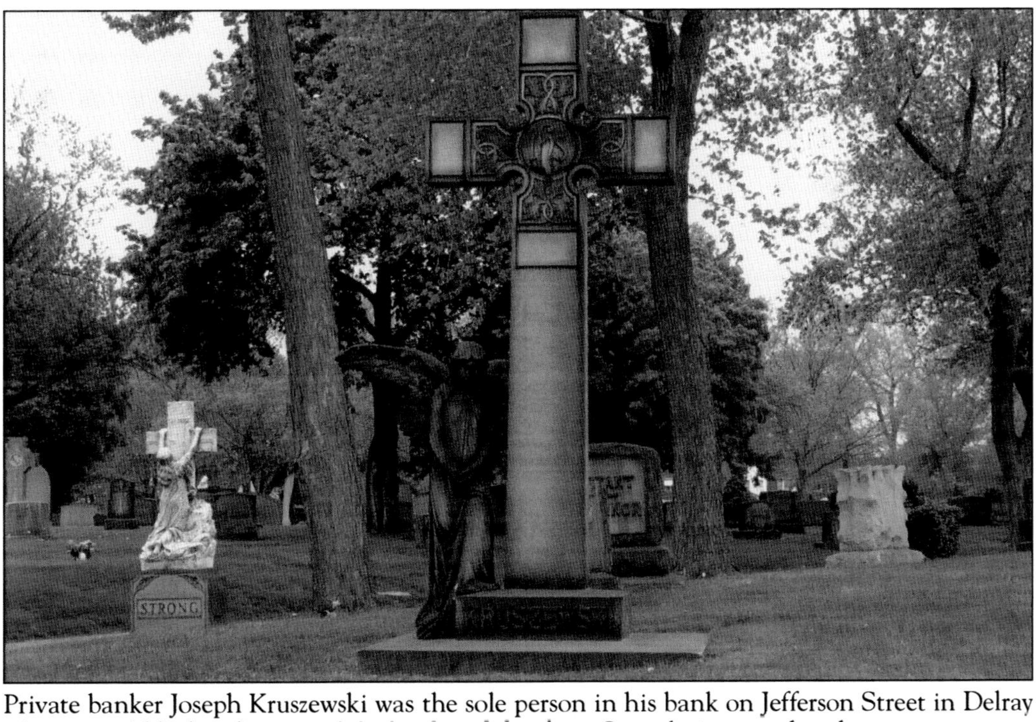

Private banker Joseph Kruszewski was the sole person in his bank on Jefferson Street in Delray when a would-be bandit entered the bank and shot him. Speculation was that the perpetrator was a disgruntled young man who grew angry over Kruszewski's advice to his much older and wealthy new bride to stop such lavish spending on him. The Kruszewski monument is in section D.

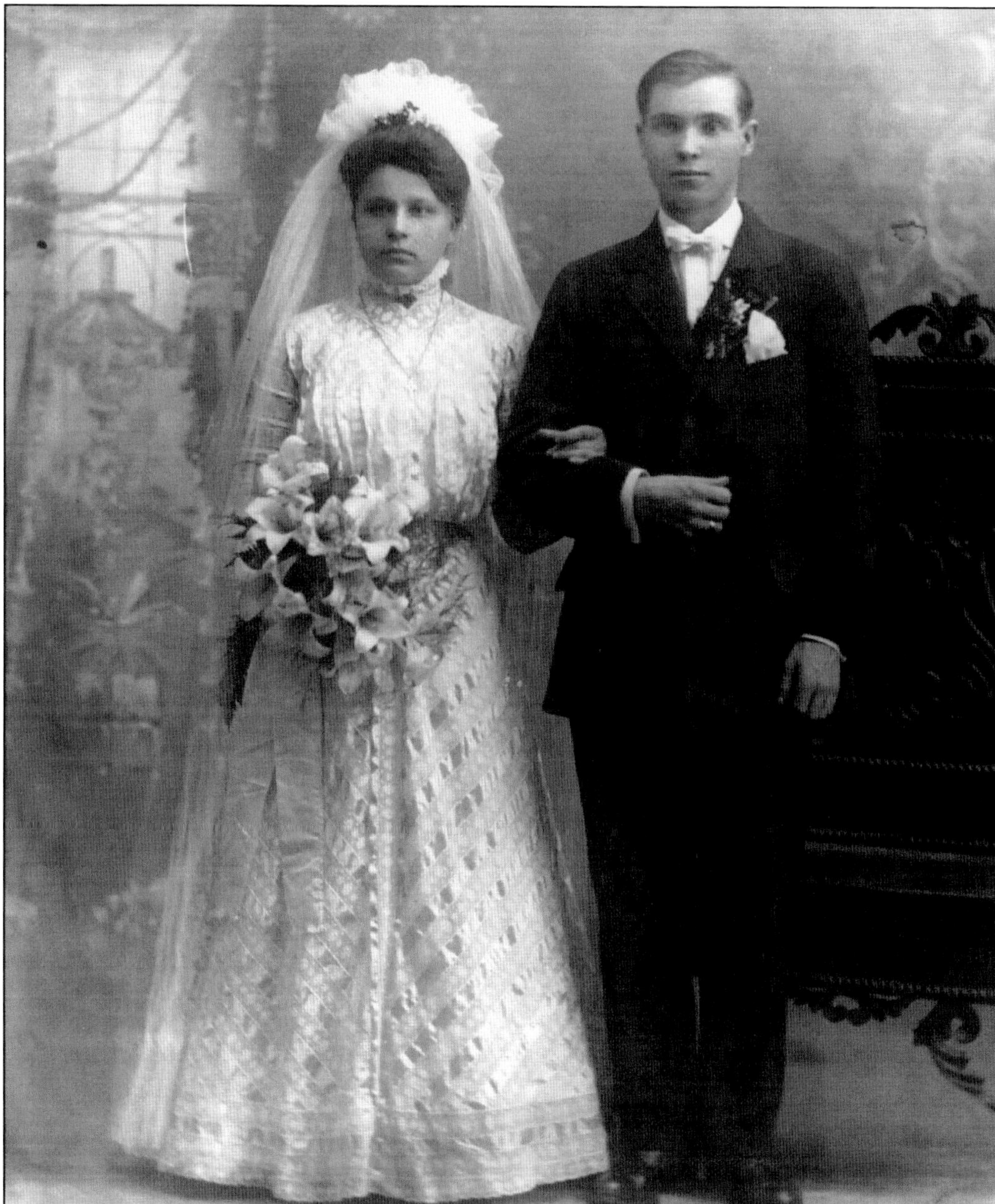

After Joseph Sitek and Katharzyna Kucyba married in 1909, they lived on Chopin Street in Detroit. They referred to their backyard as the "farm," consisting of a pear tree, a chicken coop, and vegetables. Like so many immigrants, they tried to re-create their former country lifestyle of back home into the makeup of a large city. Joseph and Katharzyna had three sons who served in World War II: Walter became a prisoner of war, captured at the Battle of the Bulge; Stanley was part of the U.S. Coast Guard's landing of Saipan; and Anthony was wounded twice in the European Theater. Joseph died from a heart attack while at work at the Ford Rouge Plant. His family laid out his body in front of a large window at the front of their home. Neighbors passed by on the front porch to pay their respects, while family came inside. They are buried in section T. (Robert Brescoll.)

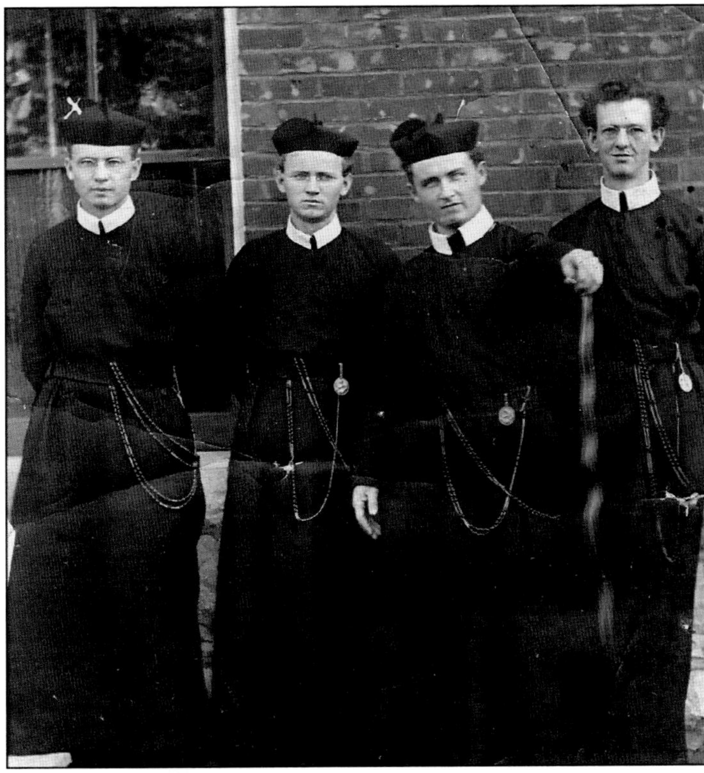

Fr. Andrew Browne (left) is one of the 138 Redemptorist priests buried at the cemetery. His appointments repetitively sent him to several cities, including four times to Detroit during his career. In 1918, Father Browne pleaded for permission to serve as chaplain during World War I, and once granted, he served in the U.S. Army for six months. He rests in section H. (Terri Johnson.)

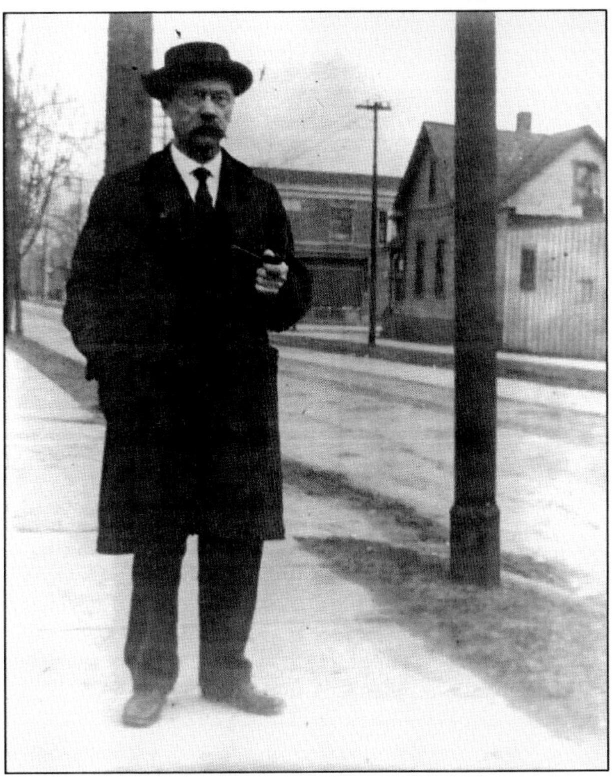

Following an old French custom, John Rousseau always celebrated New Year's Day dressed in his Sunday best and top hat, visiting neighbors from house to house for a drink to cheer in the new year. As a skilled carpenter, John carved wooden bells, a crucifix, and a communion railing at St. Anne Church that bears his name. (Gloria Kaier Rousseaux.)

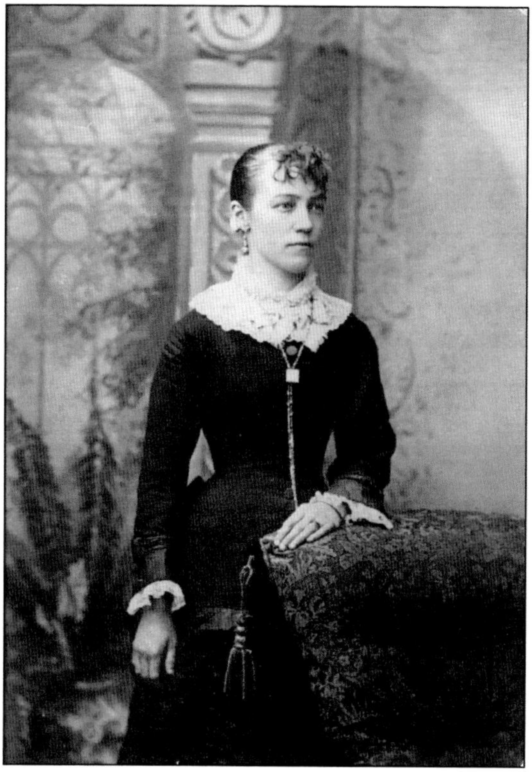

Lydia Filteau was born on August 13, 1862, to a Parisian sea captain who emigrated from France to Quebec where Lydia was born. She married John Rousseau at St. Anne Church in 1882. Lydia and John are buried in section J. (Gloria Kaier Rousseaux.)

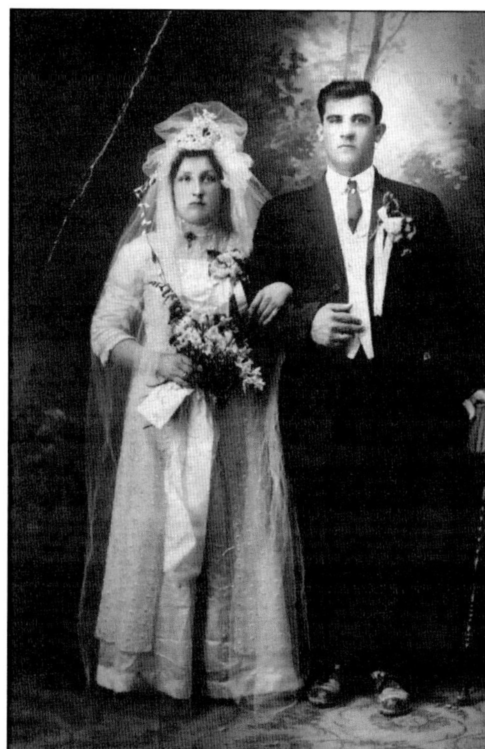

In 1911, Jovan Uglasich married Ludwika Czarnota. He was an immigrant from Serbia, and she was from Poland. Jovan was at work at the Ford Rouge Plant's steel foundry when molten sparks flew into his face, causing the loss of his left ear and sight in one eye. Jovan is buried in section S. (Nancy Dietz.)

Jovan and Ludwika had seven children. The three youngest, from left to right, Stephen, Stella, and Nellie, are standing in front of the family home on Waldo Street in southwest Detroit. A number of years later, Stephen tragically lost his life on the Fourth of July weekend. He is buried in section H. (Nancy Dietz.)

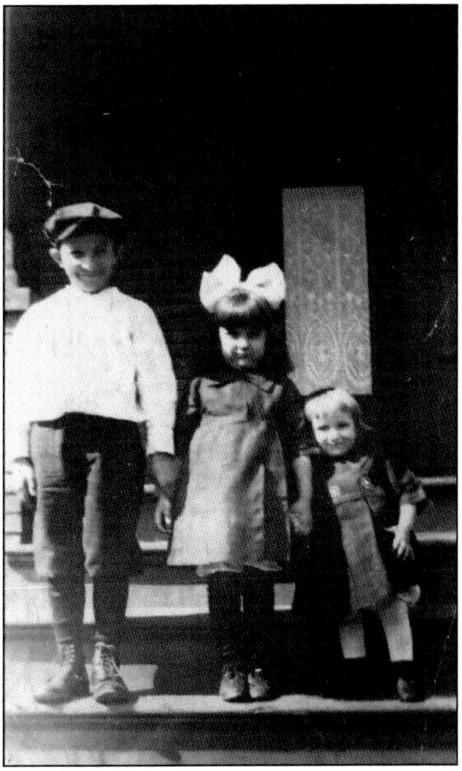

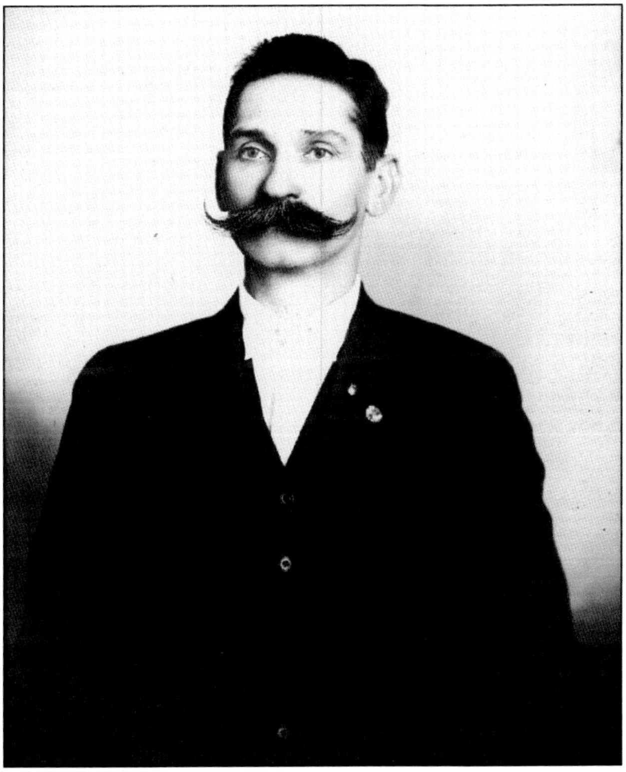

Stanley Skiba married Ludwika's sister Catherine Czarnota. Like many Polish immigrants, he settled in Hamtramck and worked at the Dodge Brothers automobile factory. On Christmas Eve 1955, an automobile struck and killed Stanley as he crossed Michigan Avenue near Junction Street. He is buried in section S. (Nancy Dietz.)

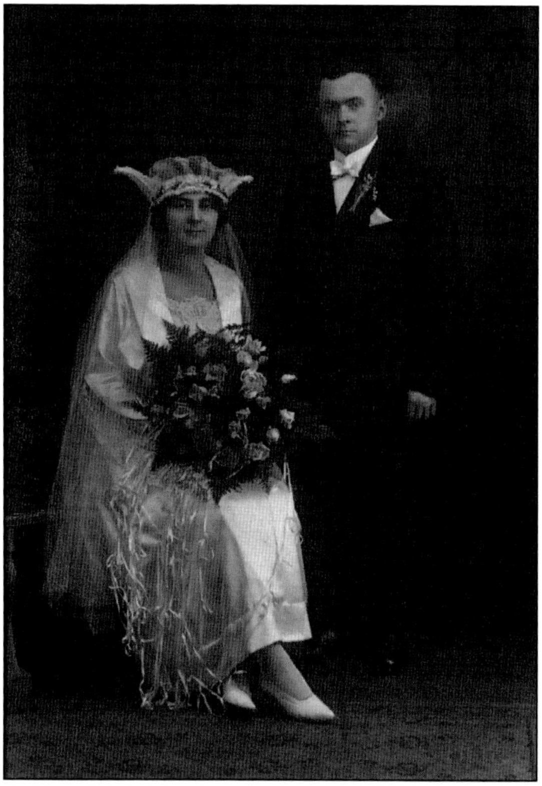

Joseph Kuszynski met his second wife, Lottie Konicki, at St. Francis D' Assisi Church where he played the violin and she sang in the choir. Joseph worked for J. L. Hudson as a printer and later worked for Gregory, Mayer, and Thon. They married in 1919. (Loraine Rzanca.)

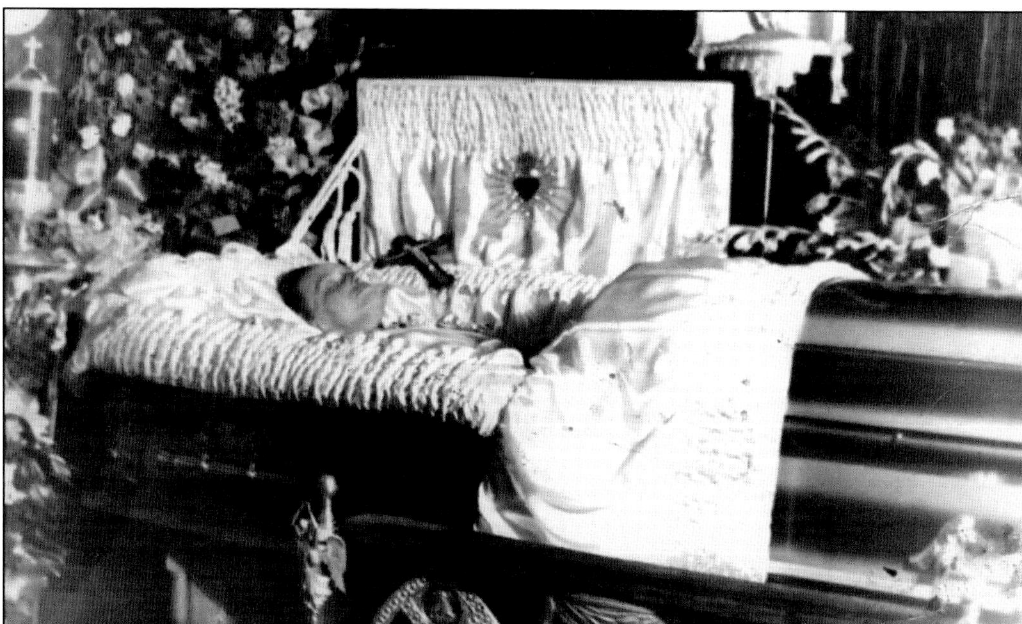

Like many men in the area, Julianna Klecha's husband, John, worked for the brickyards, first as a wagon driver and later as a truck driver. They lived on Wesson Avenue, down the street from Julianna's sister who married John's brother. Julianna was a widow for 19 years before she died on February 13, 1939, at the age of 51. She is buried in section H. (Sharon Dancer.)

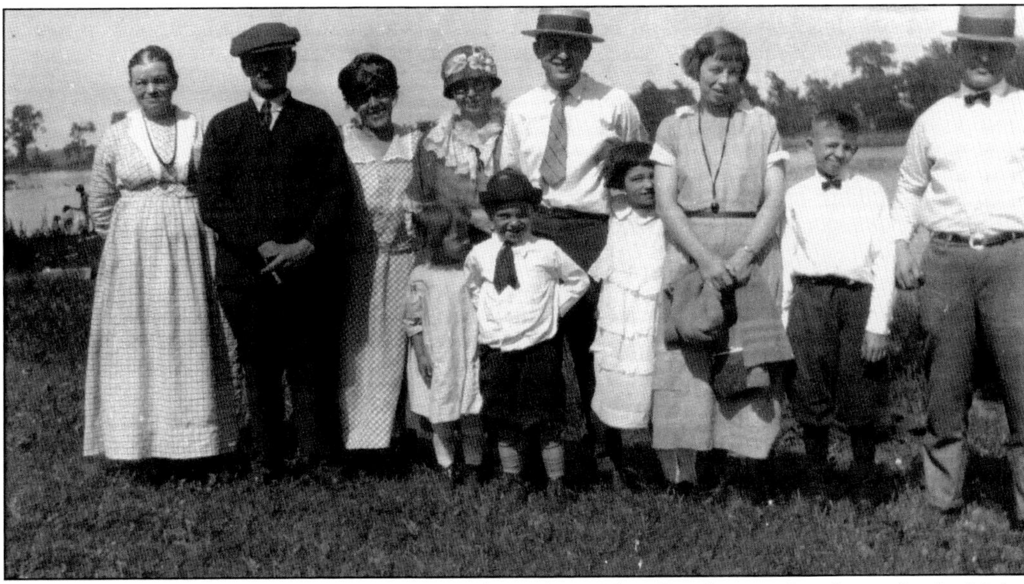

The cemetery became an unusual matchmaker when Alois Reszke met his future bride, Helen Oleynik, when both families would visit their respective family lots located adjacent to each other in section G. They married in 1926. Prior to the nuptials, Alois (fifth from left) posed for this family photograph in 1924. Alois died young, at age 37, and is buried in the Reszke family lot. (Loraine Rzanca.)

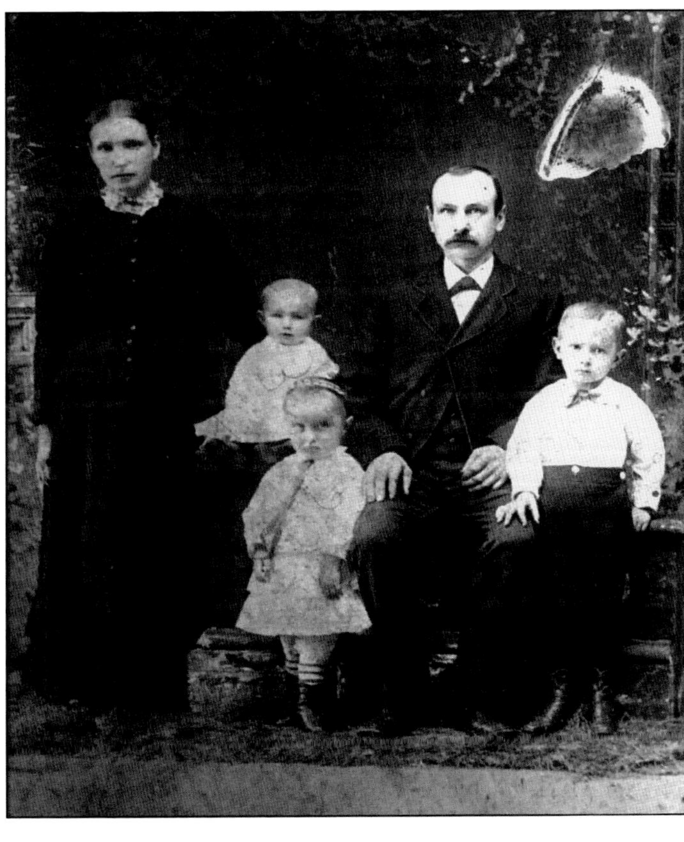

Anthony and Mary Gaffke are posing with their three young children, John (far right), Anna (standing), and Julianna (sitting). Both Anna and Julianna married brothers August and John Kelcha. Anna and August are buried in section U, and John and Julianna are buried in section H. (Sharon Dancer.)

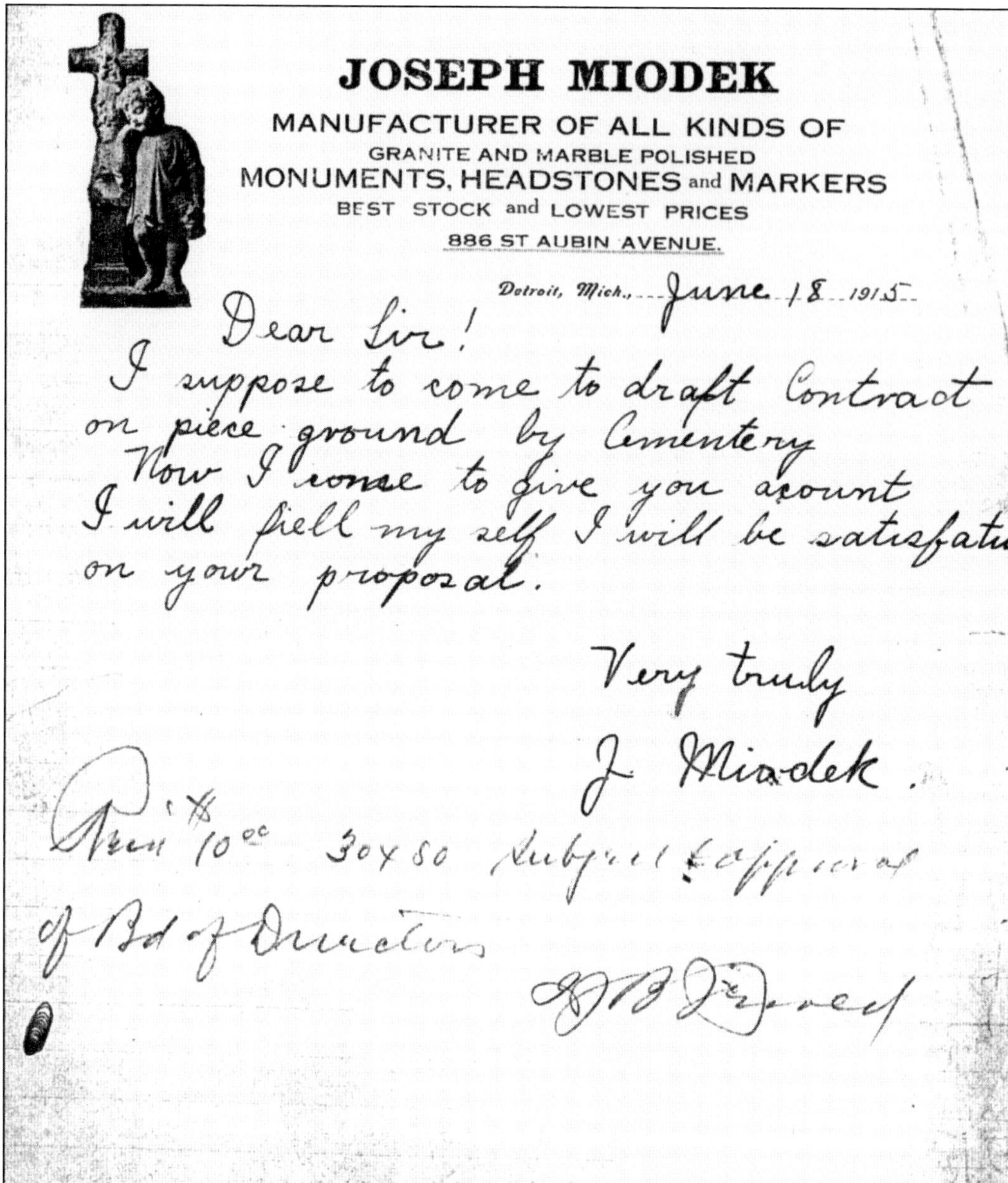

JOSEPH MIODEK

MANUFACTURER OF ALL KINDS OF
GRANITE AND MARBLE POLISHED
MONUMENTS, HEADSTONES and MARKERS
BEST STOCK and LOWEST PRICES
886 ST AUBIN AVENUE.

Detroit, Mich., June 18 1915

Dear Sir!
I suppose to come to draft Contract
on piece ground by Cementery
Now I conse to give you acount
I will fiell my self I will be satisfatio
on your proposal.

Very truly
J. Miodek.

Rent 10.00 30x50 subject to approval
of Bd of Directors
[illegible]

Joseph Miodek's growing monuments and headstones business outgrew his St. Aubin Avenue address, so in 1915, he rented cemetery land, including a barn, located south of Dix Road. After Miodek moved out, the cemetery used the barn for equipment storage. Since the low-lying land frequently flooded, making it unusable for burials, the cemetery sold it to the City of Detroit but rented the barn for $15 a month to house equipment. In March 1927, the city sent the cemetery a notice to terminate tenancy, asking them to vacate the barn that they recently purchased at a condemnation sale. The cemetery asked for and received a 60-day extension in order to build a new barn on higher ground north of Dix Road, which it did using the old barn wood. The commission of parks and boulevards turned the land south of Dix Road into Patton Park. (Holy Cross Cemetery.)

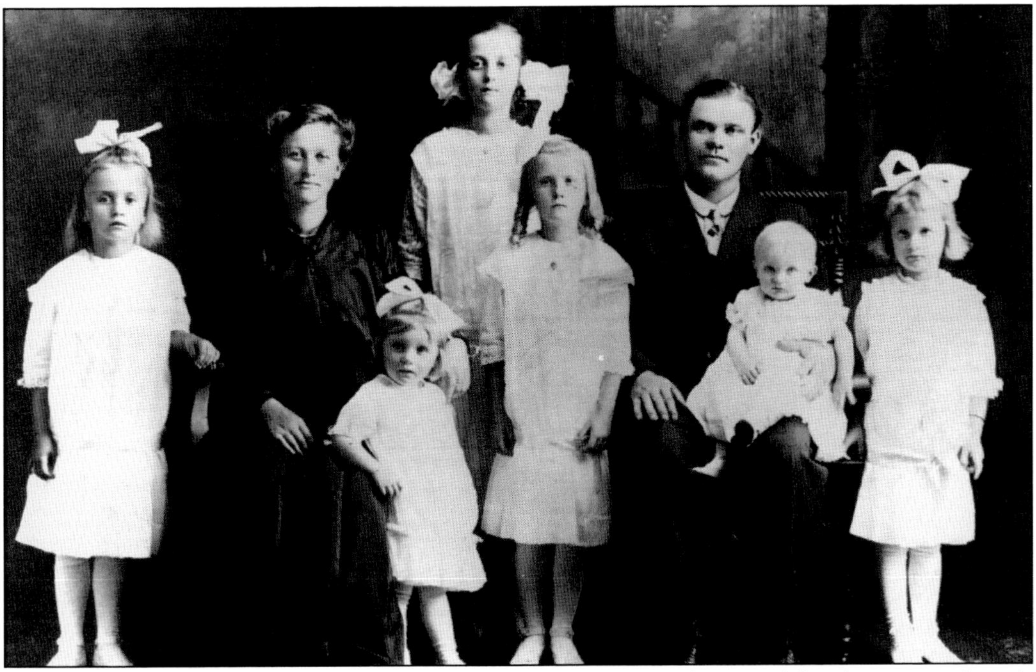

Pauline and Joseph Michalak and their six children are sitting for a 1915 family portrait. Joseph worked as a supervisor for Mercier and Larkins Brickyard. During World War II, construction of the I-94 expressway sliced through the middle of the brickyard, and construction workers, in a grand manner, blew up the landmark smokestack to make room. Pauline and Joseph are buried in section C. (Kenneth Michalak.)

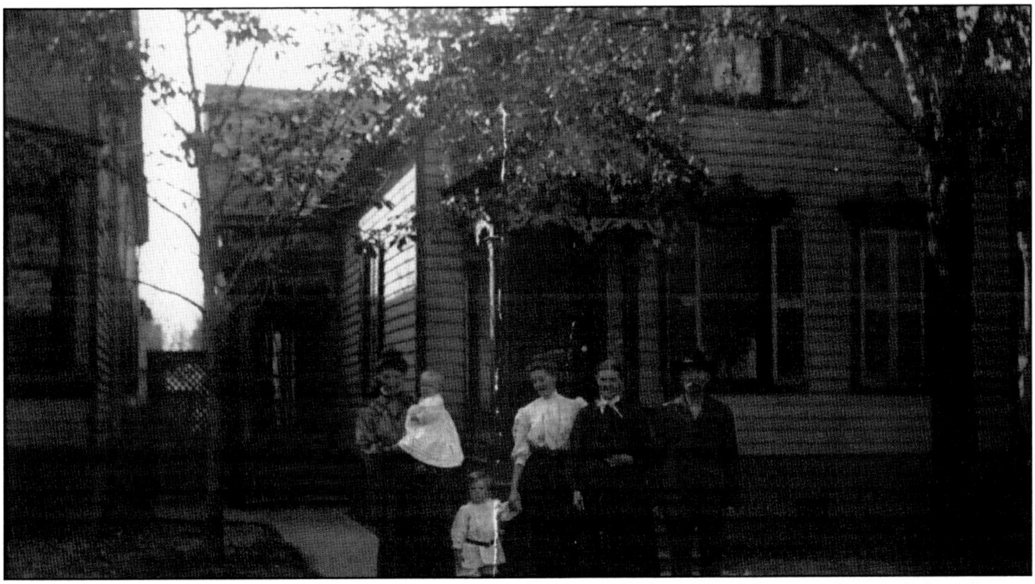

Polish immigrants Michalina and Felix Bydlowska (far right) are standing in front of their home on Tillman Street in Detroit. Michalina started a long tradition when she gave birth to twin boys in 1870. Later her daughter Frances also had twin boys. Frances's daughter Gurtie had twins, as did Gurtie's daughter Constance. Constance's daughter Lori became the fifth generation to give birth to twins. (Lori Beaty.)

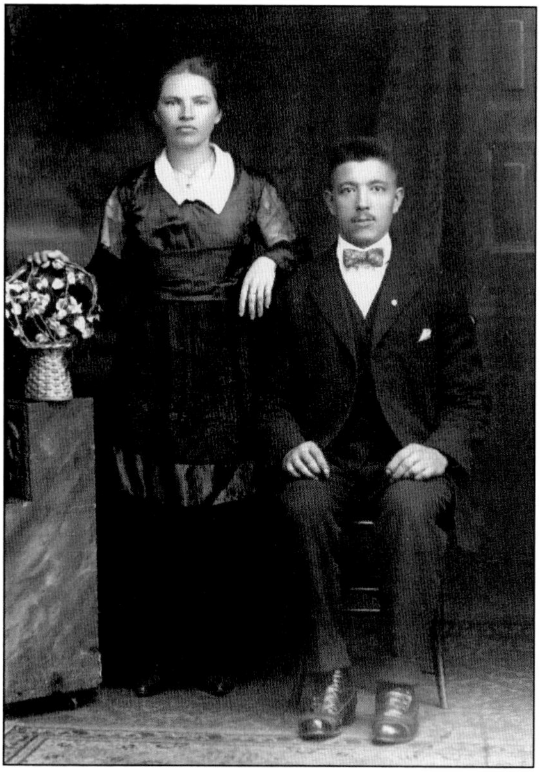

Maryianna Kapica and Stanislaw Golomb, both Polish immigrants, are posing for their 1915 wedding portrait. Stanislaw was working as a paver for Julius Porath Company, a highway contractor, when a steam shovel beheaded him in 1924. Stanislaw is buried in section P, Maryianna in section H. (Anthony Tardif.)

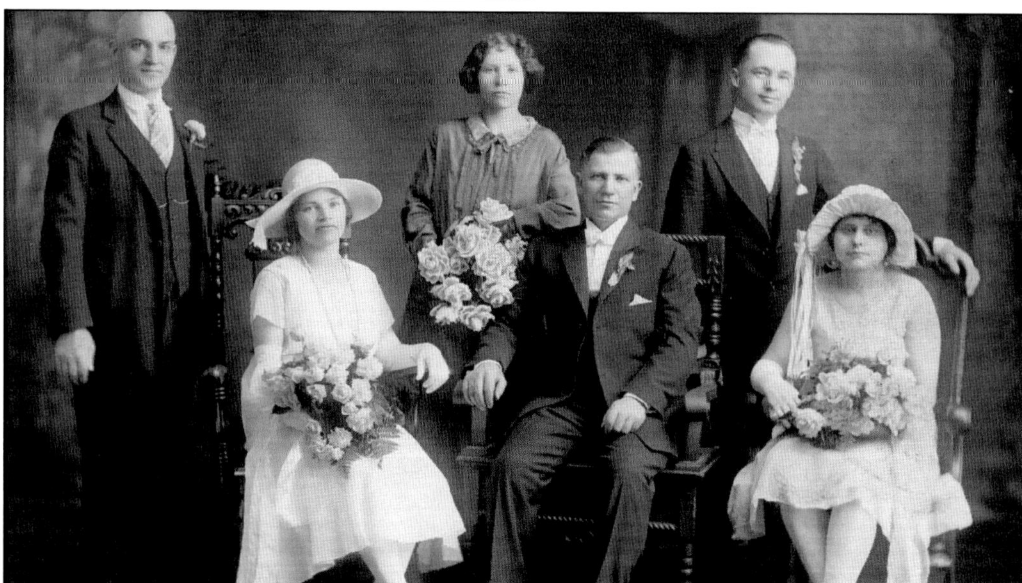

After Stanislaw's death, Maryianna (sitting left) married Jacob Sarna (sitting middle), another Polish immigrant, shown here for their 1926 wedding portrait. Jacob died on Christmas day in 1932, leaving Maryianna to raise their five children alone. Maryianna found a part-time job as a meat trimmer at Hygrade but lost her job after returning from a 1959 visit to relatives in Poland. Unable to afford a headstone for Jacob, Maryianna's daughter and son paid for the stone 50 years after Jacob's death. (Anthony Tardif.)

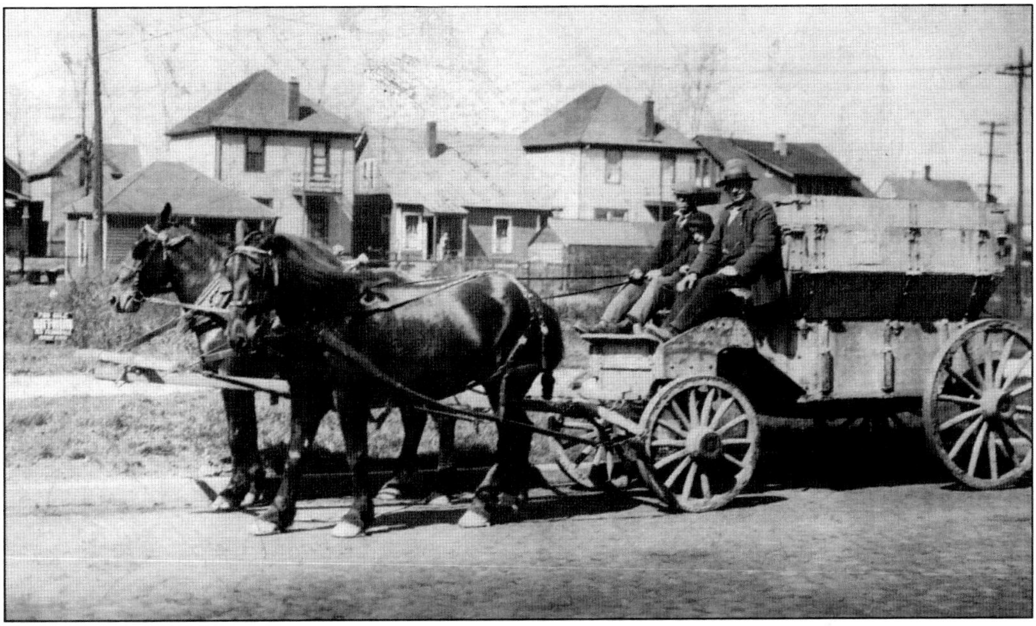

The industry boom was taking hold in 1917 at the time of this photograph, yet farms still dotted the area. Charles Kaier (right) is hauling a load of grain on cobblestoned Fort Street in his drop cart. A pull lever on the rider's side opened the bottom, dropping out the load. The "for sale" sign at the left is from William Hoffmann's realty located on Ferndale Street. Charles is buried in section B. (Gloria Kaier Rousseaux.)

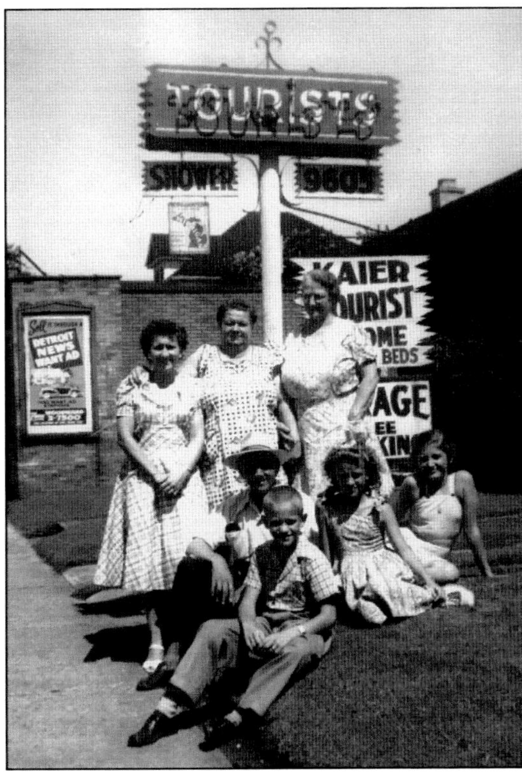

Charles and his wife, Odelie (standing, top right), ran a tourist home on West Fort Street across from Woodmere Cemetery. The tourist home bustled with businessmen and guests all year long but after World War II fell out of favor to the more trendy hotels. Odelie was 86 years old when she died in 1975. She is buried in section J. (Gloria Kaier Rousseaux.)

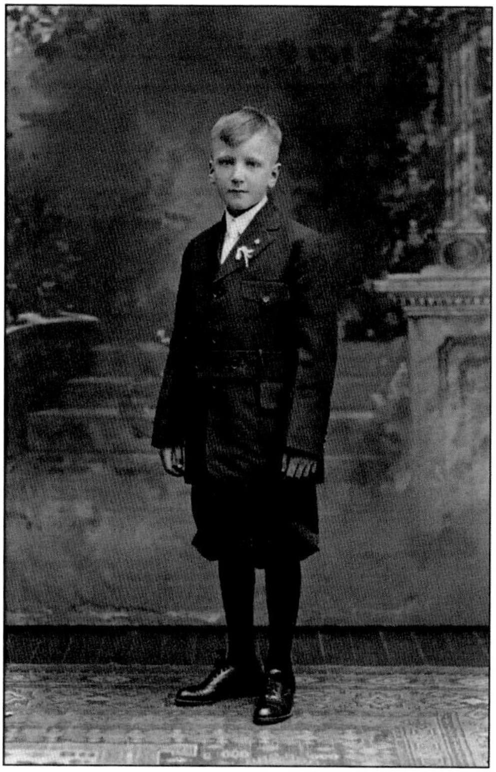

Harry Kaier was an avid duck hunter who hand-carved over 300 duck decoys that he toted with him while hunting. During one such trip, Harry's unfortunate hand placement over the gun barrel resulted in the loss of some fingers. He worked for Detroit breweries Stroh's, Ekhardt and Becker, Johnny Pfeiffer, and retired from Budweiser Company. Kaier was 66 years old when he died in 1974. He is buried in section J. (Gloria Kaier Rousseaux.)

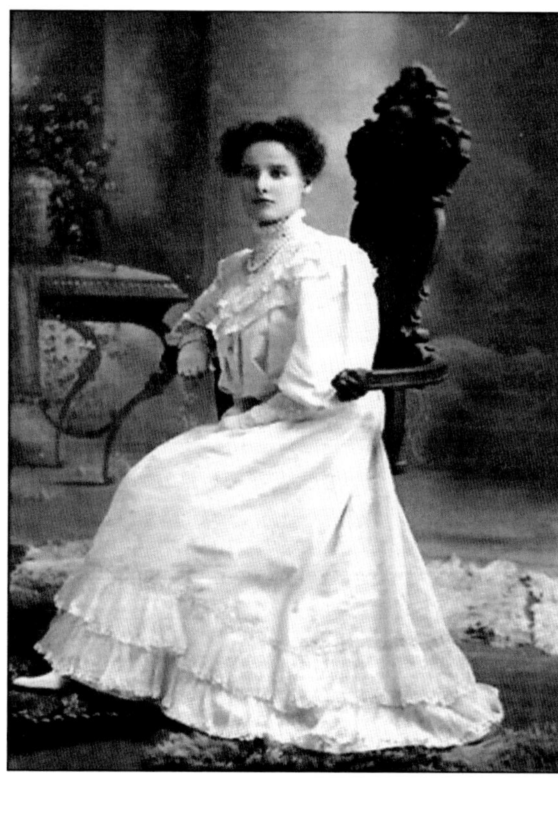

Nellie Lesniak is sitting for her November 16, 1908, wedding portrait. She went on to have 10 children, 3 of whom died at just months old: Charlie, Gertrude, and Rose lie in unmarked graves. Nellie was a remarkable woman, speaking five languages, but once she arrived in the United States from her home in Lutzca, Galicia, she never left the country. (Sharon Dancer.)

Ellen Maloney, the daughter of John and Mary Maloney and wife of George Beaulieu, gave birth to son Robert on December 17, 1913, at Detroit's Providence Hospital with the distinction of being both the first mother and child to survive a C-section birth at that hospital. Ellen and her husband, George, are buried in section C. (Shelia Beaubien.)

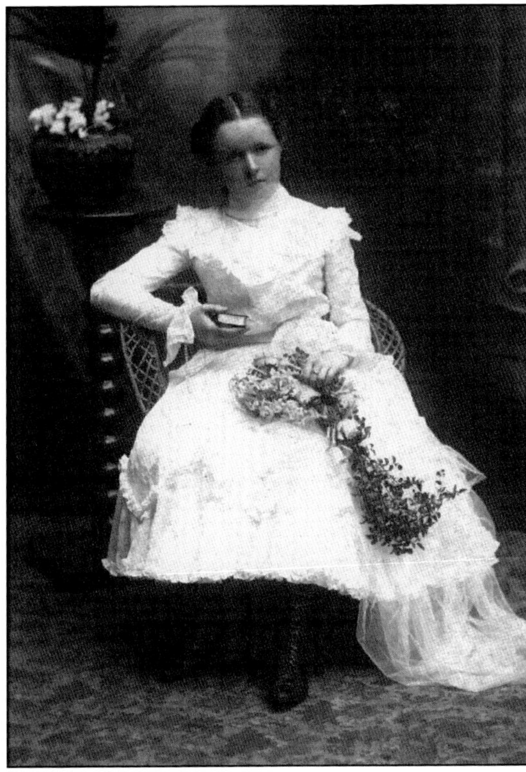

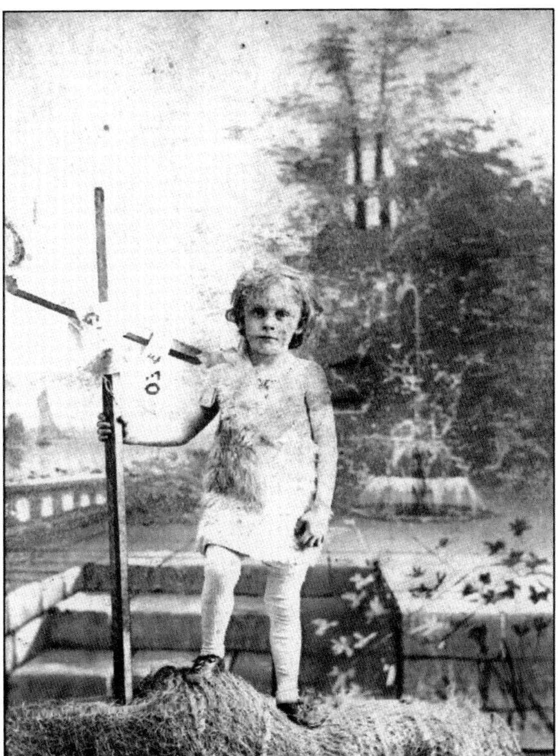

George worked for Ford Motor Company where he befriended Pete Martin, Henry Ford's first vice president. George was the best man in Martin's 1904 wedding. George is pictured here dressed as John the Baptist for his First Holy Communion. George is buried in section C. (Shelia Beaubien.)

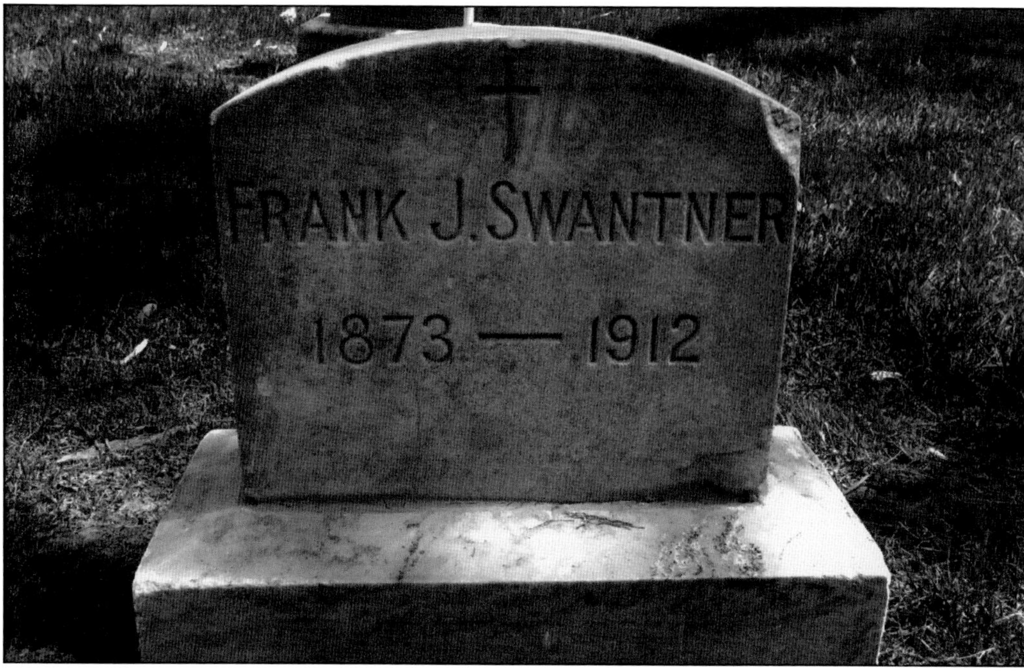

As a young man, Frank Swantner worked for Michigan Stove Works on Jefferson Avenue. When his son, Edward, was older, he opened a tire business, and together the two of them developed the retread tire for semi-trucks. Unfortunately, someone stole the patent; hence Frank and Edward never received pecuniary gain or recognition for their invention. Frank died on May 17, 1912, and is buried in section K.

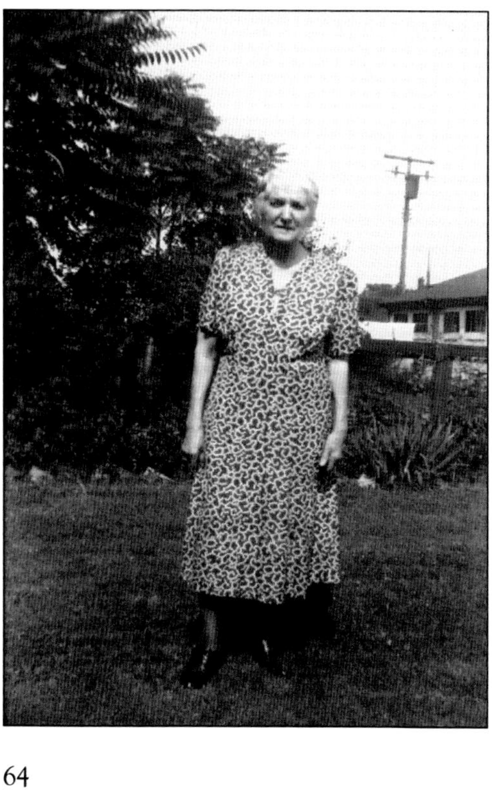

When Margaret Rhode, Emma Swantner's sister, immigrated to the United States in 1891, she wished to bring Emma with her. Emma, without money for her ticket yet eager to make the voyage, allowed her sister to pay her fare for passage, knowing that Margaret's intention was for Emma to work as a lady of the evening to reimburse her for the ticket. Emma accepted the plan but had no desire to follow through with it. Once in the United States, she chose to clean houses instead. Emma is buried in section N. (Carol Swantner.)

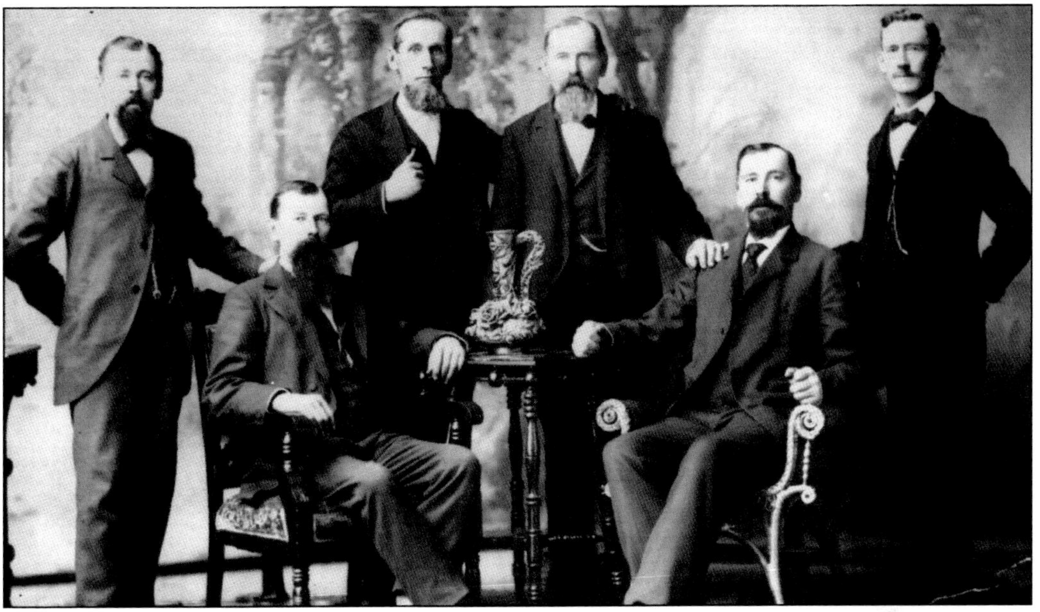

The Esper family was among the first to settle in the area known as Springwells. Jacob Esper emigrated from Prussia with his parents Peter and Catherine in 1842. Peter offered his home for the first mass held in the area and in 1846 donated land to build a German Catholic school in northeast Dearborn near Warren Avenue. Six sons of Peter Esper are, seen here from left to right, Anthony, John, Peter, Jacob, Matthias, and Michael. Jacob is buried in section C. (Lori Katona.)

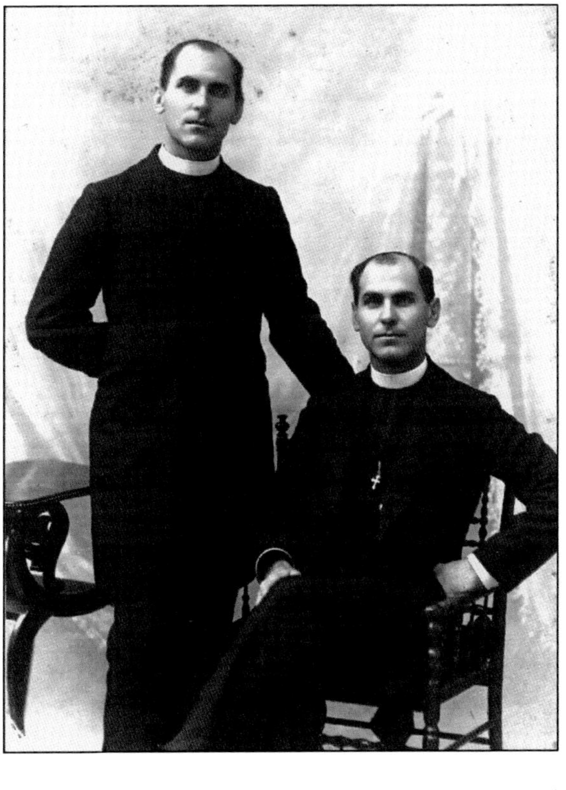

The twin sons of Jacob Esper, Peter and Michael, vowed at their first communion to become priests and were subsequently ordained on the same day in 1894. Father Peter founded St. Gabriel Church in 1915 and served there until his death in 1936. Father Michael steadfastly moved St. Boniface Church into an English-speaking parish. He died of a heart attack on the 37th anniversary of his first mass. Both share a monument and are buried in section C. (Lori Katona.)

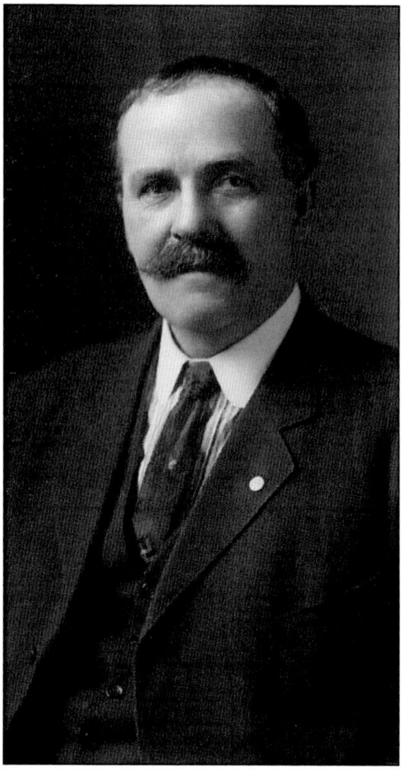

The abundant lacustrine clay found in Springwells gave rise to a multitude of brickyards. Timothy Burns and his brother ran a profitable brickyard, the Burns Brothers Brickyard. Eventually it grew to include Simon O'Shea and was renamed Burns and O'Shea Brick Company. Burns ran for alderman in Detroit. He died in 1917 at 60 years old and is buried in section B. (John Graf.)

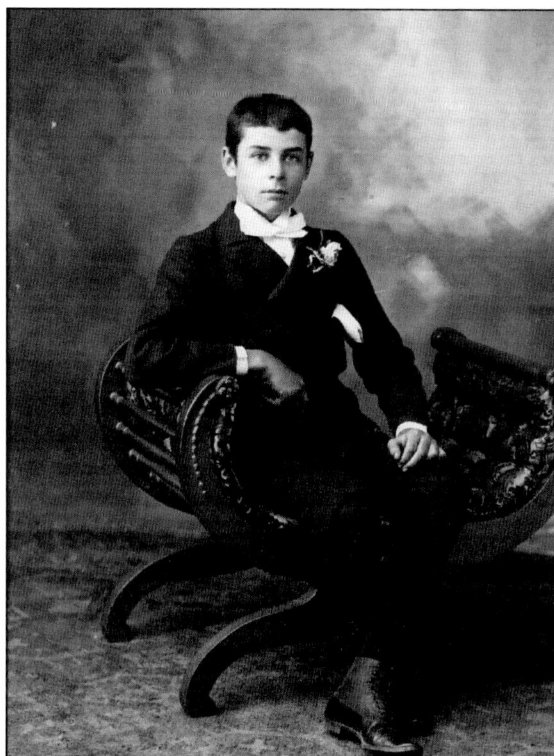

Edward Burns is sitting for this photograph in preparation for his confirmation that took place at Holy Redeemer Church. He later married Madge Doyle and began work as a stationary engineer. He traveled from location to location, maintaining the boilers that provided steam heat for buildings in Detroit and environs. He and his wife are buried in section C. (John Graf.)

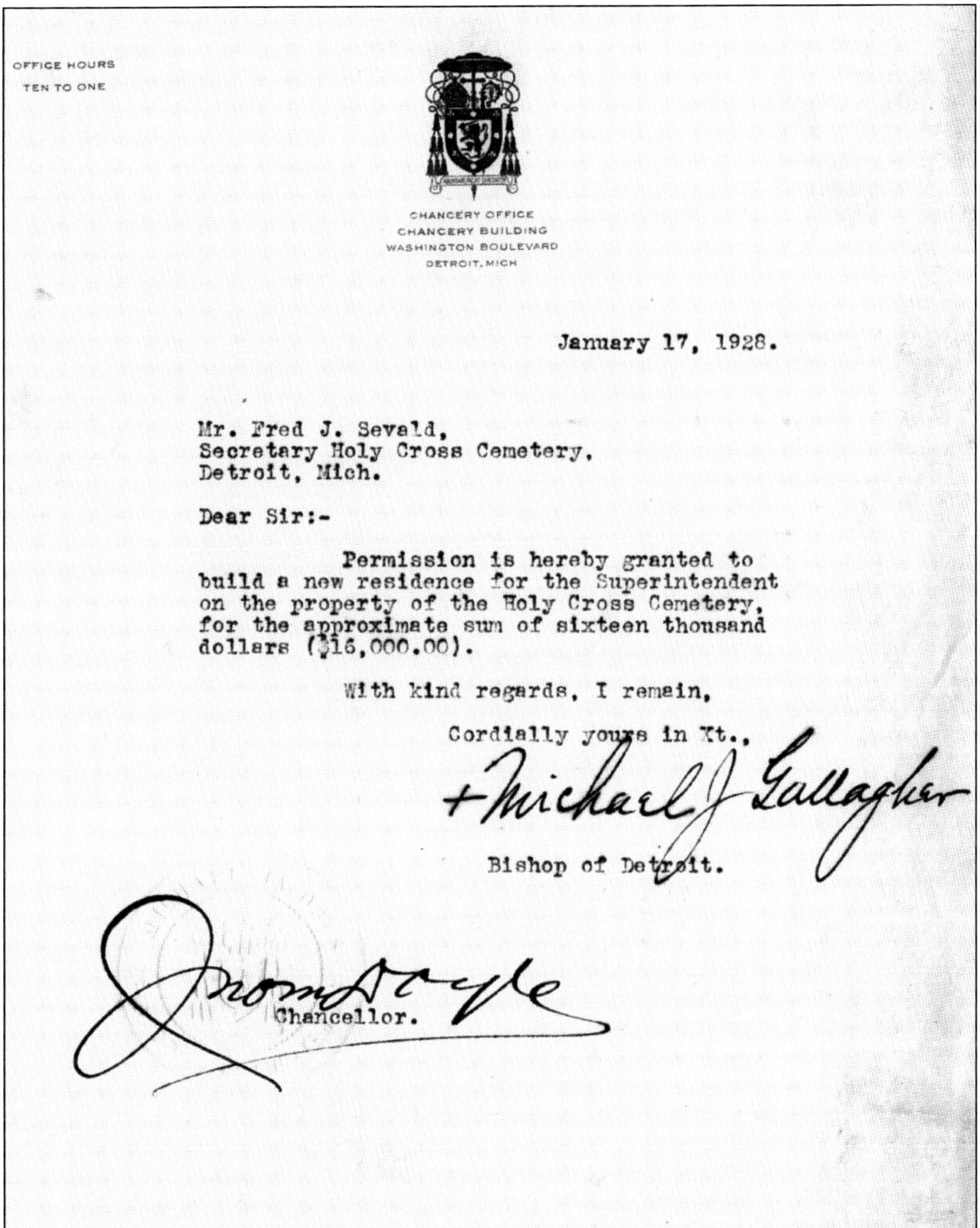

OFFICE HOURS
TEN TO ONE

CHANCERY OFFICE
CHANCERY BUILDING
WASHINGTON BOULEVARD
DETROIT, MICH

January 17, 1928.

Mr. Fred J. Sevald,
Secretary Holy Cross Cemetery,
Detroit, Mich.

Dear Sir:-

Permission is hereby granted to build a new residence for the Superintendent on the property of the Holy Cross Cemetery, for the approximate sum of sixteen thousand dollars ($16,000.00).

With kind regards, I remain,

Cordially yours in Xt.,

+Michael J Gallagher

Bishop of Detroit.

Jno M Doyle
Chancellor.

After building the office and comfort station in 1923, the association realized the need for new, up-to-date living quarters for the superintendant. Previously farmhouses located on cemetery property acted as cemetery office and housing for the superintendant, but the buildings were old and not suitable in juxtaposition to the new office. In January 1928, Bishop Gallagher signed this letter, granting the cemetery authorization to construct the new residence for $16,000. The architect firm of D. Allen Wright drew the plans for the four-bedroom, two-bathroom house. Northwood Building Company won the bid, and construction began later that year. (Holy Cross Cemetery.)

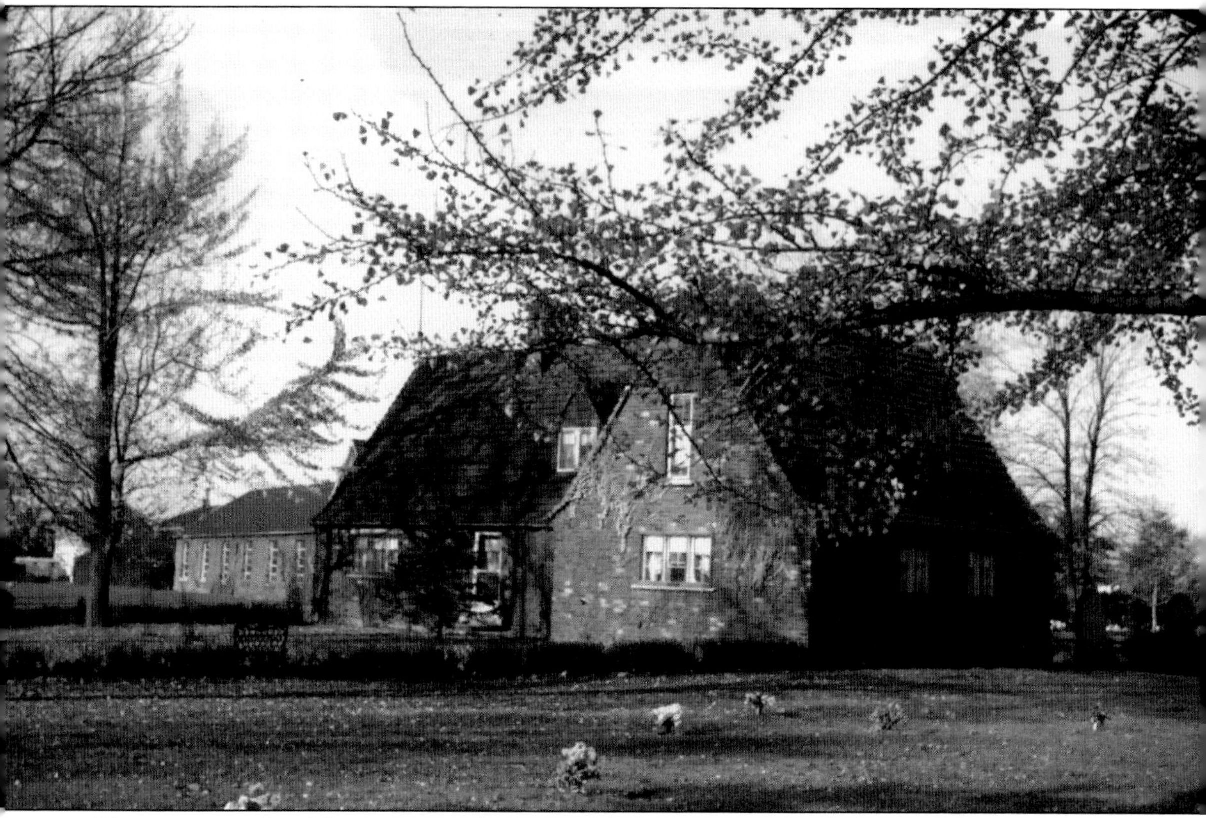

The superintendant's house was in the front of the cemetery, set back from Dix Road in section Y, behind where the old Laurain house stood, as shown in this September 1961 photograph. During installation of the wrought-iron fence in 1923, a small gate put in opened to the Laurains' front door. The same gate allowed access to the new superintendant's house by extending the sidewalk farther back. Today the little gate is not used; burials cover all evidence of the residences. Viewable to the left of the house is a portion of the chapel and garage. The access road next to the house and between the chapel served as the driveway to the house and for deliveries to the garage. The cemetery demolished the house in the early 1970s to make room for more burials. (Harry Scheuren.)

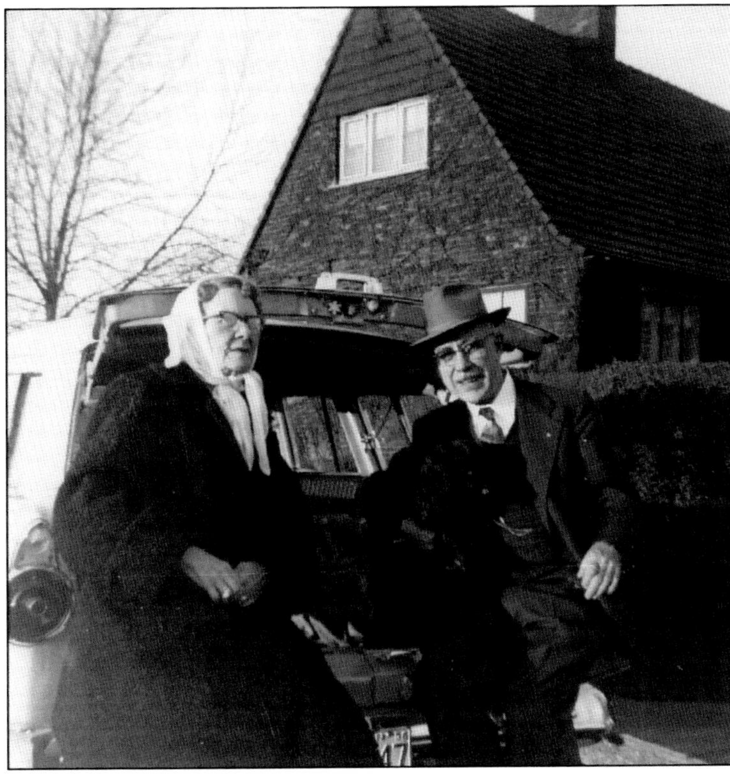

Shortly after its completion, Herman Schueren and his wife, Mary, pictured here, moved into the house. In 1920, Herman acted as secretary for the cemetery association and later was appointed supervisor. During his tenure as supervisor, Herman raised his two sons, Harry and William, in this house. Harry went on to become the cemetery supervisor and raised his son, also named Harry, here. Additionally, Schueren worked as Henry Ford's accountant at his Fairlane estate, for the Michigan Central Railroad, and the post office. (Harry Schueren.)

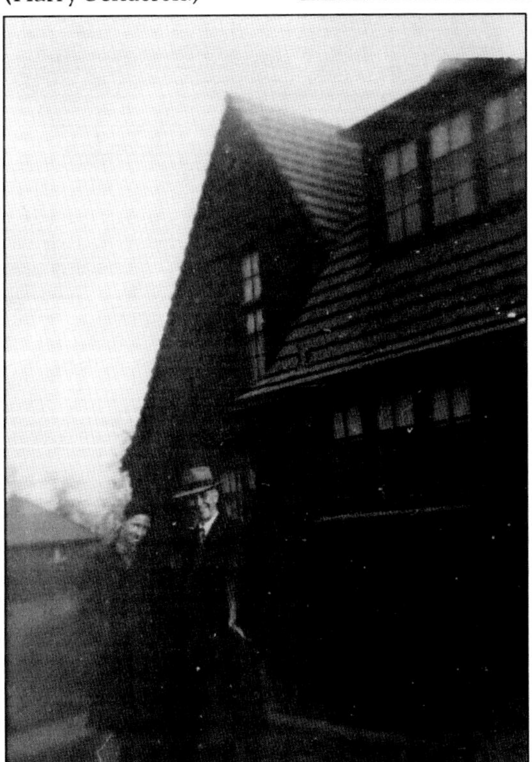

Herman Schueren and his grandson Harry Schueren are standing at the back of the superintendant's house in 1943. The comfort station is at the far left. Like his father and grandfather before him, young Harry worked at the cemetery, but in a part-time capacity. To facilitate lawn cutters, Harry and another worker received instructions to lay flat all the headstones in section P, a summer-long undertaking for them and a task the current groundskeepers are reversing. (Harry Schueren.)

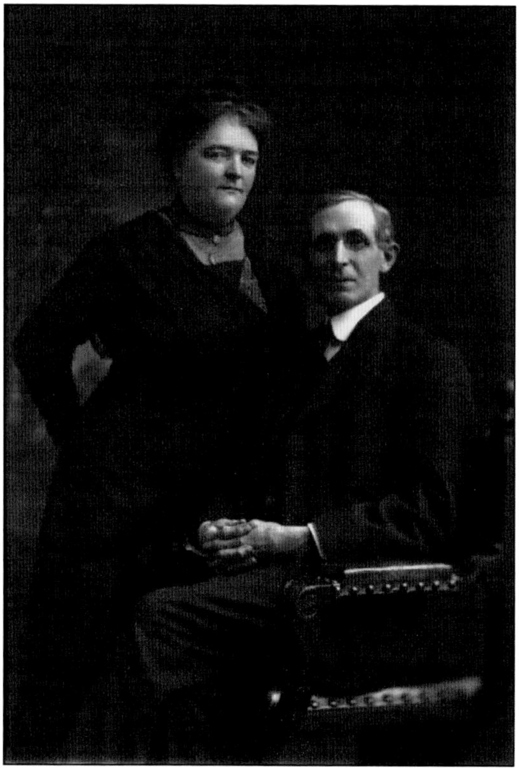

John Maloney married Mary Cullen, a "lace curtain Irish." John hailed from County Cork, Ireland, immigrating with his parents who settled in Dearbornville about 1870. He started work at the Michigan Central Railroad at the age of 12, and by age 20 was a brakeman. He retired from there as a conductor in 1917 at the age of 64. John and Mary are buried in section C. (Sheila Beaubien.)

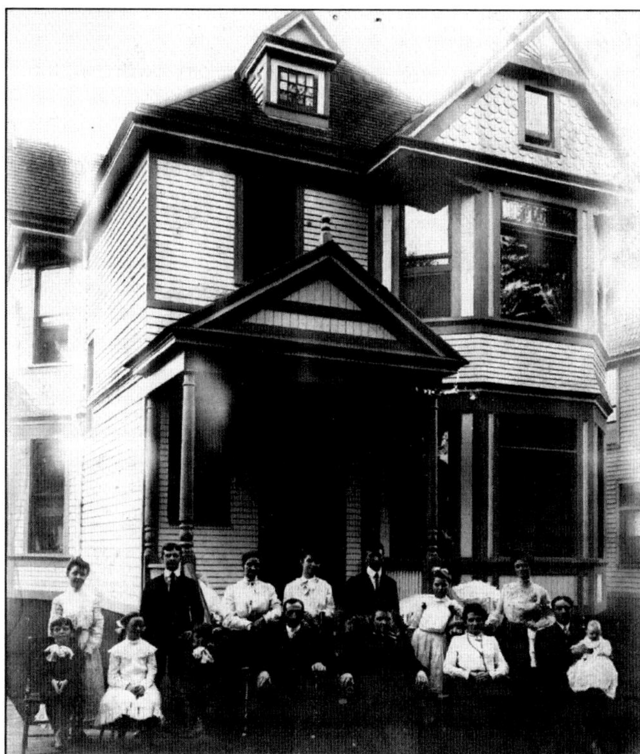

John and Mary Maloney (seated middle front) moved into this house at 737 Military Avenue, Detroit, in 1902, at the time of this photograph. It remained the last standing dwelling on the block after road crews dug the ditch for construction of the I-75 expressway and is visible from the expressway today. The home stayed in the family until 1979 when John's daughter, Ellen Beaulieu, moved into a nursing home. (Sheila Beaubien.)

The Balogh family, Andrew, wife Anna, daughter Irene, son John, and subsequently five more children made their home in River Rouge. Both Andrew and Anna were among the wave of Hungarians that immigrated to Detroit and environs in the early 20th century to seek work in its burgeoning industries. Andrew worked at the same shipyard that built the *Edmund Fitzgerald*. Anna died in 1936 and is buried in section P. (Marlyn Balogh.)

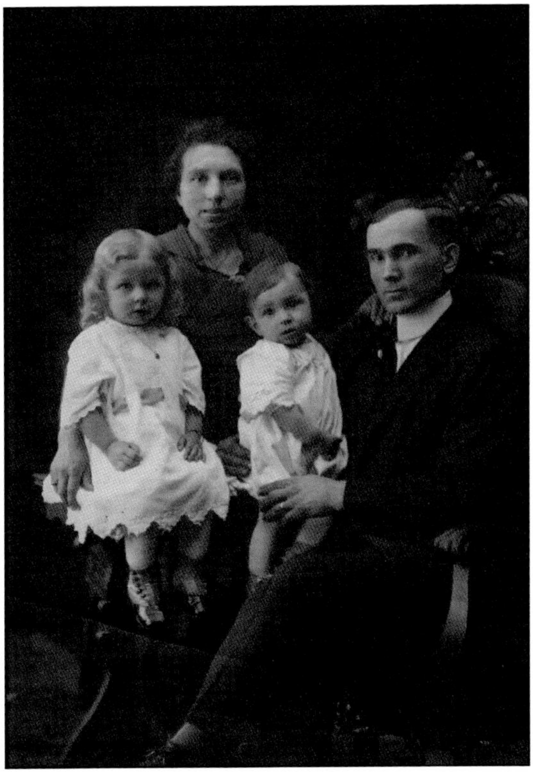

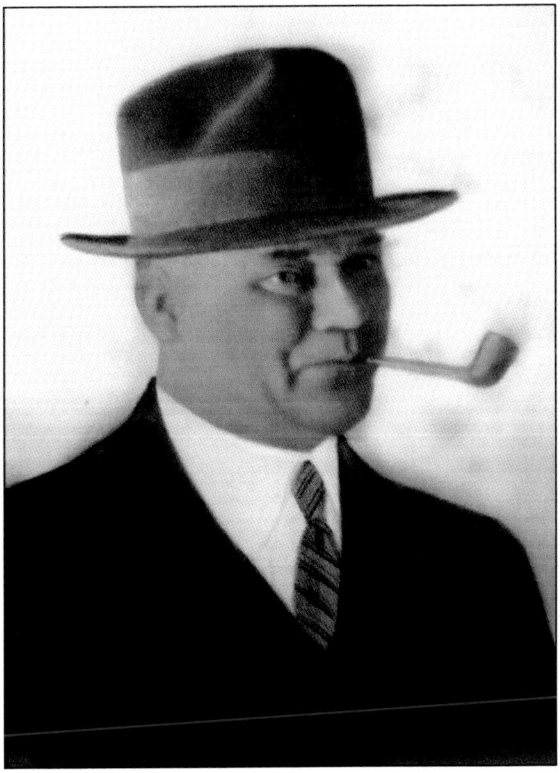

Joseph Michalak dressed for all occasions. Wanting chicken for dinner, Joseph, while wearing this vest, suit coat, hat, and tie, and with a pipe hanging out of his mouth, bent over and killed a chicken at his home located at Martin and McGraw Streets. Immediately thereafter he posed for this photograph. (Kenneth Michalak.)

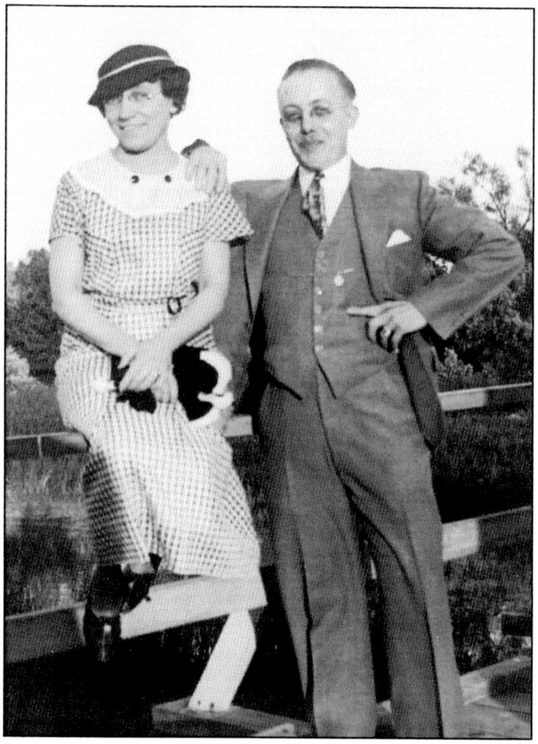

Francis Ashbaugh owned a retail dry goods store on Baker Street near Clark Park. His wife, Albertine, worked alongside her husband during the early years of their marriage but later went to work for Crowley's Department Store. Founded by a Catholic family, Crowley's drew employees of the same faith for that reason. (Gloria Kaier Rousseaux.)

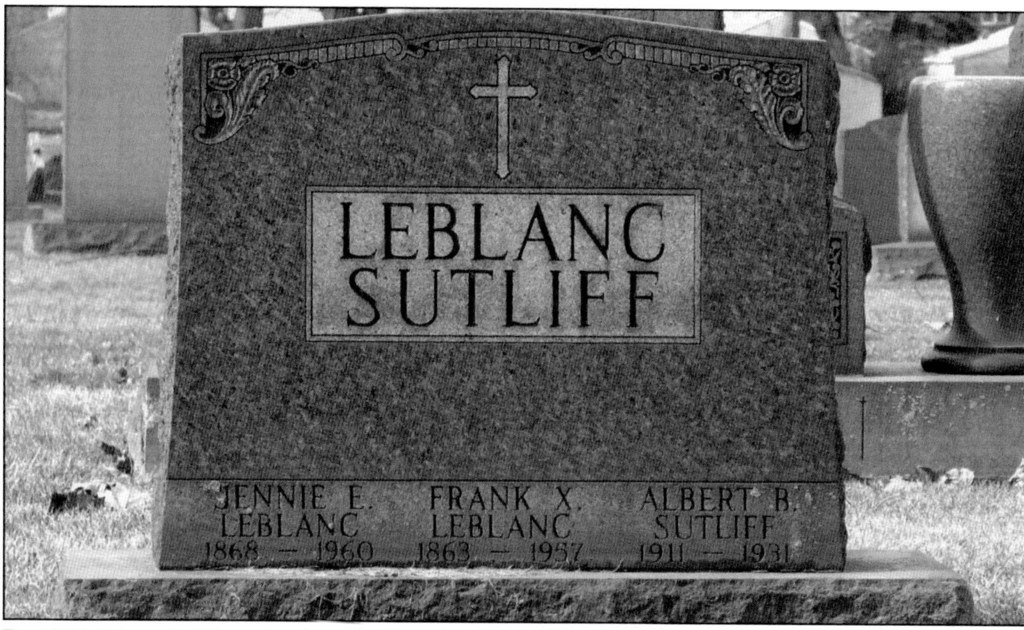

By 1801, Pierre LeBlanc had settled his family on farmland that he cleared at what is now the corner of West Jefferson and White Streets in Ecorse. His grandson, Francis X. LeBlanc, lived at that corner nearly his entire life. He was civically minded, and in addition to his ventures in the insurance and banking businesses, Francis served as Ecorse village commissioner and as president of the Ecorse board of education. Francis died in 1957 at 93 years old. He is interred in section C.

When a trolley car accident injured Frederick Krefft, Henry Ford sent his personal physician to his house to tend to his injuries. Krefft's skill and affability drew attention from Ford, who was eager to help him after his accident. During his early years, Krefft worked on bridges as an ironworker and as a firefighter at the station located behind St. Anne Church. He is buried in the Krefft family lot in section J. (Pamela Walls.)

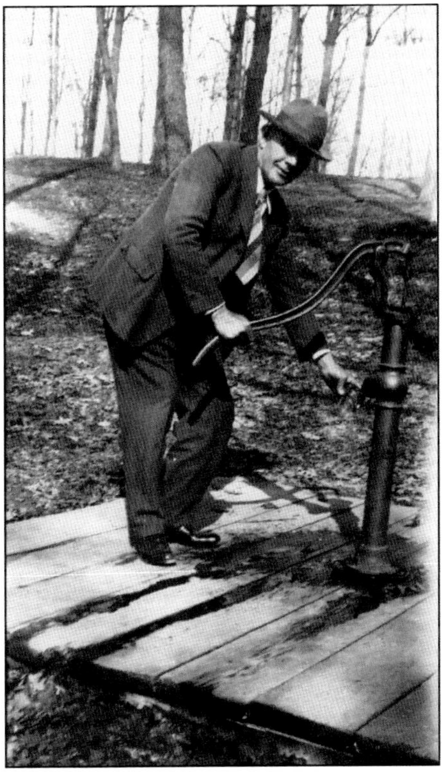

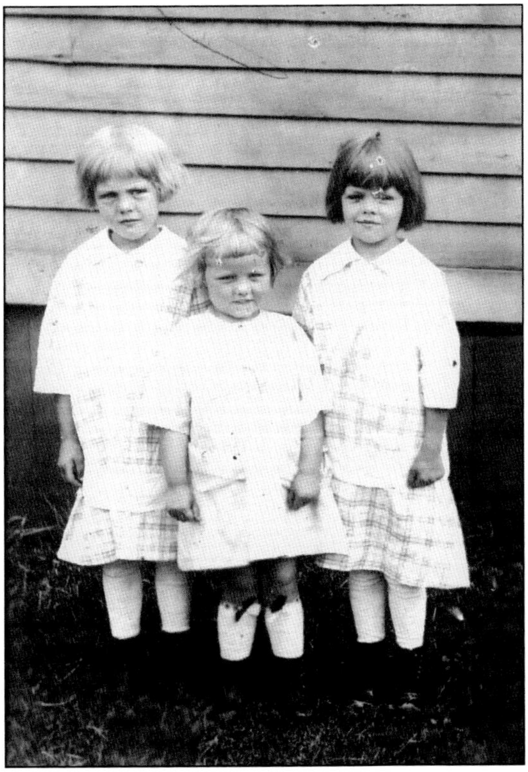

These three sisters, (from left to right) Evelyn, Mollie, and Dorothy, are the daughters of Frederick and Ella Krefft. Evelyn eventually married and had a daughter of her own. Evelyn's daughter usually slept with her, but one night, the little girl felt her mother grow cold so she crawled out of bed and scampered into bed with her grandmother. Evelyn had died during the night. Evelyn is buried in section J. (Pamela Walls.)

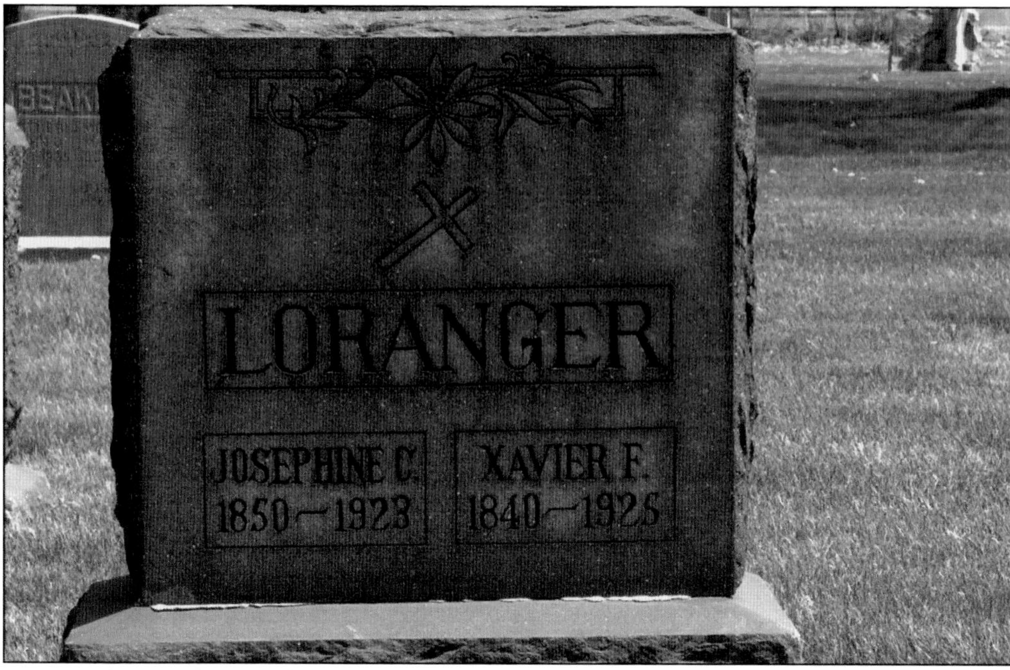

Many early French Canadian pioneers settled south of Detroit at Monroe as Francis Xavier Loranger's father, Edward, did in 1824. Francis grew up working at his father's gristmill until he married Josephine Beaubien, a descendant of another prominent early pioneer family. When Francis was ready to retire, he moved to a smaller farm in Detroit to be closer to his children. Francis and Josephine are buried in section J.

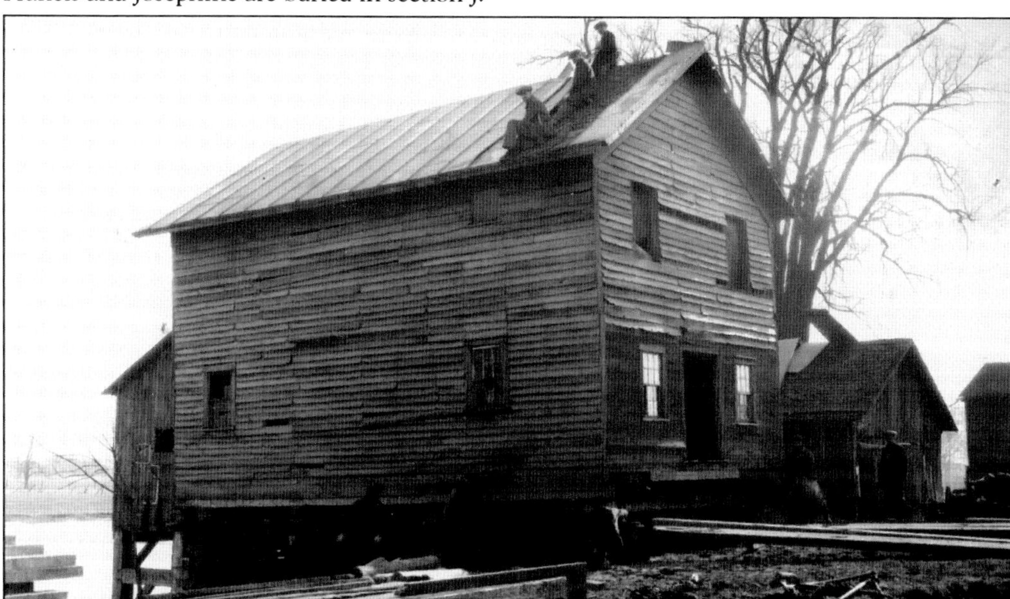

The gristmill belonging to Francis's father stood on Stony Creek at Monroe. Edward built the mill in 1832 and ran it until he was 91 years old. Here in 1929, workers are preparing the mill for the move to Henry Ford's Greenfield Village at Dearborn, where it is on display. (Monroe County Historical Museum Archives.)

Arthur Plourde was born in 1850 at beautiful Baie de Gaspé, Quebec, a maritime community at the St. Lawrence estuary, so it was natural for him to immigrate to Ecorse to work as a machinist in the William M. Dwight lumber mill, a mill that produced, among other things, lumber for shipyards. Arthur's first wife, Lilioise Dumontier, died in childbirth in 1883, and Arthur married Elizabeth Begin in 1888. Arthur and Elizabeth are buried in section G.

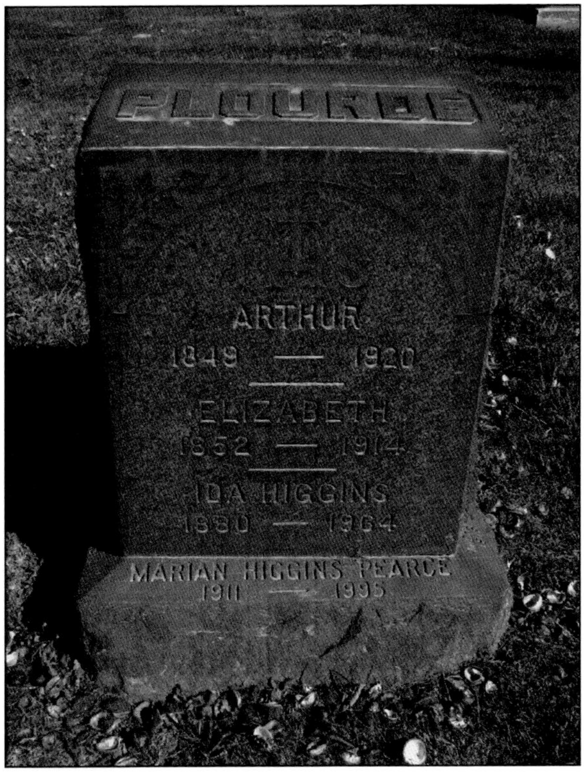

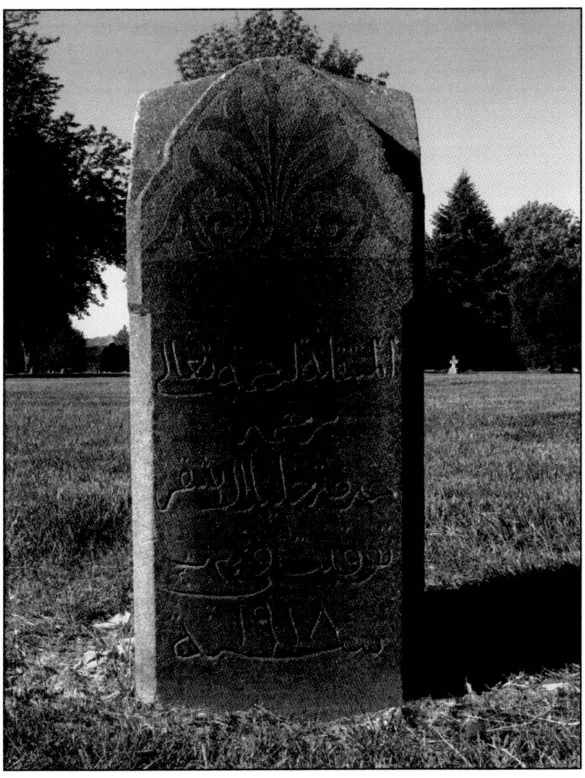

Anna Ashare was born in Syria. Her stone reads, "Departed to the Almighty, Rahmeh, wife of Khalil, family Alashkar, died on November 25, 1918." Anna's stone is the only stone in the cemetery written in Syrian. She was 29 years old when she died of pneumonia and is buried in section M. She left behind two small children.

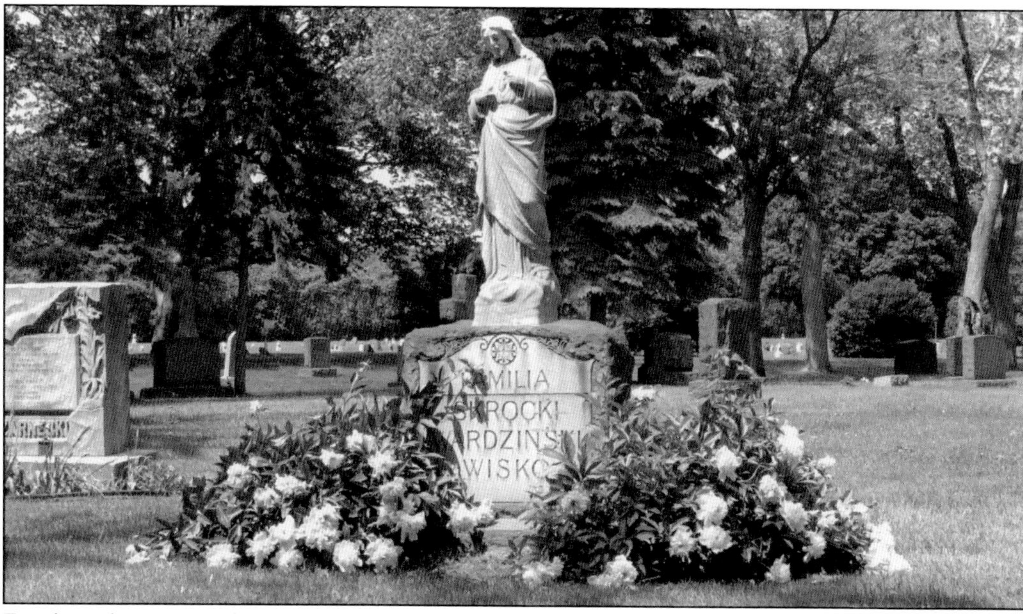

Frank and Mary Wisko lived a few houses down on Twenty-Fifth Street from Mary's parents, Adam and Katherine Skrocki. Adam, like many immigrants, came to the United States to find employment and a place to live before sending for the rest of his family. Katherine and son Julius arrived in 1893, three years after Julius. They are buried in section J.

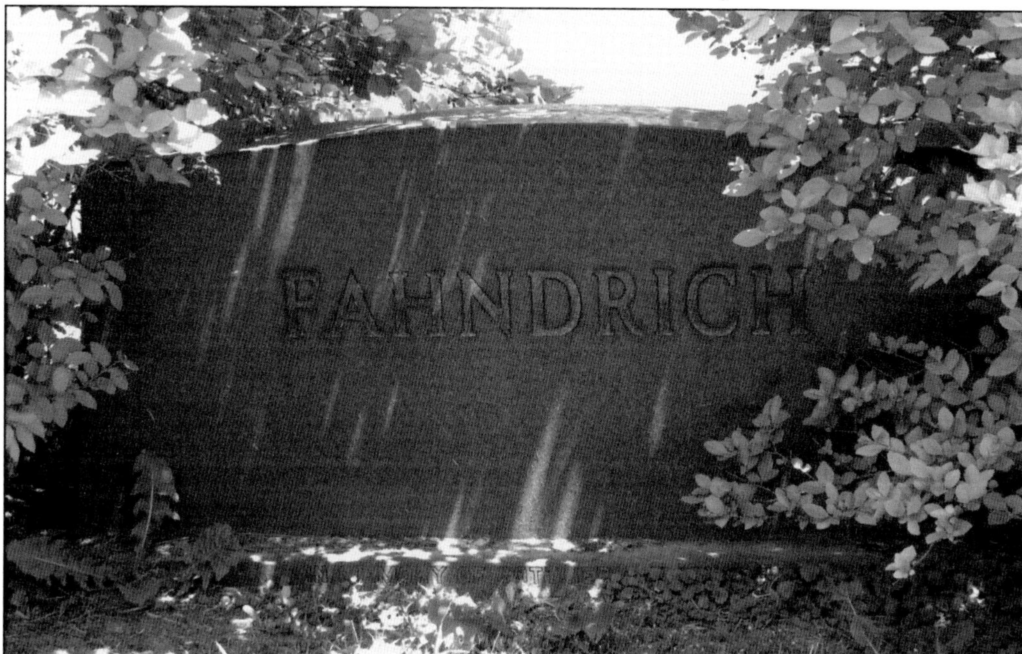

In the late 1800s, Springwells was still a large farming community. Gottlieb Fahndrich's father, Charles, a German immigrant, purchased a sizeable farm southwest of Waterman Avenue and north of Fort Street. Gottlieb followed in his father's business, tending a garden farm near Dix Road close to the cemetery. Gottlieb died in 1921. He, his wife, and three children are buried in section G.

With her mouthwatering Polish cooking, Anastasia Kuszynski filled her family with love and chrusciki that she piled high in wicker clothes baskets. Remembering Anastasia's angel wings still provokes fond memories from her relatives many years after her death. Family and friends always filled Anastasia's house, and summertime meant family picnics at the park and a reason to bake more chrusciki. (Loraine Rzanca.)

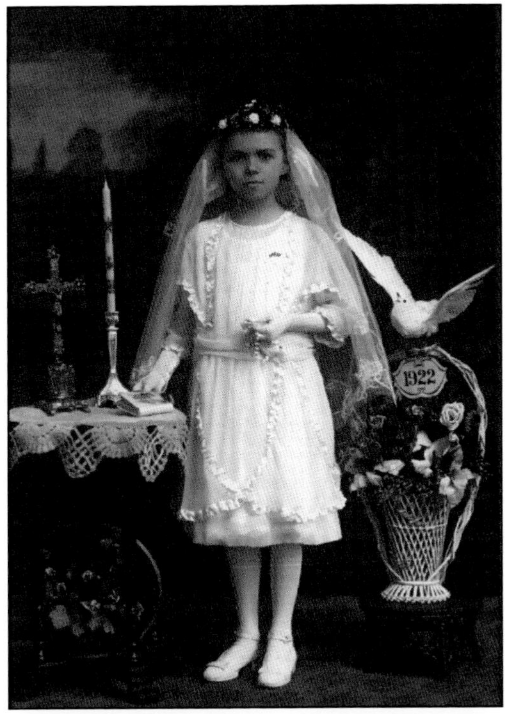

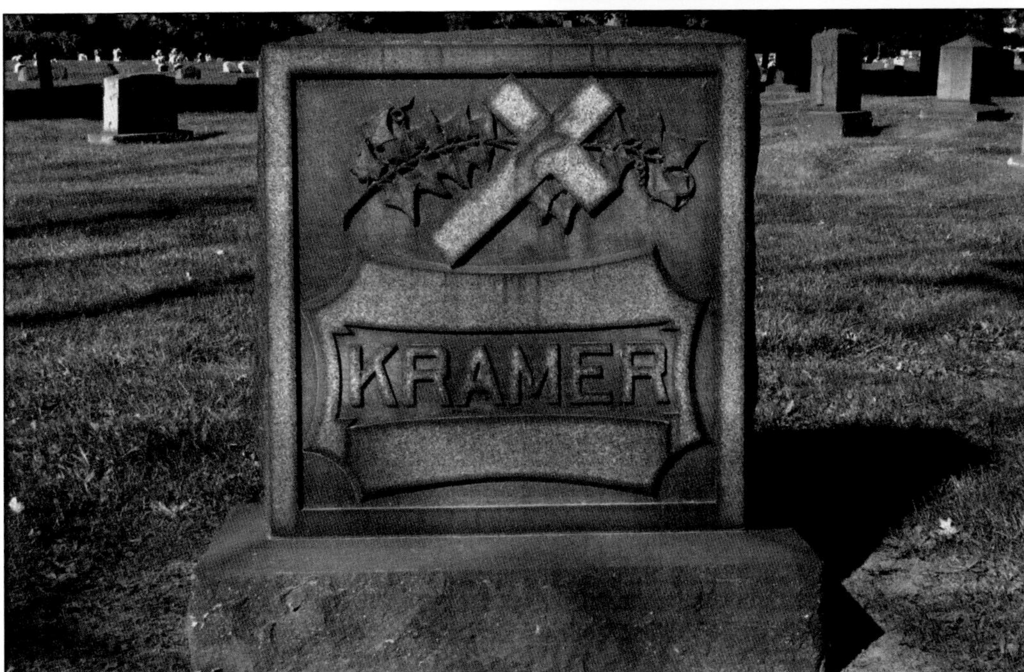

At the edge of the 10-acre Laurain property abutting Dix Road and adjacent to the Peter Reiden farm sat the farm that John Kramer rented from Richard Laurain. The property included a store, a frame house, a barn, outbuildings and two greenhouses. Kramer, a grocer, ran a general store. When the cemetery bought the Laurain property in 1911, Kramer paid the same rent to the cemetery as he did to Laurain, $125 a year. Kramer and his wife, Mary, are buried in section H.

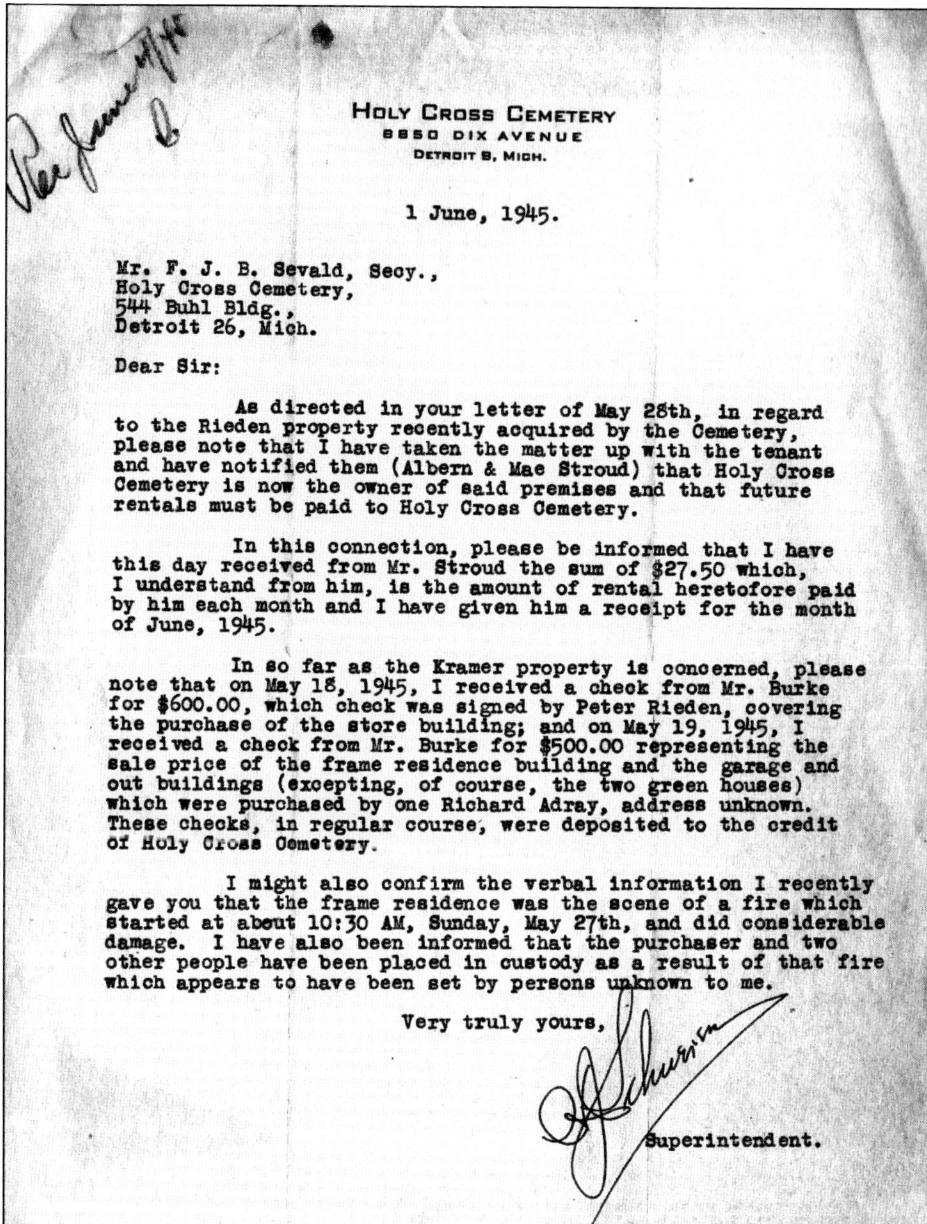

HOLY CROSS CEMETERY
8850 DIX AVENUE
DETROIT 9, MICH.

1 June, 1945.

Mr. F. J. B. Sevald, Secy.,
Holy Cross Cemetery,
544 Buhl Bldg.,
Detroit 26, Mich.

Dear Sir:

As directed in your letter of May 28th, in regard to the Rieden property recently acquired by the Cemetery, please note that I have taken the matter up with the tenant and have notified them (Albern & Mae Stroud) that Holy Cross Cemetery is now the owner of said premises and that future rentals must be paid to Holy Cross Cemetery.

In this connection, please be informed that I have this day received from Mr. Stroud the sum of $27.50 which, I understand from him, is the amount of rental heretofore paid by him each month and I have given him a receipt for the month of June, 1945.

In so far as the Kramer property is concerned, please note that on May 18, 1945, I received a check from Mr. Burke for $600.00, which check was signed by Peter Rieden, covering the purchase of the store building; and on May 19, 1945, I received a check from Mr. Burke for $500.00 representing the sale price of the frame residence building and the garage and out buildings (excepting, of course, the two green houses) which were purchased by one Richard Adray, address unknown. These checks, in regular course, were deposited to the credit of Holy Cross Cemetery.

I might also confirm the verbal information I recently gave you that the frame residence was the scene of a fire which started at about 10:30 AM, Sunday, May 27th, and did considerable damage. I have also been informed that the purchaser and two other people have been placed in custody as a result of that fire which appears to have been set by persons unknown to me.

Very truly yours,

Superintendent.

In May 1945, the cemetery sold the store building to Peter Reiden for $600, and Richard Adray purchased the residence, garage, and outbuildings for $500. Adray realized that he had made a bad deal and tried to have the cemetery buy back the property. When that failed, he asked the cemetery to sell the property for him. Again, that failed. Immediately Adray put $2,500 fire insurance on the building. On Sunday morning, May 27, 1945, the frame house mysteriously caught fire in eight different places. Once the arson squad investigated the dwelling, the police arrested Adray and took him to the Fort-Green police station. After receiving notice from the department of building and safety regarding the dangerous and abandoned dwelling, the cemetery dismantled it later that summer. The Kramer store and farm are now part of sections X and W between the chapel and Dix Road. (Holy Cross Cemetery.)

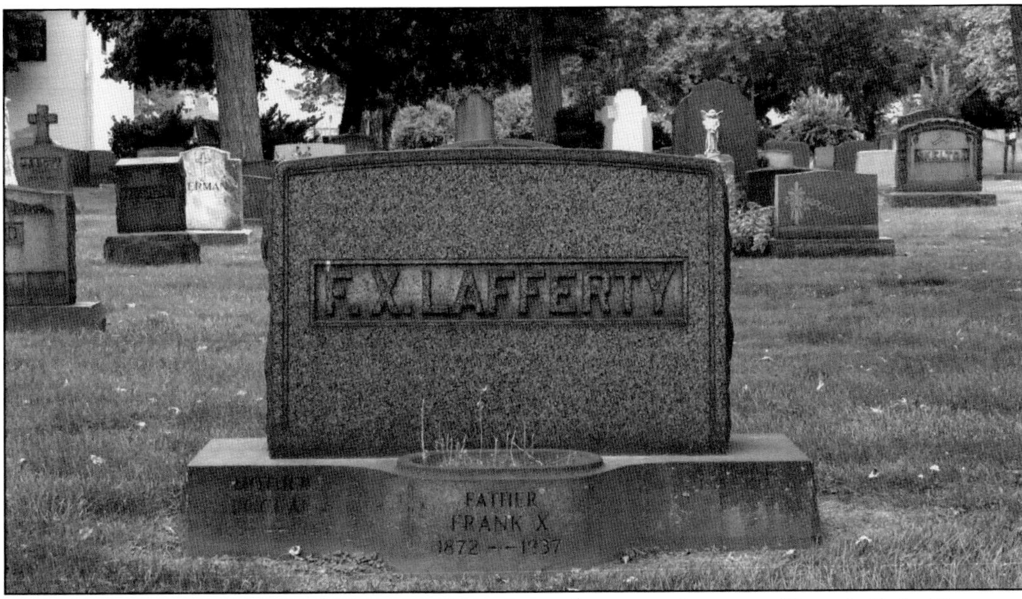

In addition to running a highly successful meat and grocery business, Francis X. Lafferty was a founder, director, vice president, and eventually president of the Down River State Bank in Ecorse. Politically aspired, he served as supervisor, treasurer, and trustee of Ecorse Township. Lafferty was born on May 18, 1872, and died on September 19, 1937. He is buried next to his wife, Luceal, in section C.

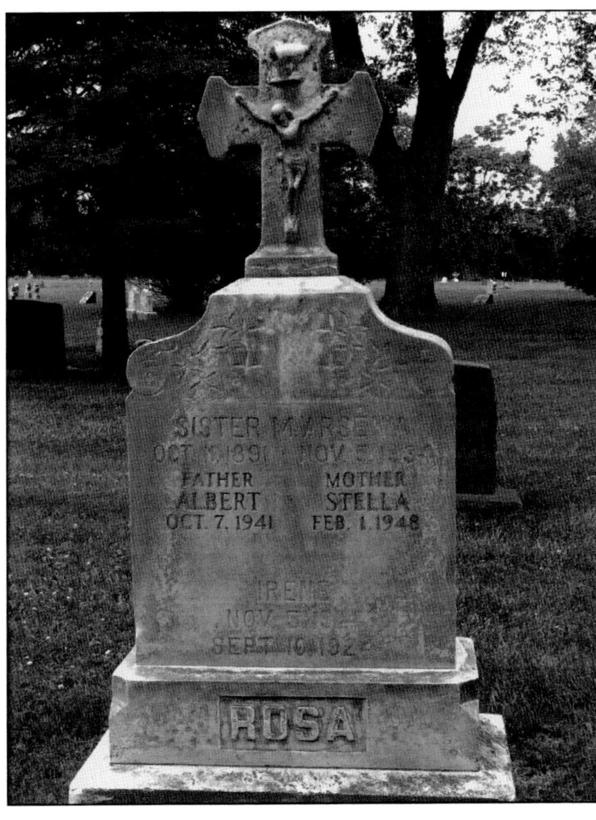

Sr. Mary Arsenia Roza is one of the few nuns buried in the cemetery. Born in 1891 as Catherine Rosa, she entered the Sisters of St. Joseph of the Third Order of St. Francis from the Ogdensburg Diocese. The motherhouse is in Wisconsin, but in 1889, the sisters established a new congregation in Kalamazoo and then moved to Nazareth on 400 acres just north of Kalamazoo. Sister Mary died in 1934 at the age of 43. She is buried in section L.

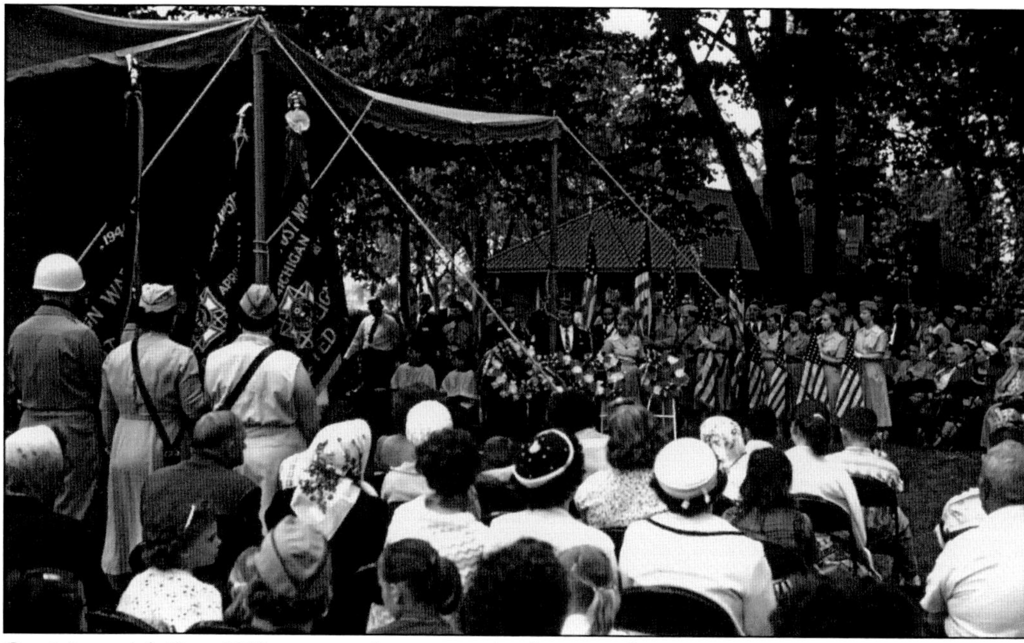

On Memorial Day 1959, a special mass took place at the cemetery to honor veterans and fallen soldiers. Hundreds of veterans and worshipers attended the outdoor commemoration underneath tents, some sitting on folding chairs while others stood. A marching band kicked off the celebration, leading a military parade down Dix Road into the cemetery. Service personnel representing every branch of the service honored fallen soldiers by placing wreaths on their graves. Before the mass began, they stacked their firearms some distance from the crowd in teepee-style, piling swivels in units of three. As with many cemeteries, this type of activity at Holy Cross Cemetery happened frequently during its prime years. (Harry Schueren.)

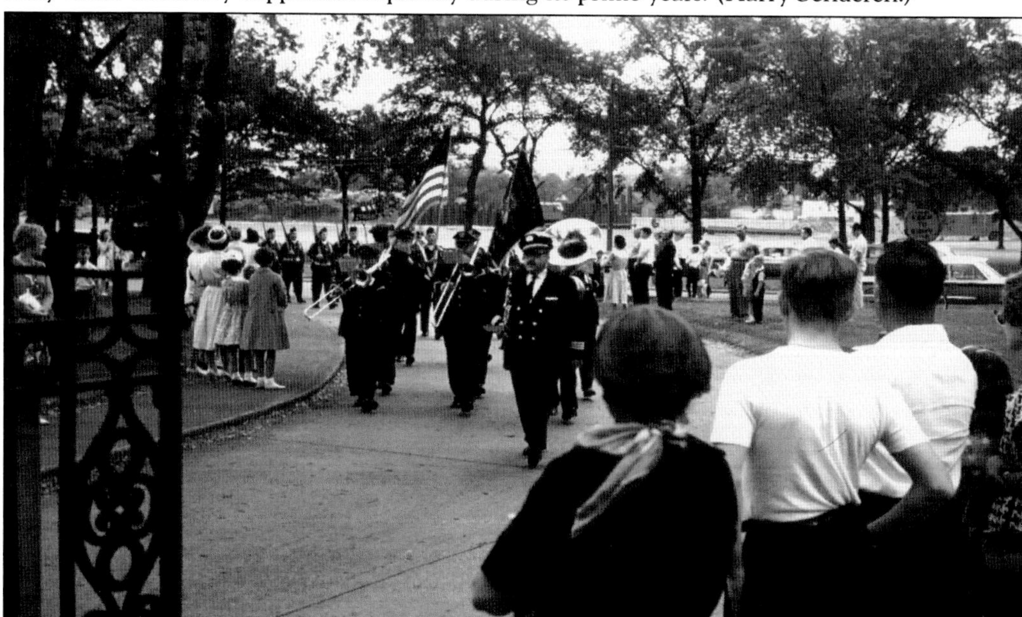

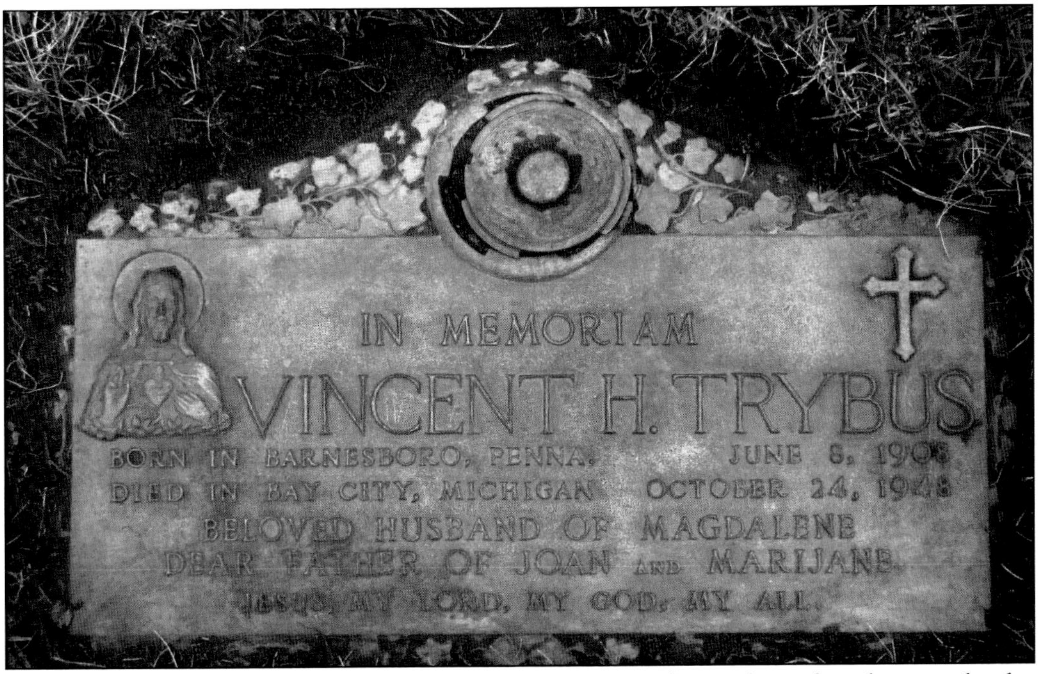

On October 24, 1958, just north of Pinconning, Vincent Trybus and two friends spent the day scouting for the perfect spot for their next month's planned deer-hunting trip. On the way home, the three men stopped in Pinconning to buy some renowned Pinconning cheese. As they crossed the three-lane highway, Trybus, unaware of an oncoming automobile, stepped from the center lane and right into its path. He died at Mercy Hospital in Bay City. He is buried in section T.

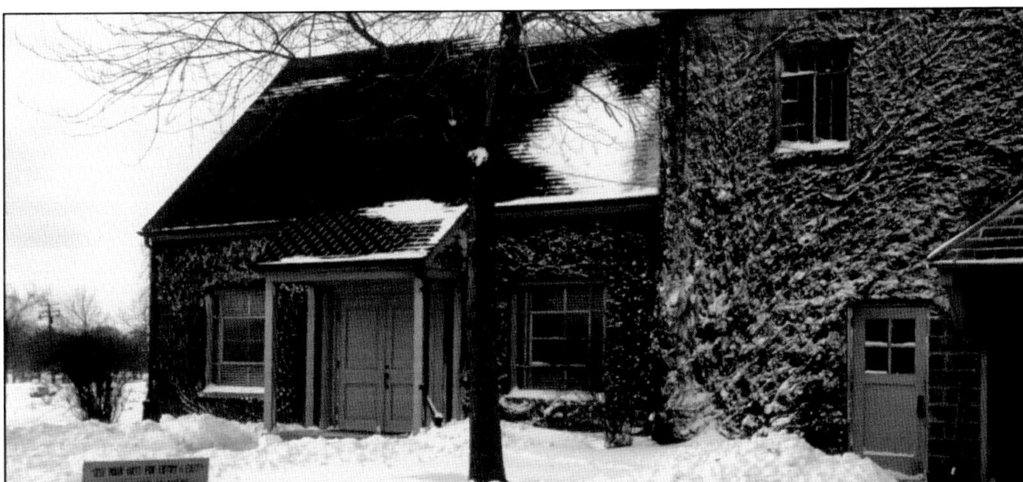

Heavy snow in 1961 did not prevent the cemetery from everyday business. The posted sign reminds drivers of the 10-mile-per-hour speed limit. The shoveled driveway leads to an entry door and garage entrance no longer in use. (Harry Schueren.)

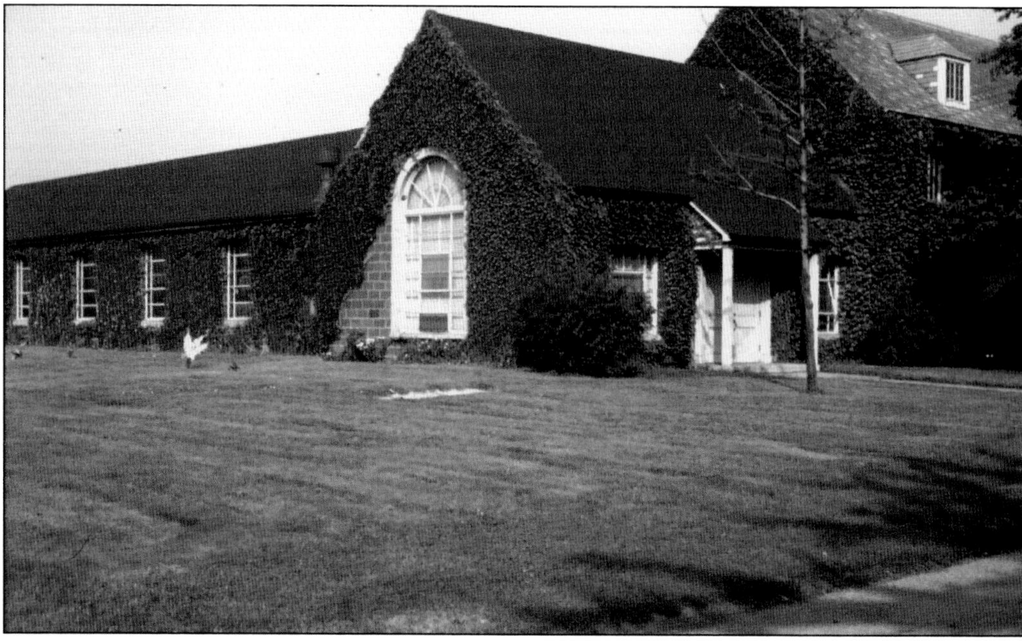

In 1960, vines covered the chapel and garage. Not yet built are the cremation niche to the left of the chapel window, and the fishpond to the left of the chapel doors. Foley's monuments built the columbarium against the comfort station wall in 1996, but moved it to its more appropriate location against the chapel wall in 1999. Timothy Daniels built the fishpond, complete with goldfish, in 2000. (Harry Schueren.)

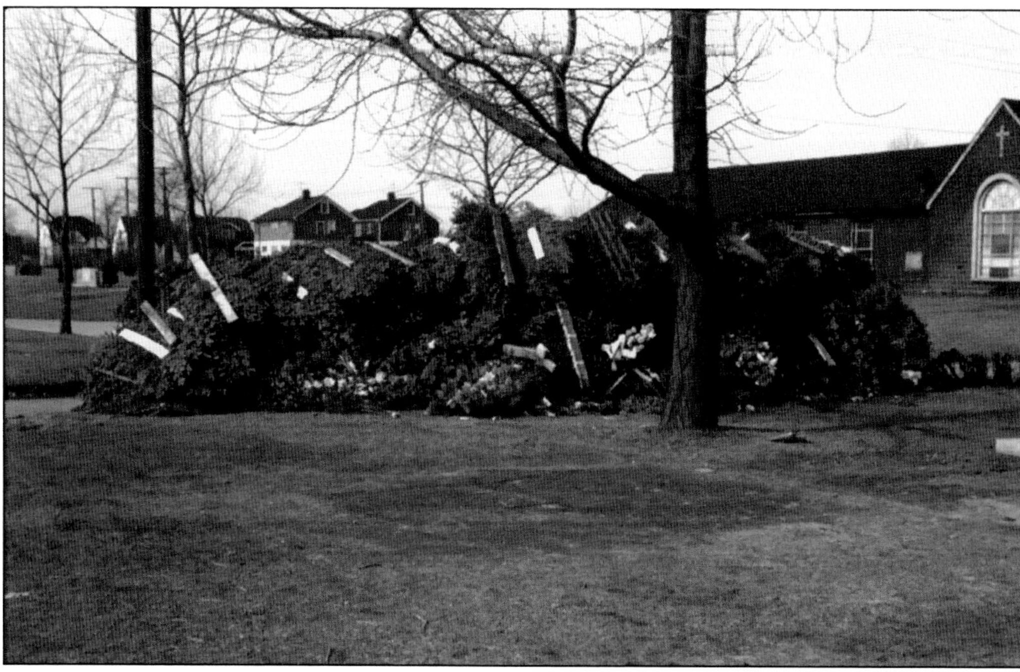

In March 1961, Christmas grave blankets lay piled near the service road in section Y, ready for removal. The chapel, seen in the background, lacks its current white color, and the stained-glass window is not yet installed. (Harry Schueren.)

Three

Characters Worth Noting

Holy Cross Cemetery is not the final resting place of governors or generals, but it can boast having noteworthy characters of its own. As Detroit expanded, so did judicious businessmen making their way as bankers, attorneys, politicians, entrepreneurs, and even rumrunners. The cemetery's incorporation founders were a remarkable group in their own right. Their progenitors settled Detroit, they were sons of immigrants or immigrants themselves, and they were farmers, plumbers, insurance salesmen, attorneys, and capitalists. Detroit's incipient growth allowed individualistic opportunity, and many embraced the chance. Ancestral landowners became involved in politics, and politicians amended laws and charters. Bankers established their businesses, as did rumrunners and underworld figures. Circumstances of war produced pioneers of design and architects, ready to help the men and women fighting overseas. Historical evolvement necessitated a transition for manufacturers to meet the demand of consumers. A business owner could go from selling carriages to automobiles in the matter of a year's time. The swelling population brought the need for more churches and clerics, many of whom left their mark on the community. The diversity of Detroit's influx of multinational immigration set the stage for remarkable and interesting lives. Many of these people have come to rest at Holy Cross Cemetery.

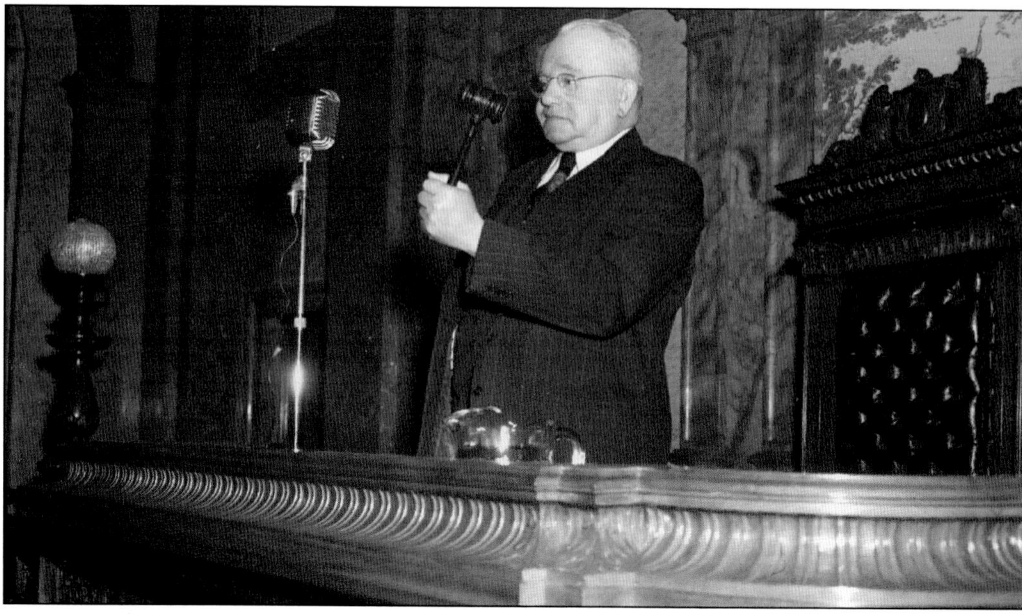

In 1915, John Kronk entered Detroit's political scene at age 32, becoming one of Detroit's 42 aldermen under the old ward system. In 1919, he was elected one of the original nine members of the common council when Detroit's power structure changed under a new city charter. Kronk owned a bar at Michigan and Junction Avenues, which he gave up, saying, "The liquor business is disagreeable at any time, but when a man is in politics it is impossible." (Walter P. Reuther Library.)

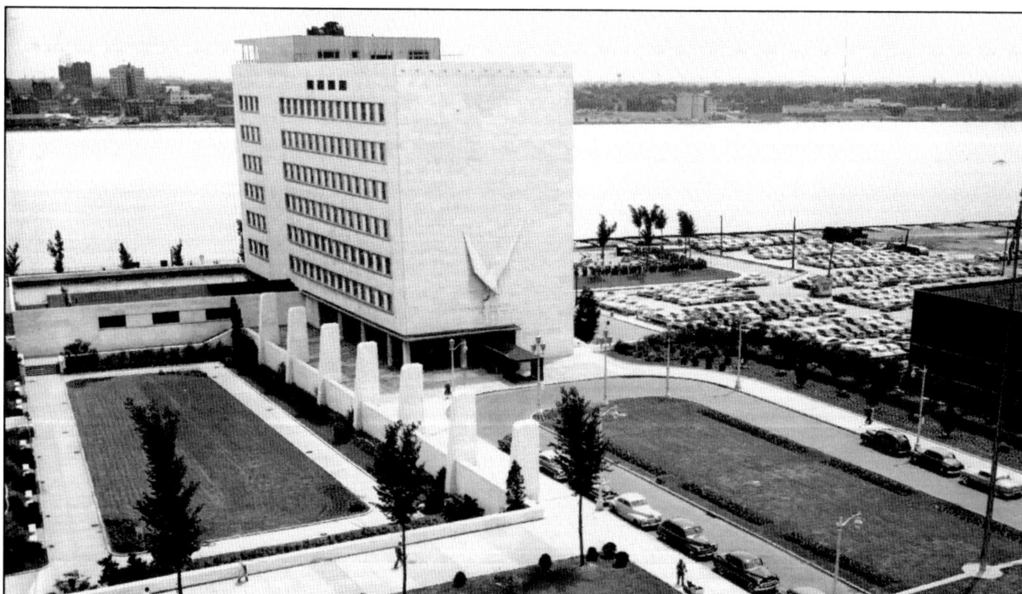

Kronk wore many hats during his tenure as councilman. Among his accomplishments were his long-sought Detroit Veterans' Memorial (above) completed in 1950. Kronk was instrumental in the location of Detroit City Airport; the widening of Woodward, Michigan, and Gratiot Avenues; and from his Detroit United Railway days, the Kronk Five-Cent Fare, an ordinance that kept streetcar fares from increasing and saved streetcar riders $5 million. (Walter P. Reuther Library.)

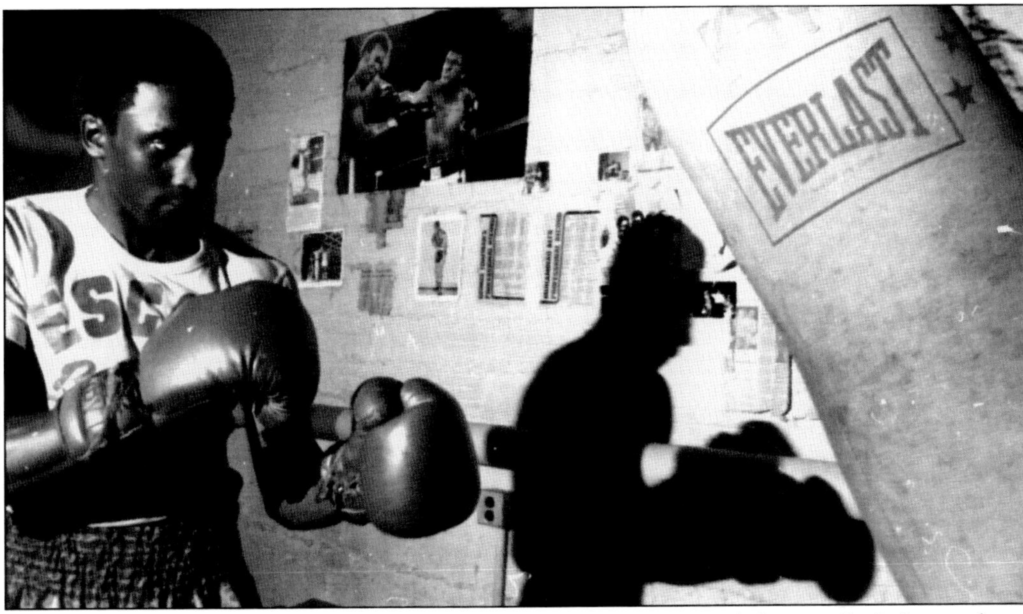

The councilman indefatigably worked for a community center in Atkinson Park for residents, and when completed, the council elected to name it in Kronk's honor. The Kronk Recreational Center was the first recreation center in Detroit. Kronk Gym, located in the basement of the center, produced world champion boxers such as Tommy Hearns (above), Evander Holyfield, and Hector Camacho. (Walter P. Reuther Library.)

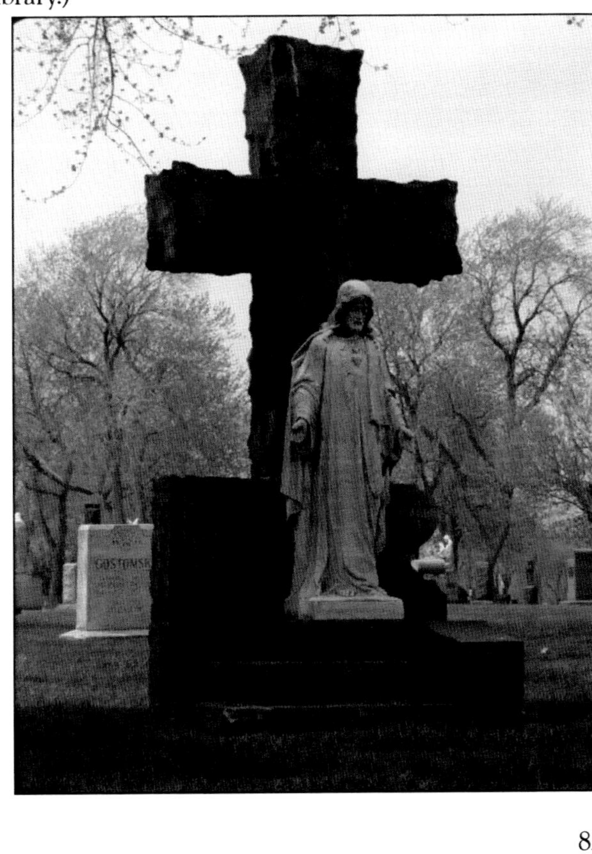

Kronk suffered a heart attack and died on February 23, 1954, while on vacation at Hot Springs, Arkansas. He had been looking forward to the vacation as a respite from the strains of his political obligations. His one-mile-long, 160-automobile cortege was the largest city officials had seen. Some 500 people followed the procession to the cemetery. The Kronk monument is in section F.

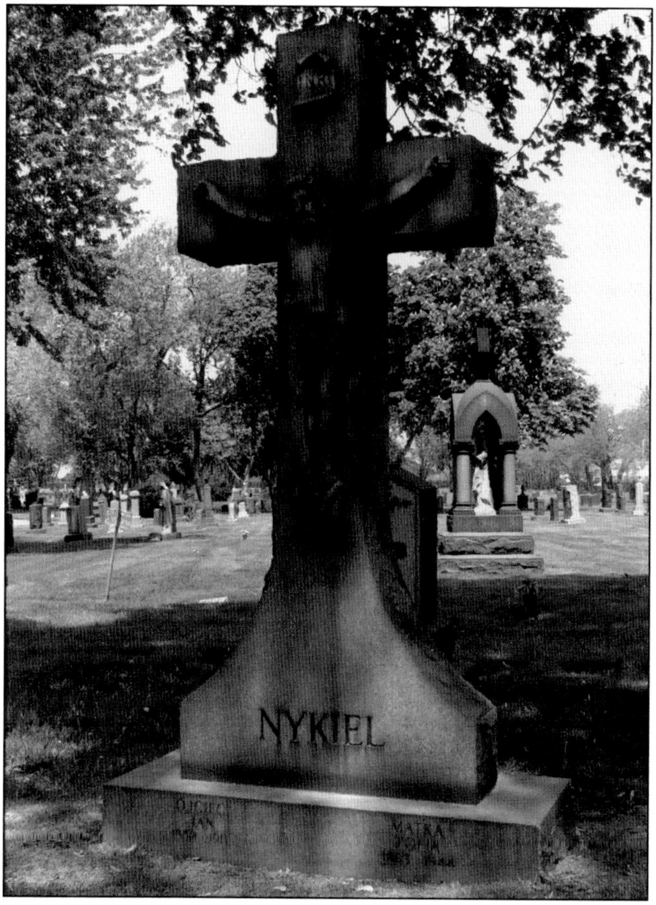

On June 27, 1928, two mafia men from Chicago visited August Nykiel at his saloon on West Jefferson and insisted that he step outside. Mike Dipisa, angered over Nykiel's refusal to cut him a share in his blind pig, pulled out a pistol and shot Nykiel. River Rouge constable Edward McPearson, in the bar to serve a citation on another matter, gave chase, exchanging gunfire with the two fleeing mobsters, killing Dipisa. The police later captured the second gunman and charged him with murder. Police tried to link Nykiel's murderers to a slaying several months earlier at the Detroit Tigers clubhouse, owned by Nykiel, on Peterson Avenue. Nykiel was part owner of the Detroit Tigers semiprofessional football team named after the professional baseball team of the same name. Before Nykiel's ownership, the team was known as the Detroit Heralds. Nykiel was laid to rest in section G.

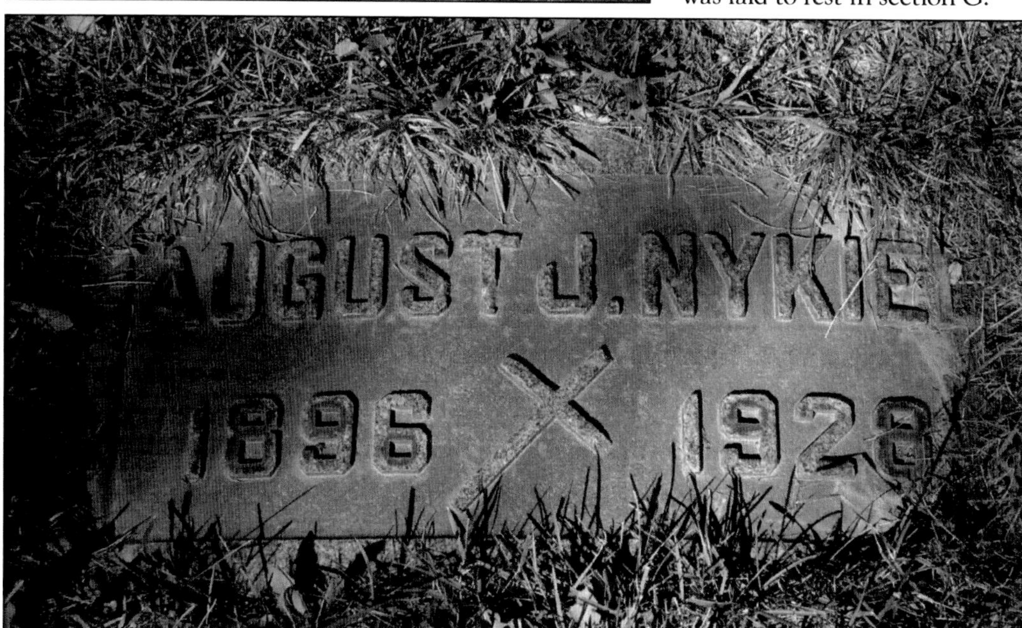

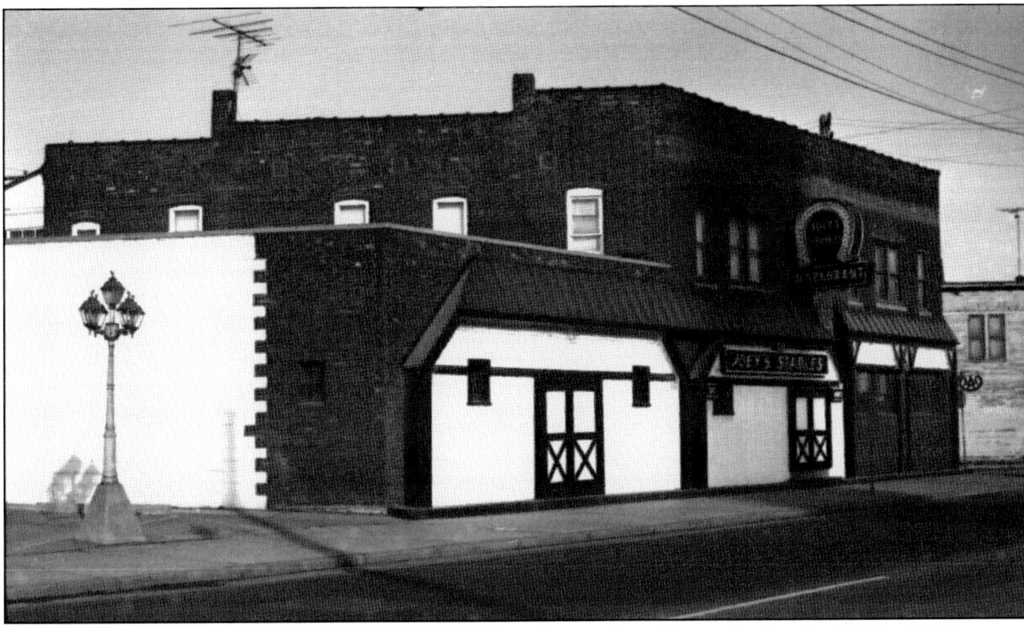

Joseph, August Nykiel's brother, expanded the saloon after August's death and in 1933 turned it into a restaurant that he named Joey's Stables. During its heyday, the fine-dining restaurant served many prestigious and notorious names from the Detroit area. A rum-running tunnel ran from the restaurant's basement under Jefferson Avenue to a building near the river that the Nykiel family owned. After Joey's Stables closed in 1981, the restaurant's sign was removed to the Rouge River Historical Museum. Joseph died in an automobile accident on the I-75 expressway in 1986. He is buried in the family lot in section H.

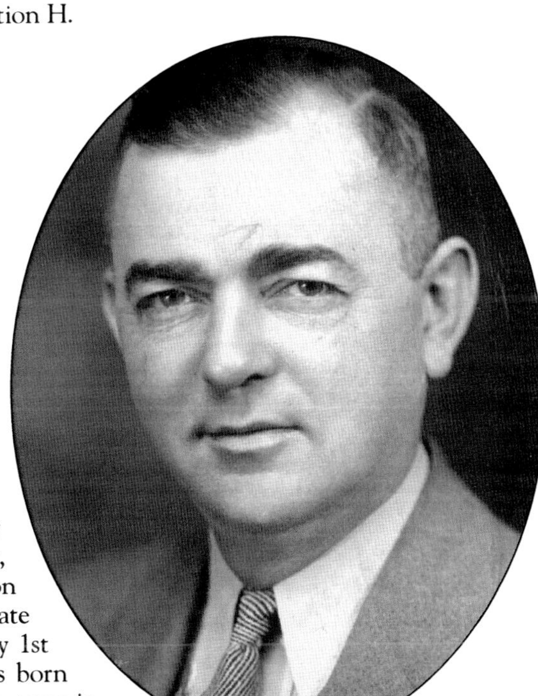

John Nichczynski was in his second year as state senator from the 21st district, Detroit, when he died in 1934. He ran on the Republican ticket for the Michigan State House of Representatives in Wayne County 1st district in 1926 and 1930. Nichczynski was born near Poznan, Poland, on April 20, 1889. His grave is in section H. (Archives of Michigan.)

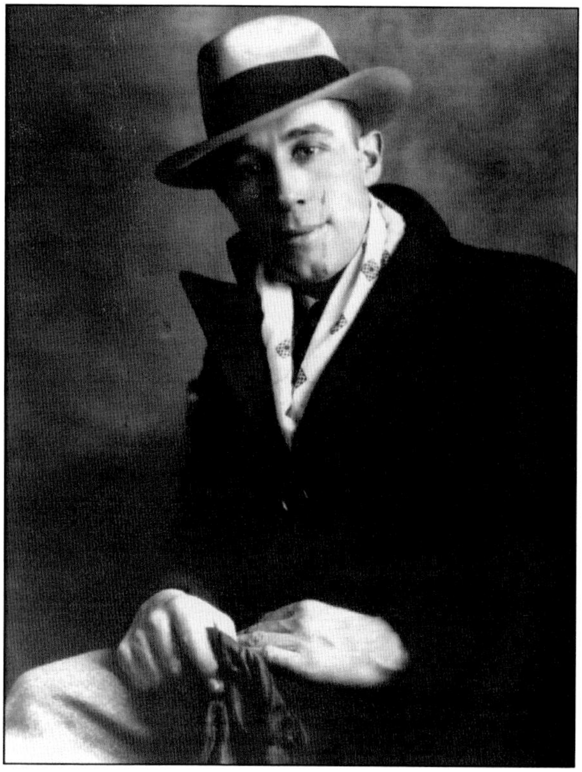

Frank Kaier ran a blind pig in the basement of his house on Fort Street while his wife played the piano and entertained the customers. Frank's run-ins with the Purple Gang found him in deep water more than once. In 1931, five members of the Purple Gang attacked Kaier in retribution for hijacking a shipment of their liquor. No one recalls how Frank received the scar on his face. He lived to the age of 96 and is buried in section B. (Gloria Kaier Rousseaux.)

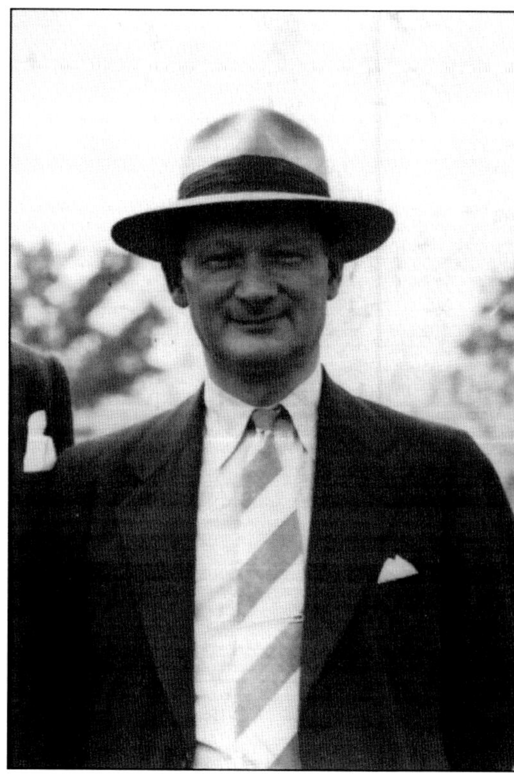

Born in Austria, Henry Dattner studied engineering at the University of Vienna, arriving in Michigan in 1907. In 1941, Michigan governor Murray Van Wagoner appointed him chair of the Compensation Commission, having previously appointed him to the Michigan Racing Commission. Henry was a member of the Michigan State Fair Commission; was also a director of the Blair Distilling Company in Kentucky, which his construction company built; and owned a summer home on Palm Island, Florida, next door to Al Capone. Dattner, an active Democrat, served as a presidential elector for Michigan in 1936. (Robert Goodchild.)

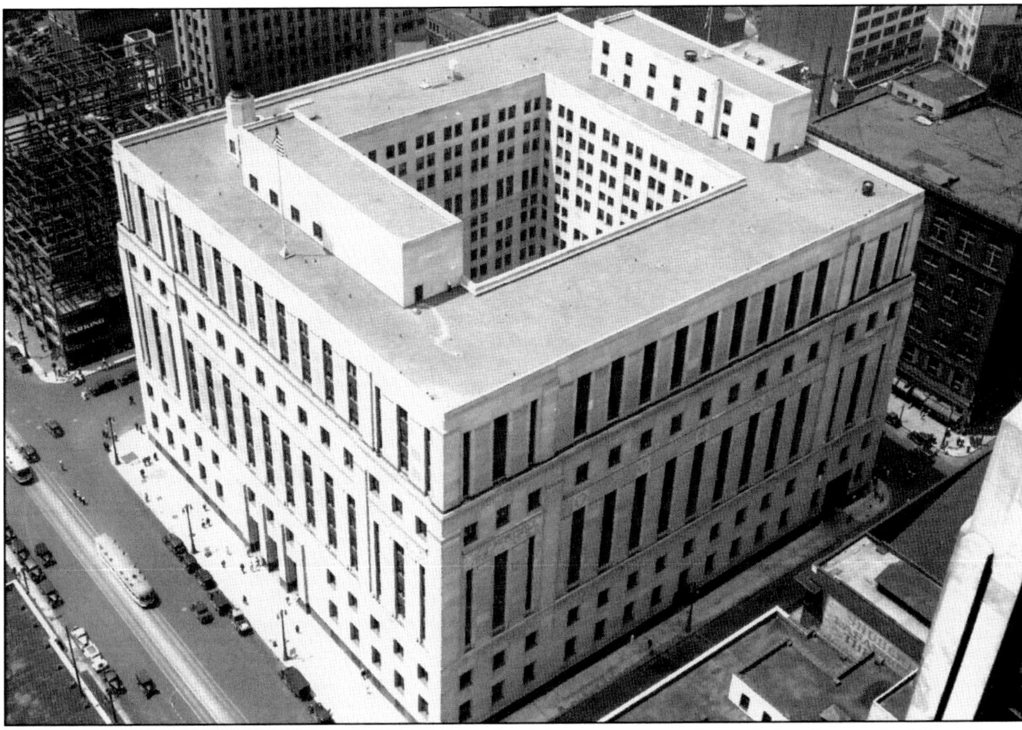

Working as a government contractor, Dattner's reputation was that of the fastest builder of post offices in the country. Locally he was responsible for building the Detroit main post office on Fort Street (above) and the Lincoln Park and Hamtramck post offices. (Walter P. Reuther Library.)

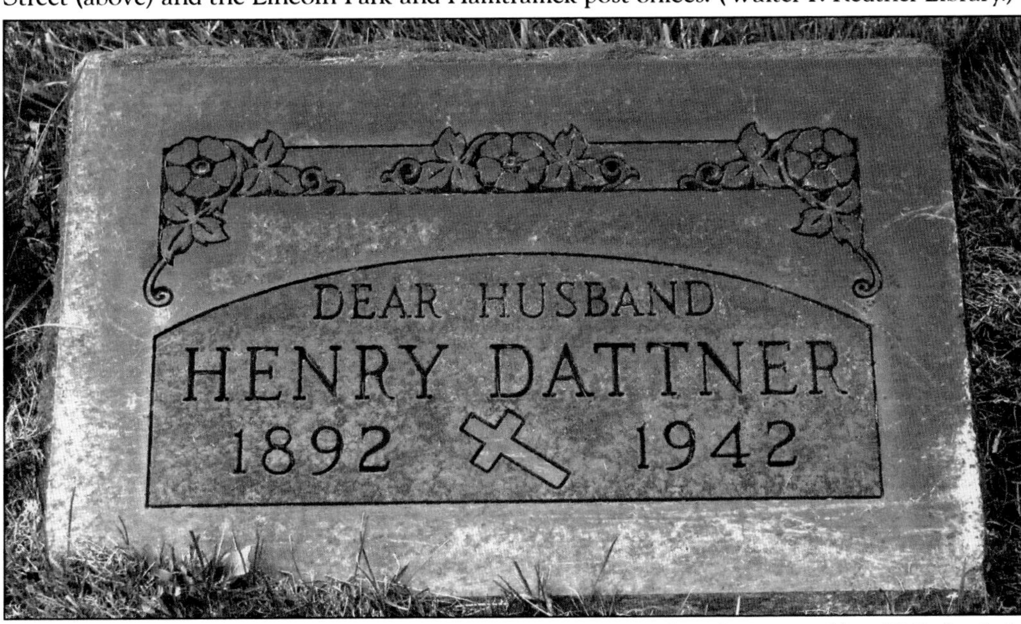

Dattner held several government construction contracts, and at the time of his 1942 death he was building a U.S. Army barracks and other buildings at the U.S. Army Air Corps base near Vincennes, Illinois. While touring the site with his superintendent, his automobile collided with another automobile, fatally injuring Dattner. He is interred in section P.

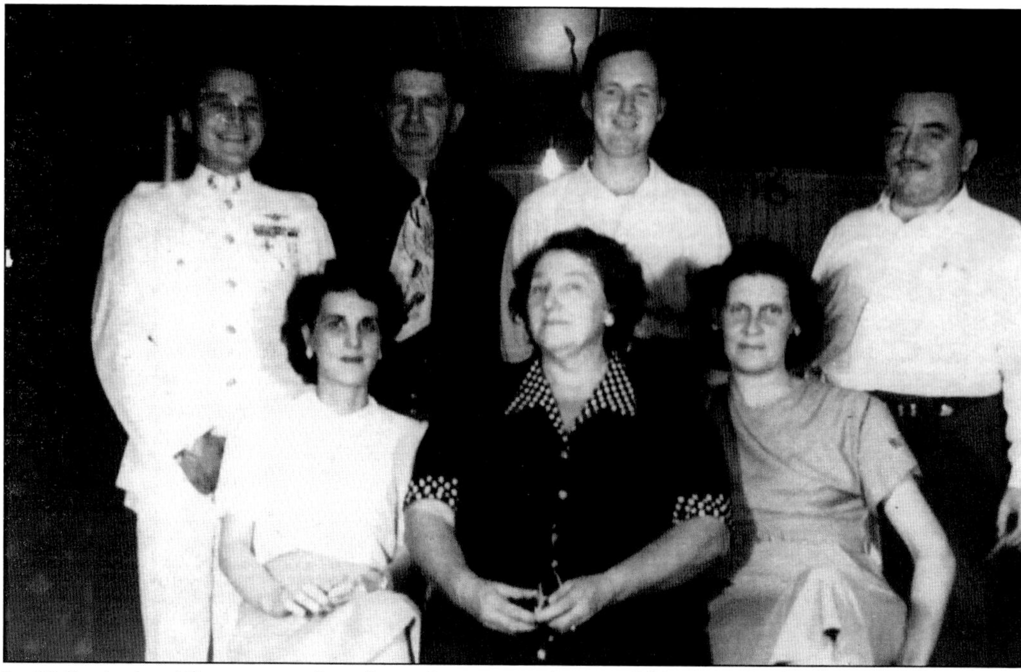

In 1961, Arthur Ternes, standing far right, received a papal blessing for his civic work. In 1944, he organized the Dearborn Chamber of Commerce and acted as its president for its first three years. Ternes established the Dearborn Good Cheer Club, devoted to providing Christmas gifts for needy children, and organized the Dearborn Boys Club, serving on its board of directors for 20 years. (David Reckinger.)

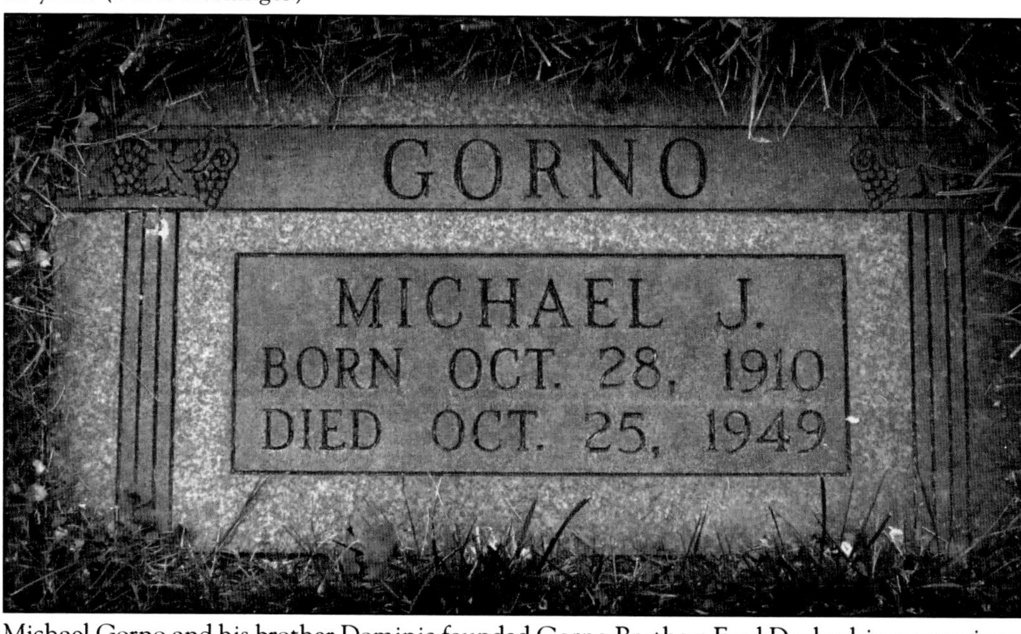

Michael Gorno and his brother Dominic founded Gorno Brothers Ford Dealership, a prominent automobile dealership in Trenton and the downriver area. Gorno served as vice president for the dealership, and for another interest, the White Star Trucking Company. Gorno was buried on what would have been his 39th birthday and is interred next to his brother in section T.

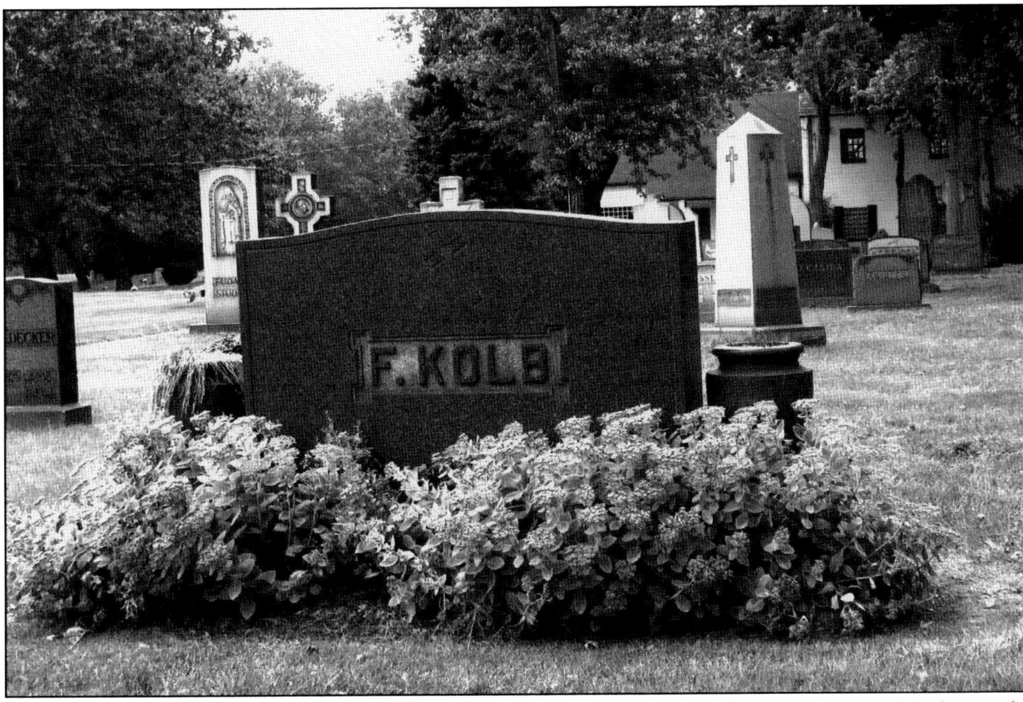

Francis Kolb lived and worked on a farm that his father settled after arriving in Michigan by way of New York from Prussia in 1820. Francis remembered as a young boy helping cut trees on their property to make railroad ties for the Wabash Railroad as it branched out through the Taylor, Lincoln Park, and Ecorse areas. The railroad hired his father, Joseph, to protect the rails from restless Native Americans who were displeased with the noisy encroachment on their hunting grounds. Francis eventually entered the banking business, becoming a director of the State Savings Bank, which later became Security Bank. When his son Alfred died in 1927, he commissioned the Raubar Granite Company to make and erect the monument located in section C. In 1953, Francis donated a section of the family farm for the building of St. Cyril of Jerusalem Church, which is located on Pardee Road in Taylor. St. Cyril merged with St. Paschal Baylon parish in 2007 to become Our Lady of Angels Church. (Holy Cross Cemetery.)

998-9

Dated at July 22 19 27

To Superintendent HOLY CROSS CEMETERY,
DETROIT, MICH.

This is to certify that I have purchased a marker and Monument *from* The Raubar Granite Co. *and I hereby authorize you to place the foundation for same at the Grave of* ALFRED KOLB

who died on 1927 *and is buried in Grave No.* ...... *Lot* 71 *Sec.* C

Signature [illegible]

(Monumental manufacturer will make sketch and mark sizes plainly on reverse side of this slip.)

FORM NO. 20

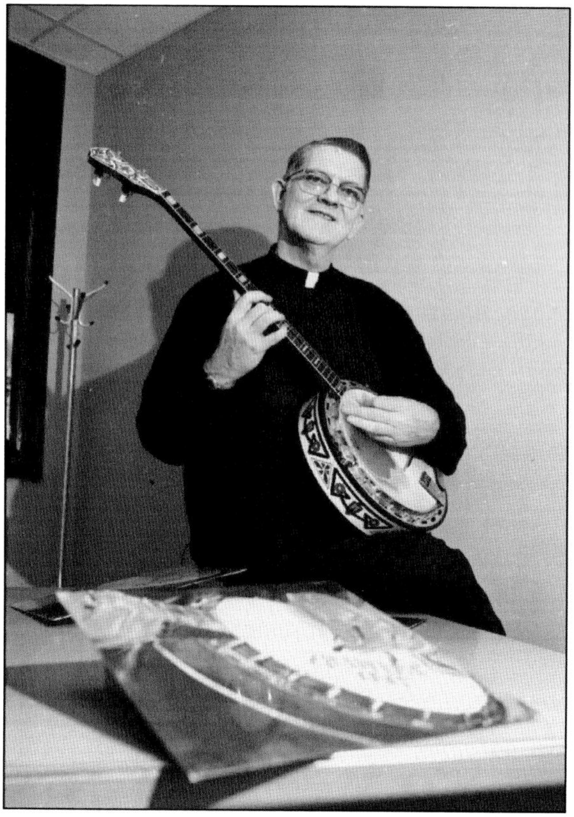

The "banjo playing priest," Fr. Joseph Dustin, inherited his musical talents from his vaudevillian parents. Throughout his career with the Redemptorist fathers, he entertained before audiences, feeling that he was helping people through his music. At one time, he played in a group with an Episcopalian priest, an African American Baptist minister, and a Jewish rabbi; their nickname was the Clerical Four. As an accomplished jazz musician, he could not read music but picked it up by ear. Father Dustin recorded three albums, the first two recorded by Riverside Records, and the last under his own label, Redemptorist Records. Whatever earnings came from concerts or album sales he donated to the Redemptorist missions in Brazil and Thailand. He appeared on national television shows such as *To Tell the Truth*, *What's My Line?*, and *The Tonight Show*. He was an honorary member of the New Orleans Jazz Company. Father Dustin died on September 28, 1989, and is buried in section E.

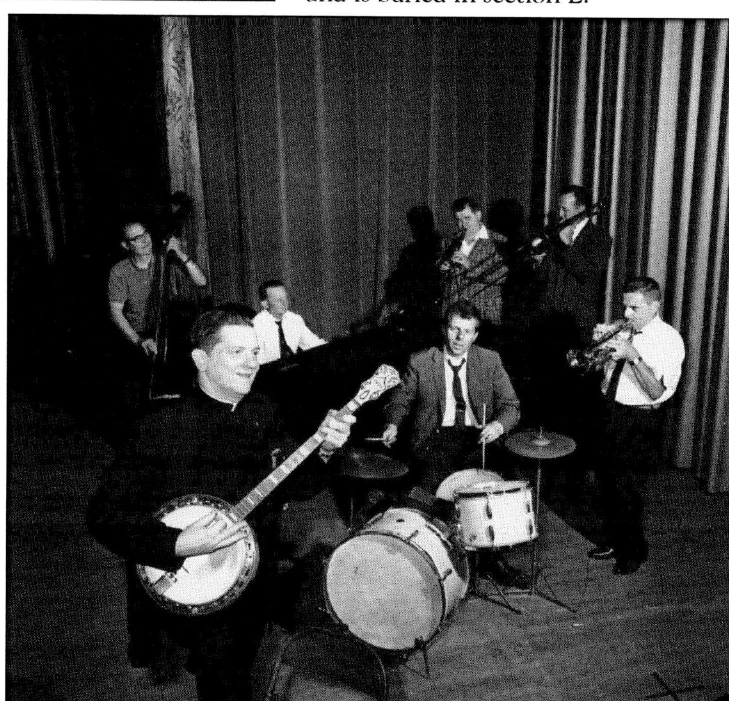

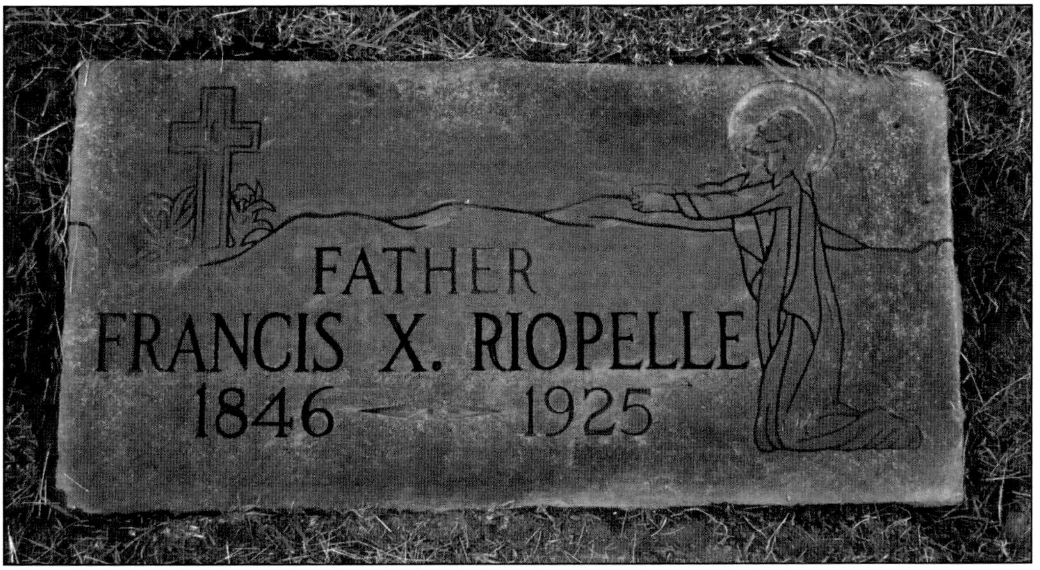

Francis X. Riopelle was a shrewd businessman who never contracted a business transaction by credit. His father, Alexander, passed down to Francis several hundred acres of land, making Francis one of the wealthiest people in the downriver area. Francis served three terms as treasurer of Ecorse Township. He was 79 years old when he died in 1925. Francis is buried in section B next to his parents.

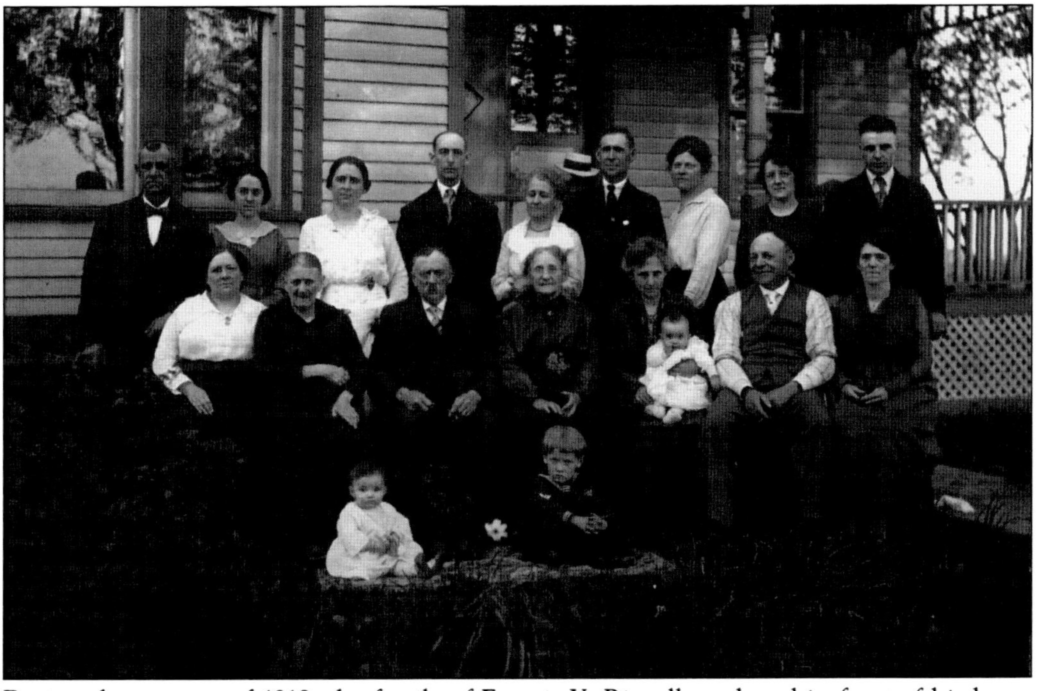

During the summer of 1918, the family of Francis X. Riopelle gathered in front of his home located at the corner of Fort Street and Montie Road in Lincoln Park for this photograph. Francis, or F. X. as he was called (seen middle row, seated third from the left), lived his entire life on the same corner, land that his fifth-great-grandfather settled on in the early 18th century. (Thomas Torango.)

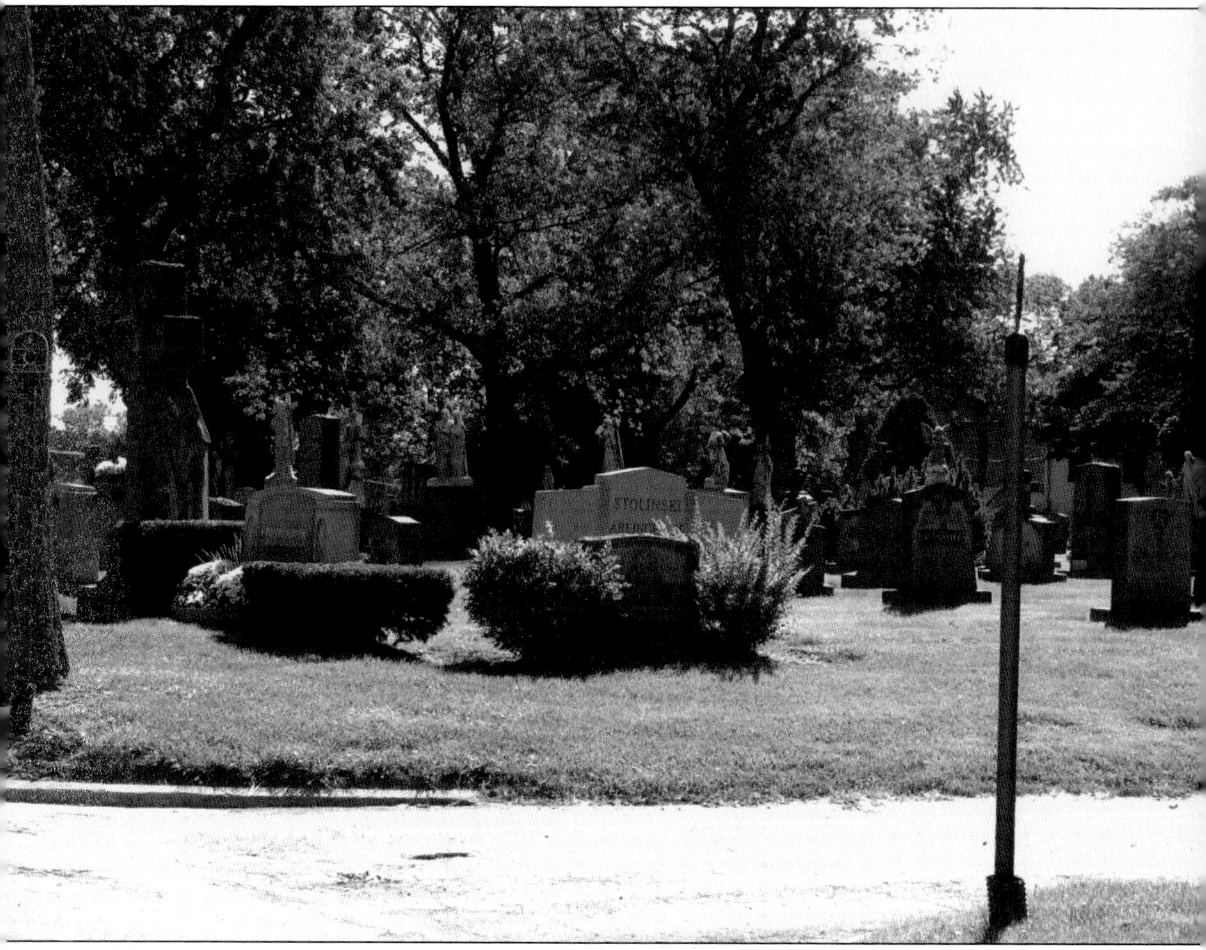

Midnight in a cemetery, a jittery priest, startling sounds, a dropped flashlight—that was the scene shot at this corner for the 1987 mystery film *The Rosary Murders*, starring Donald Sutherland and Charles Durning. Based on a novel written by William X. Kienzel and filmed entirely in Detroit, the movie included scenes at the Hart Plaza waterfront, Ford Motor Company, Pegasus Bar in Greektown, and located at the corner of Junction Street and Vernor Highway, Holy Redeemer Church, both interior and exterior scenes. Kienzel, who attended Holy Redeemer and graduated from the University of Detroit, became a priest and author and used Fr. Robert Koesler, played by Donald Sutherland, as a mystery-solving priest, with *The Rosary Murders* as the first in a series of Father Koesler novels. Kienzel used southwest Detroit as the setting for several of his books.

Four

Lost Too Soon

During its early years, Holy Cross Cemetery held more baby burials, especially stillborn, than adult burials. Inclement weather and a long drive to the closest Catholic cemetery, Mount Elliot, located on Detroit's east side, presented a hardship on farmers whose fields needed tending. After the cemetery's dedication in 1840 and its two-acre size firmly established, the cemetery saw a rapid increase in adult burials. Many of these burials were the result of illness, war, pandemics, primitive medical care, or tragic circumstances of lives lost too soon.

One such tragedy happened on a Sunday evening in June 1907. A young man, distraught over the wayward ways of his wife, who was about to leave him, slit her throat and then his own at the foot of their bed, while their two young daughters, ages seven and five, lay on the bed watching the terrible scene. Too terrified to move, the two young girls clung to each other until daylight when the oldest one mustered the courage to run next door to summon help. The family buried the couple together in section B.

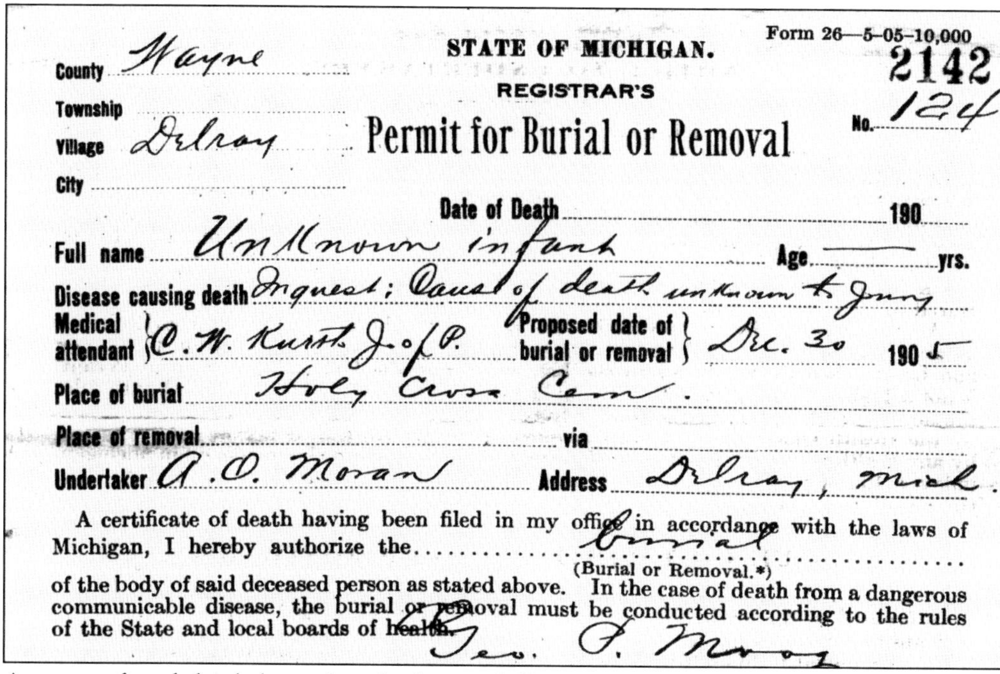

Form 26—5-05-10,000

STATE OF MICHIGAN.

2142

REGISTRAR'S

Permit for Burial or Removal

County Wayne

Township

Village Delray

City

No. 124

Date of Death 190

Full name Unknown infant Age —— yrs.

Disease causing death Inquest; Cause of death unknown to Jury

Medical attendant C. W. Kurth J. of P.

Proposed date of burial or removal Dec. 30 1905

Place of burial Holy Cross Cem.

Place of removal .... via ....

Undertaker A. O. Moran Address Delray, Mich.

A certificate of death having been filed in my office in accordance with the laws of Michigan, I hereby authorize the burial (Burial or Removal.*) of the body of said deceased person as stated above. In the case of death from a dangerous communicable disease, the burial or removal must be conducted according to the rules of the State and local boards of health.

Geo. P. Moran

A woman found this baby under a bush near Jefferson Avenue and brought it the cemetery for burial. The burial permit offers no clue as to the name, sex, age, date of death, or cause of death, just simply the date of burial, December 30, 1905, at 3:00 p.m. Frequently lot owners offered a section of their lots for this type of burial. (Holy Cross Cemetery.)

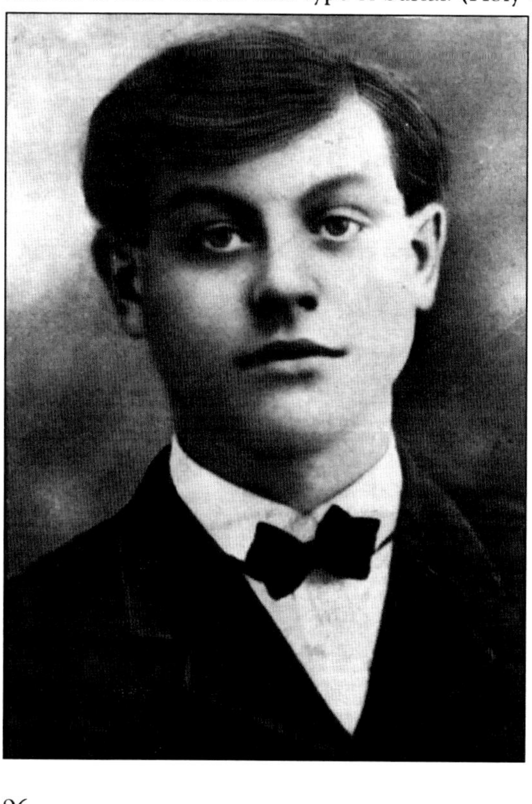

As a young man, 19-year-old Joseph Kusz worked as a hand for the Detroit and Cleveland Steam Navigation Company, a steamship line used by company executives as an alternate form of travel between Detroit and Cleveland. Preferred over train travel, the steamship allowed well-to-do executives an opportunity to throw wild parties. While at work on the docks, Joseph's clothes became drenched, chilling him and triggering deadly pneumonia. He died on August 12, 1905, and is buried in section B. (Kenneth Michalak.)

Alexander and Mary Mero buried two babies, Jane and John, in the same grave, each sharing a different side of the same headstone. Daughter Jane, short for Angeline, died at 13 months old in 1873, while son John, died at 12 months old in 1877. Aside from the names and dates, each side of the stone bears identical markings. The cross represents salvation, while the crescent moon represents purity and innocence. The five-pointed star of Bethlehem represents divine guidance and protection for their souls. This symbolism held special meaning for their parents. The stonecutter phonetically spelled the surname to fit on the stone and save costs, a very common practice. Office records show the name spelled as Meureau and Marue. Other unrelated documentation shows Merrow, Mirrow, and Miro as phonetic derivatives. The children are buried in section B.

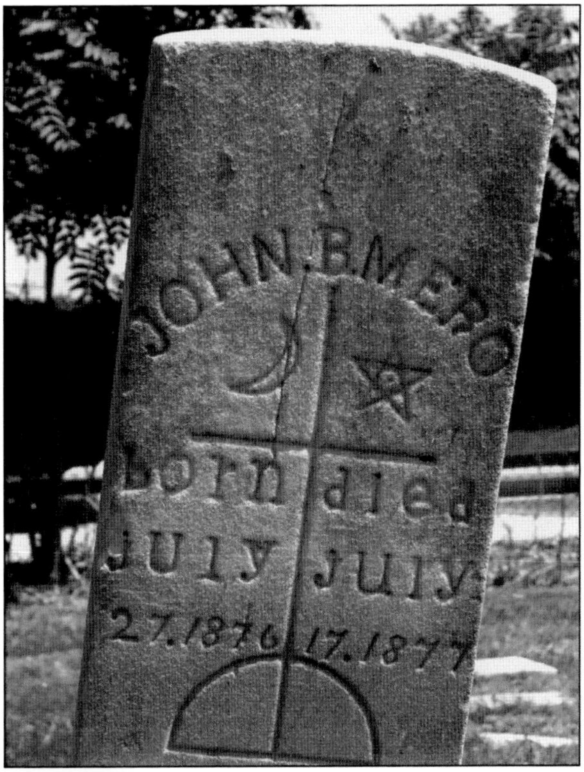

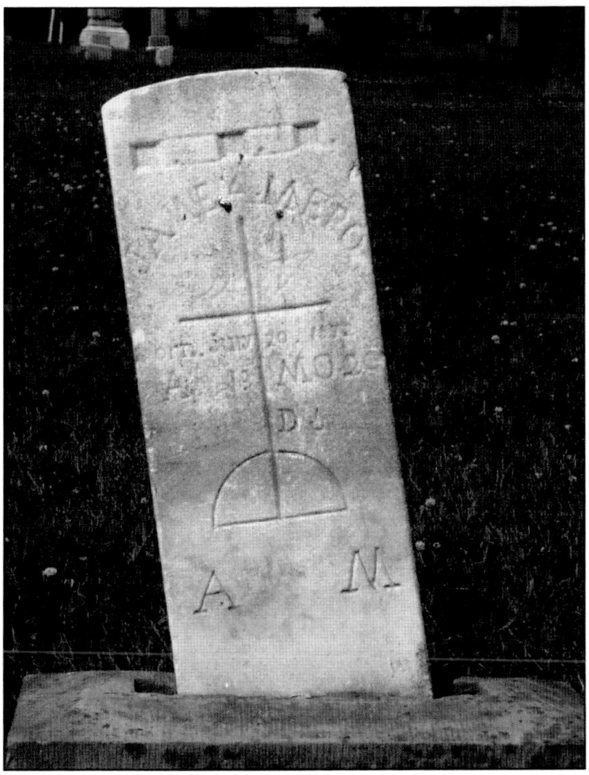

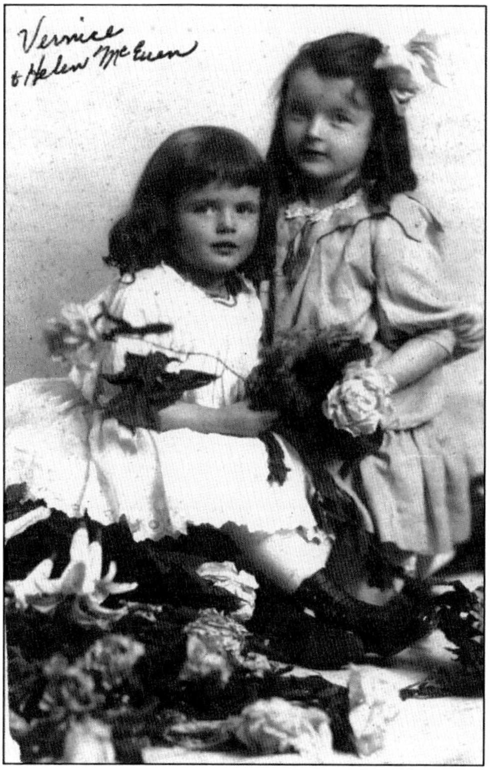

Helen and Vernice McEuen's mother, Margaret, reluctantly agreed to take care of her husband's sister, a nun, ill with tuberculosis, at her husband's insistence. Her worst fear, becoming ill herself, came true, as she succumbed to the disease leaving behind her two small girls. Regrettably, Helen and Vernice died of the same disease. Their aunt, who was the nun, survived. All three are buried in section H. (Sheila Beaubien.)

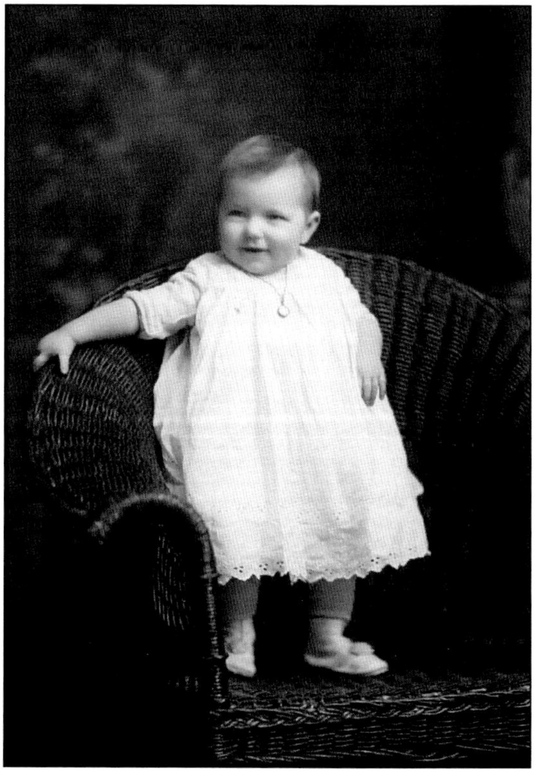

This sweet little baby, Helen Burger, died when the great influenza epidemic of 1918 spread across the globe. She was born in 1917 and died just before her first birthday in 1918. This photograph was taken to celebrate her first birthday. She was the daughter of Stephen Burger and Clara Burns and buried in section D. (John Graf.)

George and Barbara Wolf lived on a farm along Pardee Road in Springwells, a gift from Barbara's father. From 1888 to 1913, Barbara gave birth to 11 children. Their first born, Maggie, died at eight days old. The next seven children lived to adulthood, enjoying the bounties of the farm and their mother's excellent cooking, a reputation she had until her death. (Vera Kolotila.)

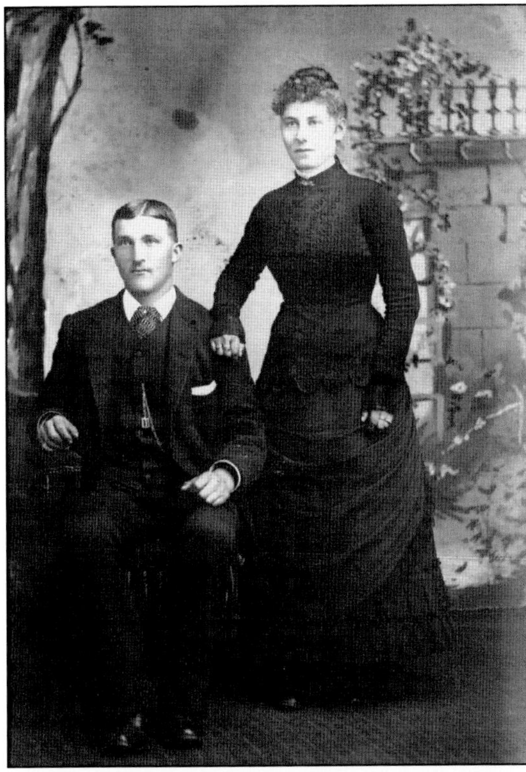

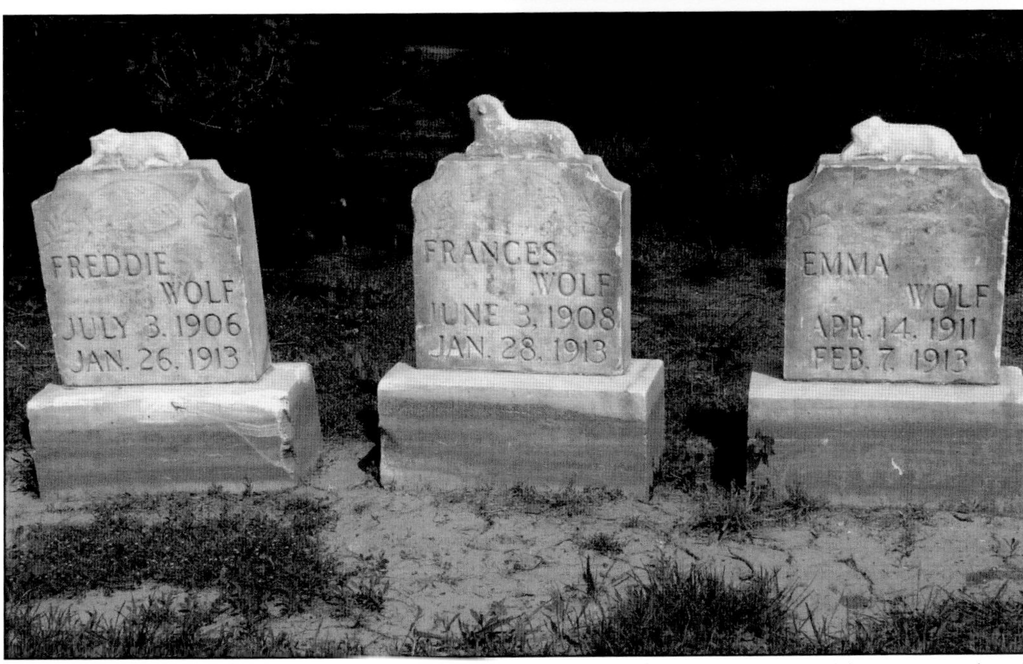

Scarlet fever hit the Wolf family hard in 1913, taking their three youngest children. An outbreak took the life of five-year-old Fred on January 26, 1913. Two days later, a daughter, four-year-old Frances, died. Some 10 days later on February 7, 1913, one-year-old Emily surrendered to the disease. The children are buried in section L. (Vera Kolotila.)

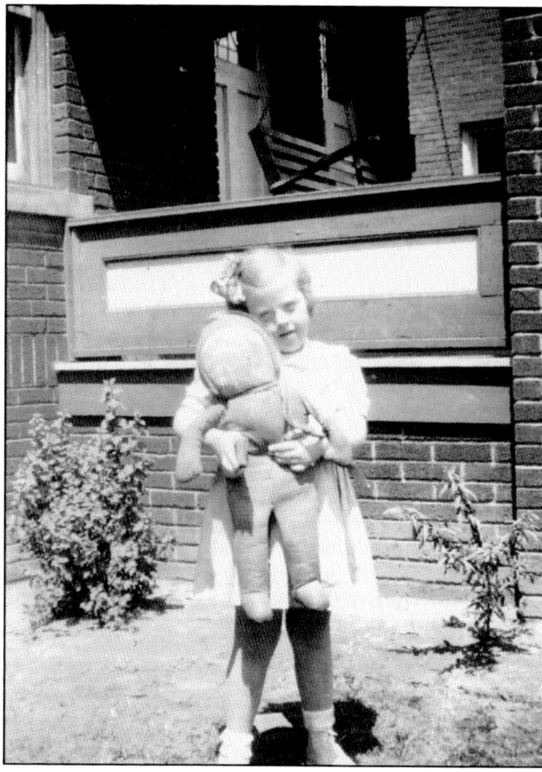

Little Marilyn Ann Burr, a lovable child with Down syndrome, is standing with her favorite teddy bear in front of her home in Detroit. She was just eight years old when she died from scarlet fever, a common disease of the early 20th century that affected mostly children from age 2 to 10. She is buried in section J. (Pamela Walls.)

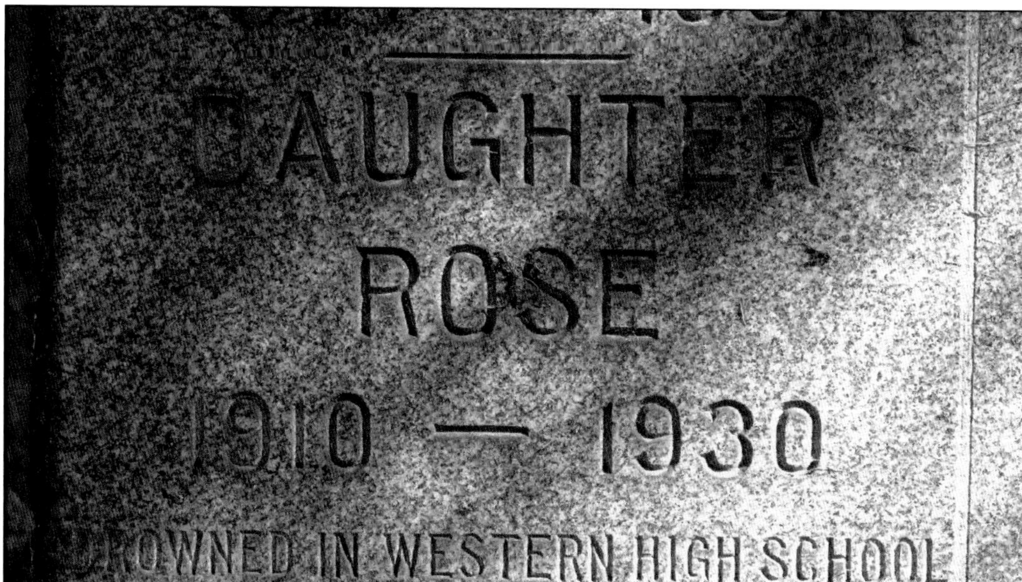

Always with a cheerful disposition, 19-year-old "little mother" Rose Zagar cared for her bedridden mother, ailing father, and nine brothers. As a break from household duties, Rose, a poor swimmer, spent Monday evenings learning to swim at Western High School. Overcome while in the deep end, she sank below the surface less than two minutes, just long enough to prevent her resuscitation. Rose's mother died the following year, and her father and a brother the year after that. She is buried in section C.

The Fourth of July weekend in 1936 was pleasantly warm and sunny, with no indication of the deadly heat wave that would strike the nation a few days later. Steven Ugalish and three friends intended to celebrate the holiday weekend fishing, so when his friends stopped by early on July 3 to get him, he told his mother that he loved her, piled into the automobile, and took off for the gas station. Some 30 minutes later, the police knocked on his mother's door with terrible news. (Nancy Dietz.)

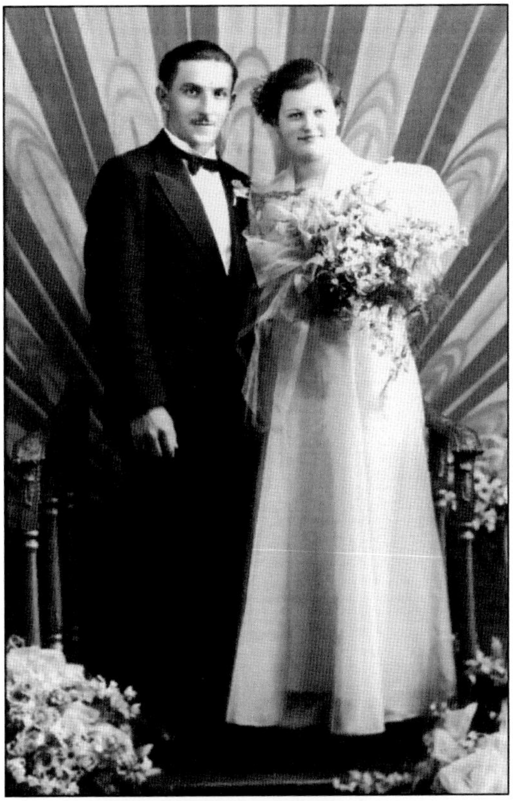

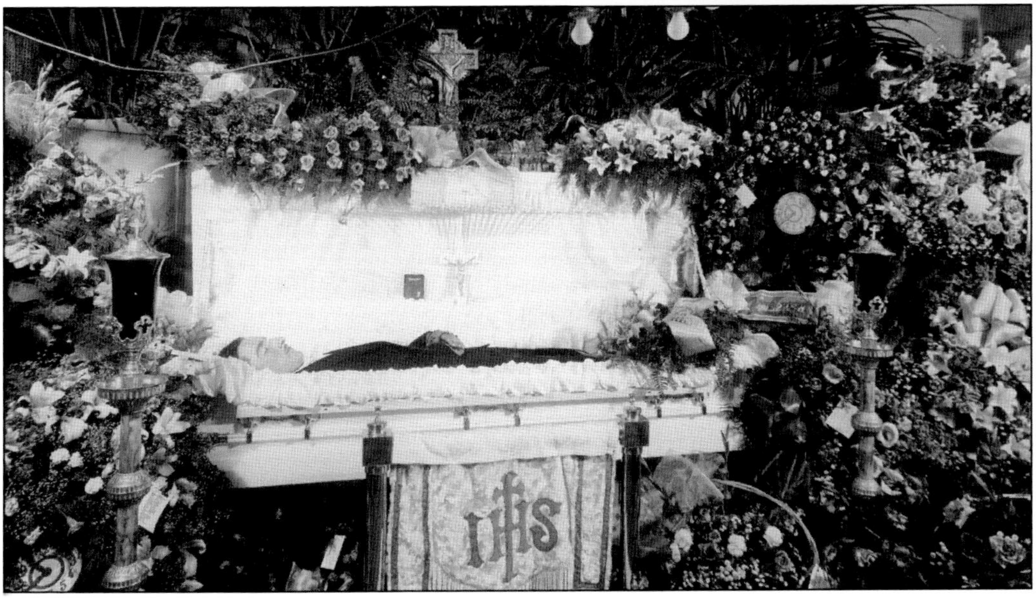

As they pulled into the gas station, they interrupted a robbery in progress, and as any young men with ideals of heroism would do, they chased the would-be robber into an alley hoping to apprehend him. In an inconceivable move, the thief raised his gun over his shoulder and wildly shot behind himself, hitting and killing 23-year-old Stephen. Stephen's valiant efforts allowed the police to capture the thief. He is buried in section H. (Nancy Dietz.)

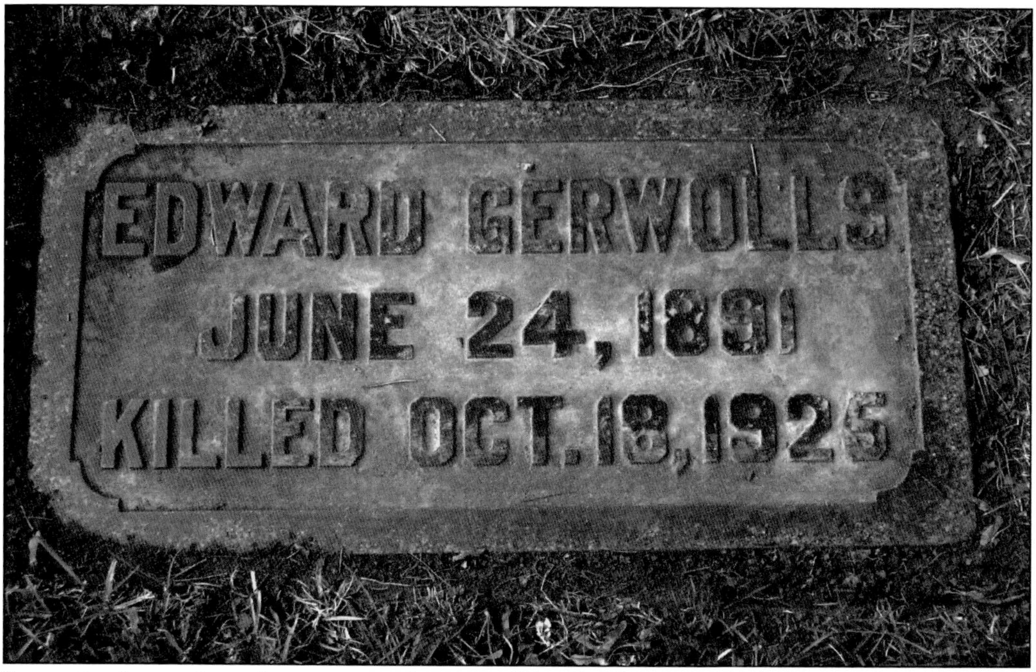

Returning home from their summer home at Woodland Beach north of Monroe on Sunday evening, October 18, 1925, were Edward Gerwolls, his wife Stella, 11-year-old daughter Dorothy, and Edward's niece Mildred Gerwolls. Perhaps tired and eager to get home from the long weekend, Edward, not hearing the crossing alarm bell ringing, unsuccessfully attempted to outdistance a Toledo interurban car across the tracks on West Road in Trenton. The force of the collision sent their car 100 feet past the crossing. Edward, Stella, and Dorothy died instantly, while Mildred, not so badly injured, was released from the hospital two days later. All three Gerwollses are buried in section J.

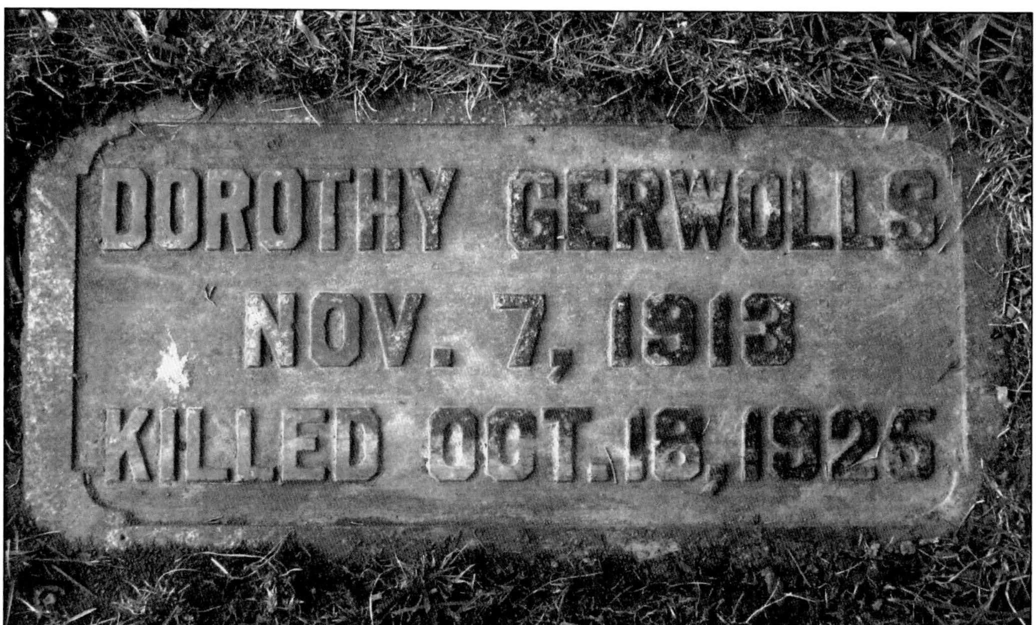

In 1933, sophomore Vincent Kadi was an outstanding fullback for the University of Detroit's football team. His exceptional kicking plays earned the nickname "Quick Kick" Kadi by his teammates. Kadi was a brilliant student and in the summer of 1934 was engaged by Detroit broker Dennis Allison to tutor his children at his country estate near Lapeer, Michigan. (University of Detroit.)

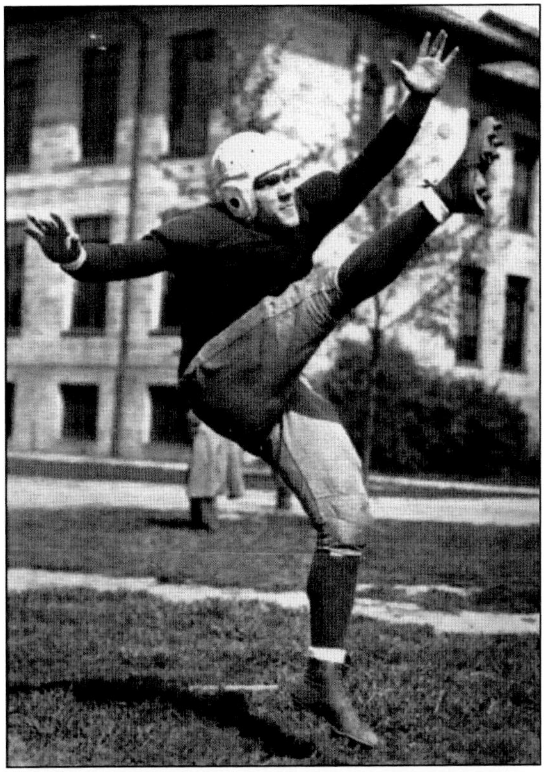

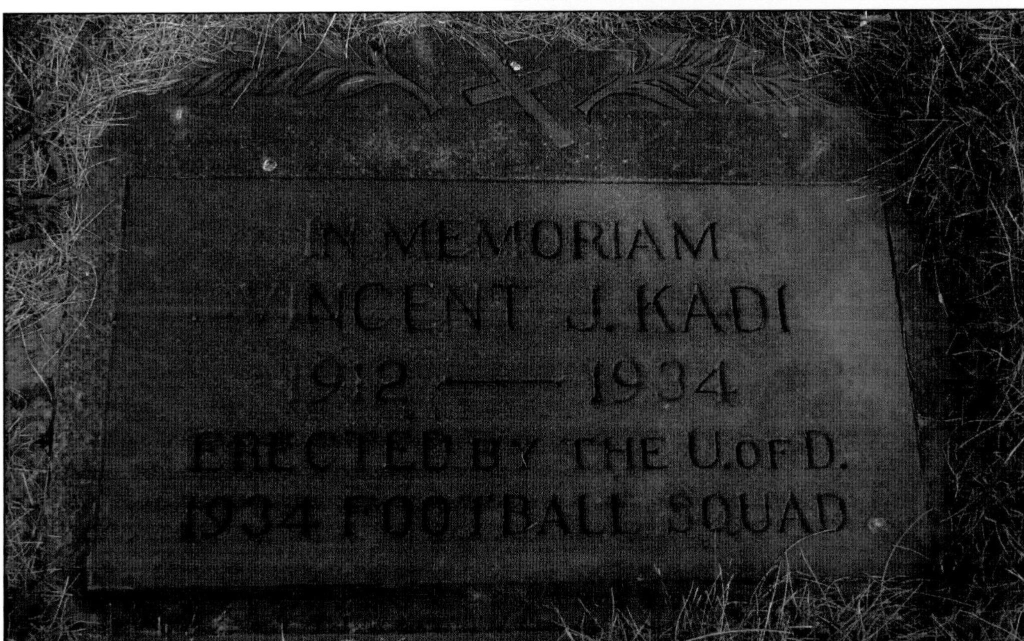

During an early-morning ride with his young pupils, Kadi's rearing horse threw him to the ground, breaking his neck and killing him instantly. His teammates acted as pallbearers for the funeral, afterward purchasing this headstone in remembrance of their teammate and friend. He is buried in section H.

Dorothy Staelens' obituary said the 10-year-old died from a heart attack on January 4, 1935. She died at Detroit's Children's Hospital after a three-week stay for treatment of acute inflammation of the heart. Dorothy's father, Theophile, immigrated from Belgium to Lansing, where he worked for REO Motor Car Company, later moving to Lenawee County where Dorothy was born and finally to Detroit. Dorothy is buried in section S.

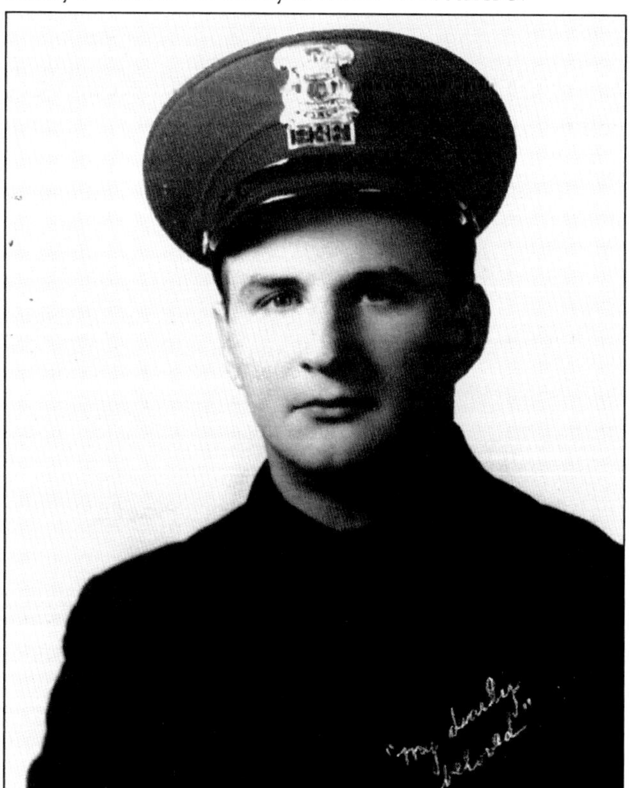

On June 6, 1943, 26-year-old Detroit police officer from the 2nd precinct, Mitchell Lipinski, lost his life while on duty. He attempted to disperse a group of rowdy men standing in front of a tavern on the corner of Trumbull Street just down from the old Briggs Stadium, when one of them pulled out a revolver and shot him. (Michele Matuszewski.)

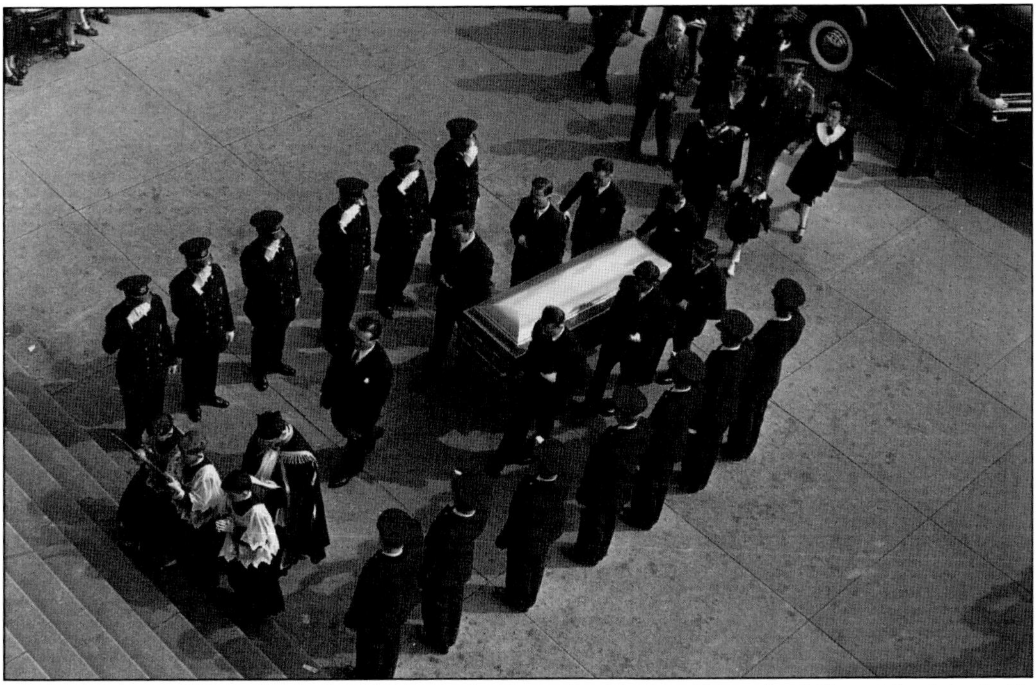

Fr. John Chrobak is leading Mitchell's casket into St. Hedwig Church, followed by Mitchell's brother holding the hand of Mitchell's little daughter Laurentine. Behind them are Lipinski's mother, his brother and sister, and then hundreds of family, friends, and police officers. Mitchell's wife, Veronica, absent from the service, had been rushed to Grace Hospital early that morning where she gave birth to their daughter, Michele. (Michele Matuszewski.)

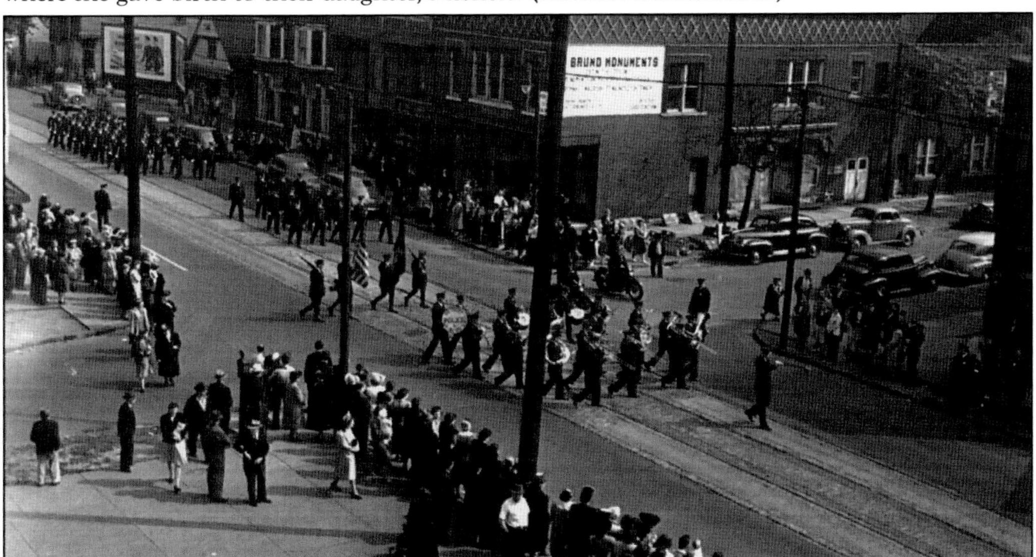

Crowds of people stopped and watched patrolman Lipinski's funeral cortege as it traveled down Junction Street on its way from St. Hedwig Church to the cemetery. Two platoons from the Detroit police and the police band escorted the mourners for the two-and-a-half-mile-long procession. The family stood on one side of Mitchell's grave while the platoons stood on the other as the bugles played taps and a gun salute broke the silence. (Michele Matuszewski.)

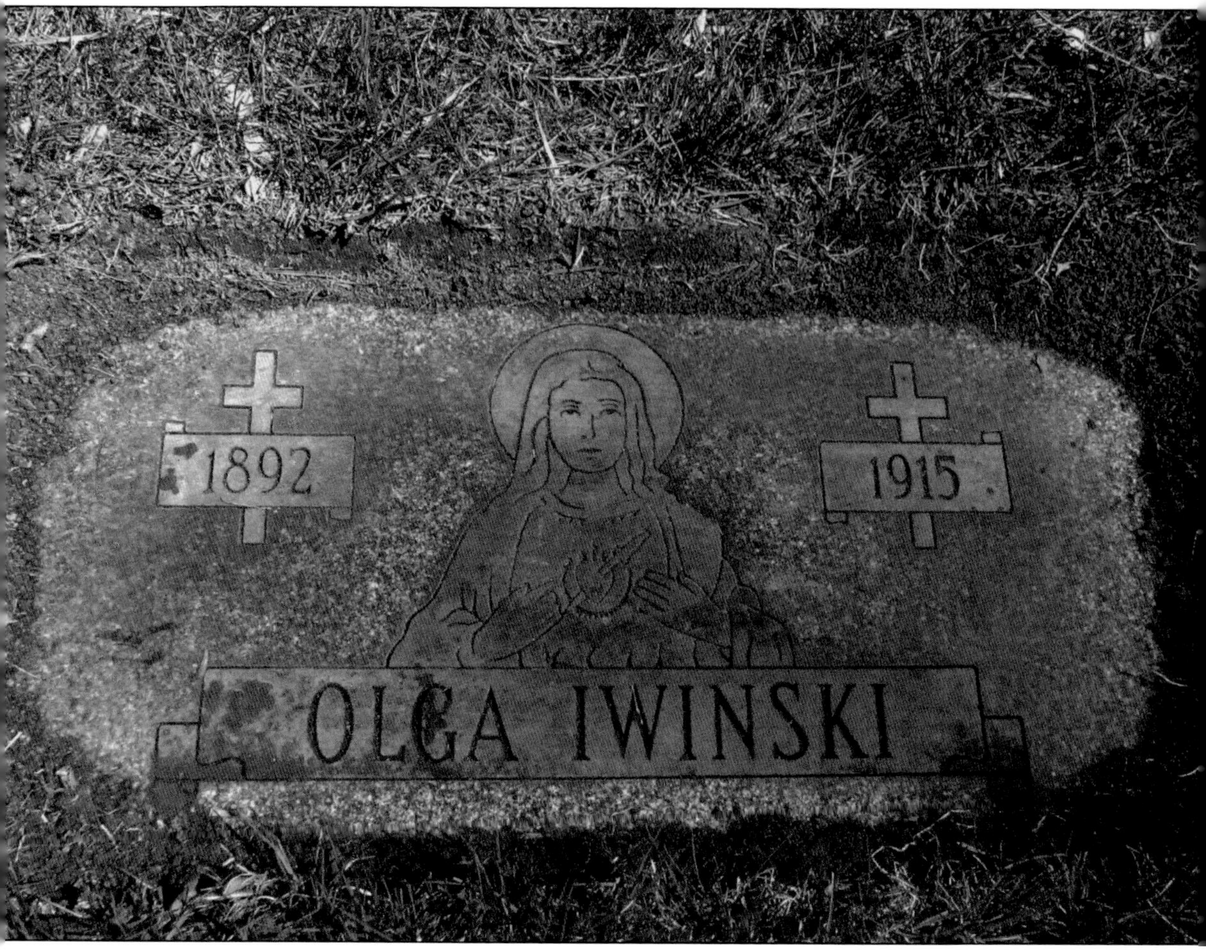

Independence Day in 1915 dramatically changed from celebration to grief for the Iwinski family when the motorcar that Olga Iwinski, her brother Julius, and his wife, Clara, were riding in was crushed by a train at Green Avenue at the Wabash and Pere Marquette Railways. Olga, Julius, and Clara were returning home from a holiday party with Joseph and Nettie Fabyszak when a freight train barreled through the unattended crossing instantly killing Olga, Joseph, and Nettie. Julius lost his right arm the following day. The holiday saw four accidents involving motorcars and trains at crossings, all with fatalities, yet they were half the number of accidents from the previous year's holiday. The police surgeon touted the decrease in accidents due to Detroit's citizens becoming sane during holiday festivities. Clara and the Fabyszaks' funerals were held together. Olga is buried in section K.

Five

THOSE WHO STOOD IN HARM'S WAY

Thomas Jefferson said, "The price of freedom is eternal vigilance." Although there is no designated military section at Holy Cross Cemetery, there are servicemen and servicewomen from all major United States conflicts (peaceful times as well) since the Civil War buried here. Of the eight Civil War soldiers buried in the cemetery, only one, Theophile Girard, has a military stone. Francis Busha served his country during the Civil War but lies in an unknown, unmarked grave in section B. By far, the most represented conflict is World War II, their deaths indicative of the cemetery's prime years. Many of these Greatest Generation heroes have family stones that do not indicate their military service or simply tell their branch of service. Theodore McKalko's stone reads US55475792 and C20071395, his serial numbers from the United States and Canada militaries. The office recorded ex-servicemen burials until 1943 in a separate binder, since then the office indicates a military burial with an orange card in the index file.

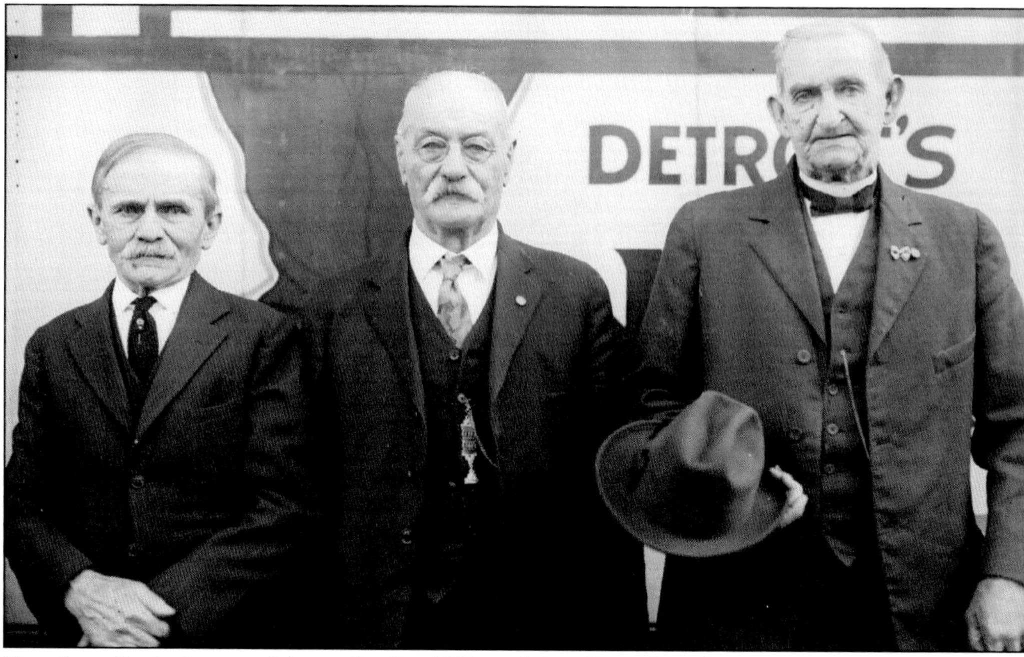

Napoleon Pepin is one of the eight Civil War soldiers buried in the cemetery. Pepin (middle) is standing between two fellow soldiers at the Grand Army of the Republic National Encampment held in 1891 at Detroit. He served in the Michigan 22nd and 29th Infantry Regiments, Company D. Pepin is interred in section M.

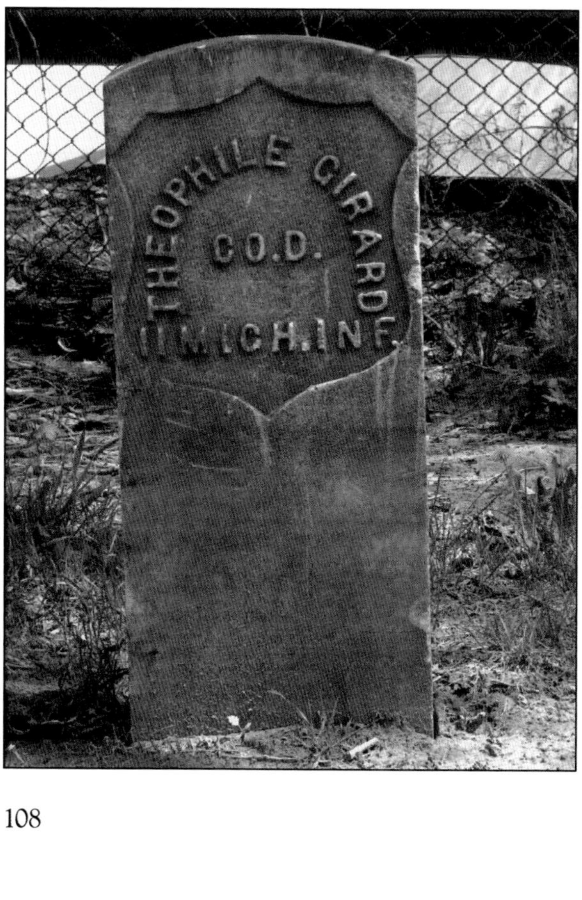

Theophile Girard's military stone is the only Civil War stone in the cemetery. Girard, a native Canadian, joined the 11th Regiment Michigan Infantry, second organization, in January 1865 at Jackson. His company guarded the Chattanooga and Knoxville Railroad in Tennessee, mustering out at Nashville in September 1865. He is buried in section K.

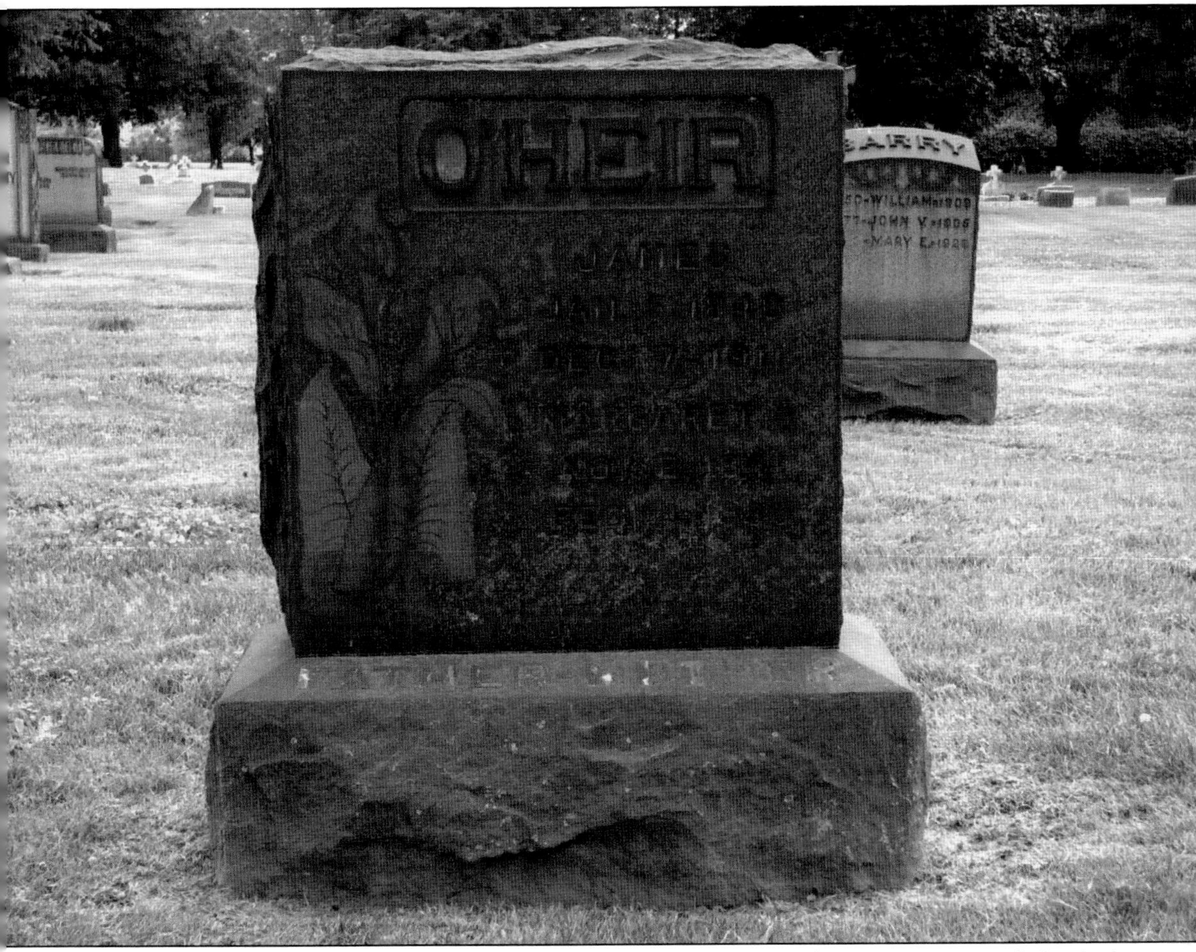

Spurred by the Civil War, James O'Heir, an eventual lifetime military man, entered the 2nd Regiment, United Sates Artillery Regular Army in 1860 in New York. Born in Limerick, Ireland, the six-foot-one-and-a-half-inch-tall, red-haired, blue-eyed sergeant must have been a commanding presence to his men. While on duty at Gloucester Point, Virginia, a horse kicked O'Heir on the bridge of his nose, an injury that plagued him for several years. O'Heir spent the bulk of the Civil War years at Brownsville, Texas, returning to Fort Hamilton, New York, in December 1865 where he met and married Margaret Cosgrove in 1867. O'Heir retired from the U.S. Army in 1890. He buried three of his small children at the Fort Wayne Cemetery, who were later removed to Woodmere Cemetery, and once again to Holy Cross Cemetery. O'Heir and his family are buried in section H.

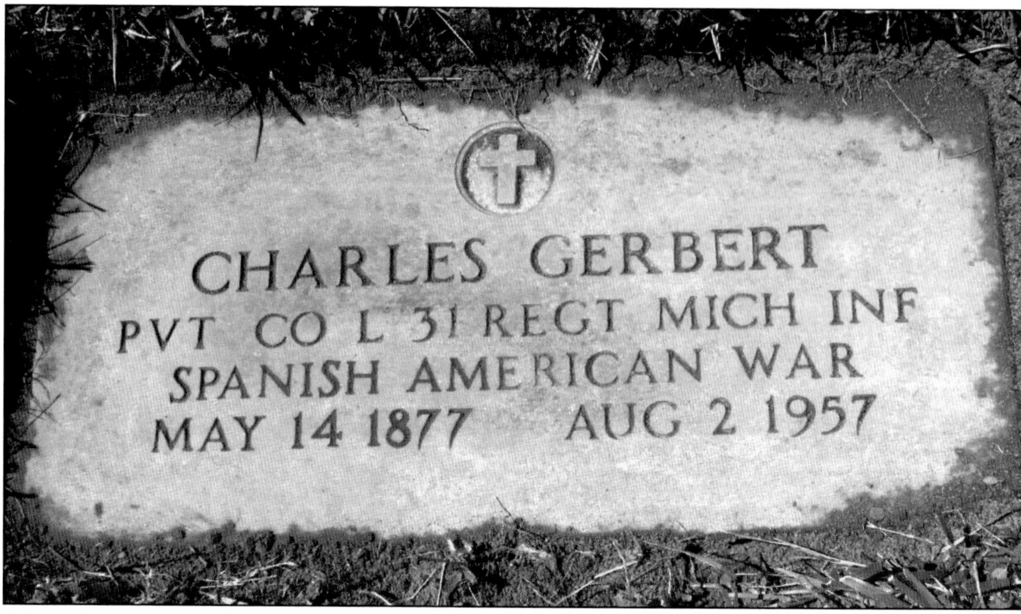

After the sinking of the USS *Main* in Havana, Cuba, on February 15, 1898, the rally cry resounded across the nation "Remember the Main!" Pres. William McKinley's proclamation calling for 125,000 volunteers to fight the war with Spain prompted Charles Gerbert to enlist, and in January 1899, the private of Company L, 31st Regiment of the Michigan Infantry landed at Cienfugeos, Cuba. His orders were to maintain order and protect property. Gerbert came home in May 1899. He is buried in section J.

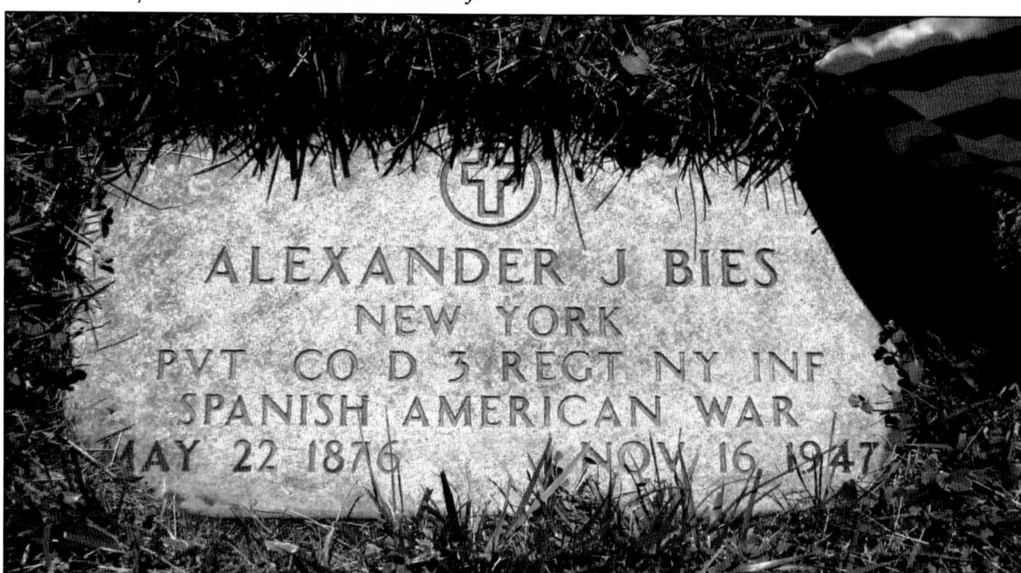

Also hearing 1898's "Remember the Main" rally cry, Alexander Bies enlisted and served with Company D, 3rd Regiment Infantry from Oswego, New York. During his regiment's deployment to Camp Alger in Virginia, Alexander developed otitis that left him deaf in one ear and partially deaf in the other. Bies suffered from vertigo and shell shock, prompting him to seek treatment at a National Home for Disabled Volunteer Soldiers, the precursor of the Veterans Administration. Bies rests in section J.

The influenza pandemic of 1918 killed an estimated 43,000 United States servicemen in World War I. Thomas and Della O'Brien lost two sons during that year. Son Thomas, a four-year Detroit policeman, entered the military and in less than one week died at Camp Custer. Seven months later, son James died at Fort Benjamin in Harrison, Indiana. Another brother, John, stationed with Gen. John J. Pershing in France, survived the epidemic. The brothers are buried in section D.

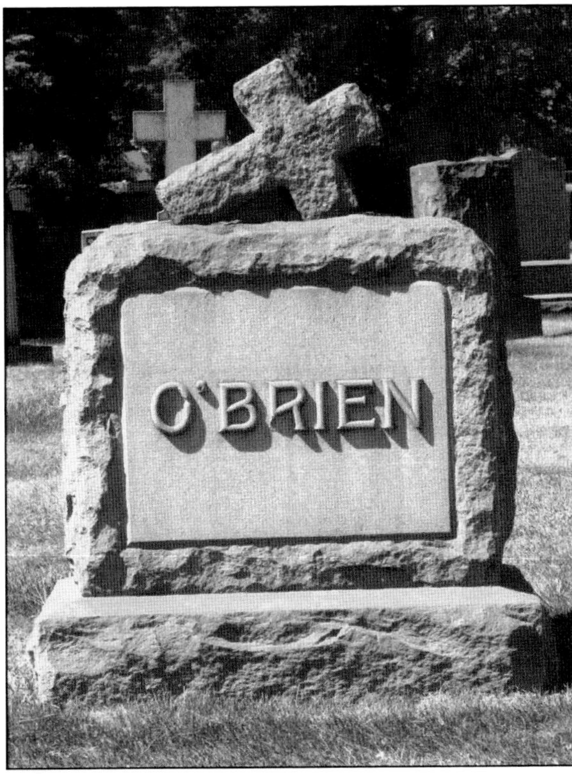

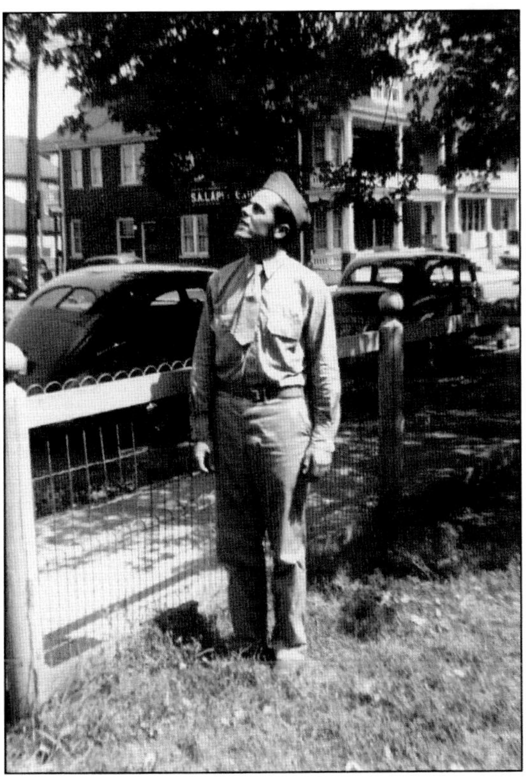

John Markey, the "Fighting Irishman," drove a truck on the Burma Trail in the China-Burma-India Theater during World War II. The hot, steamy road wound itself from India across Burma to China, allowing the Allies to send war supplies and materials to China in anticipation of building an army and naval base there. John died in 2002 and is buried in section D. (John Graf.)

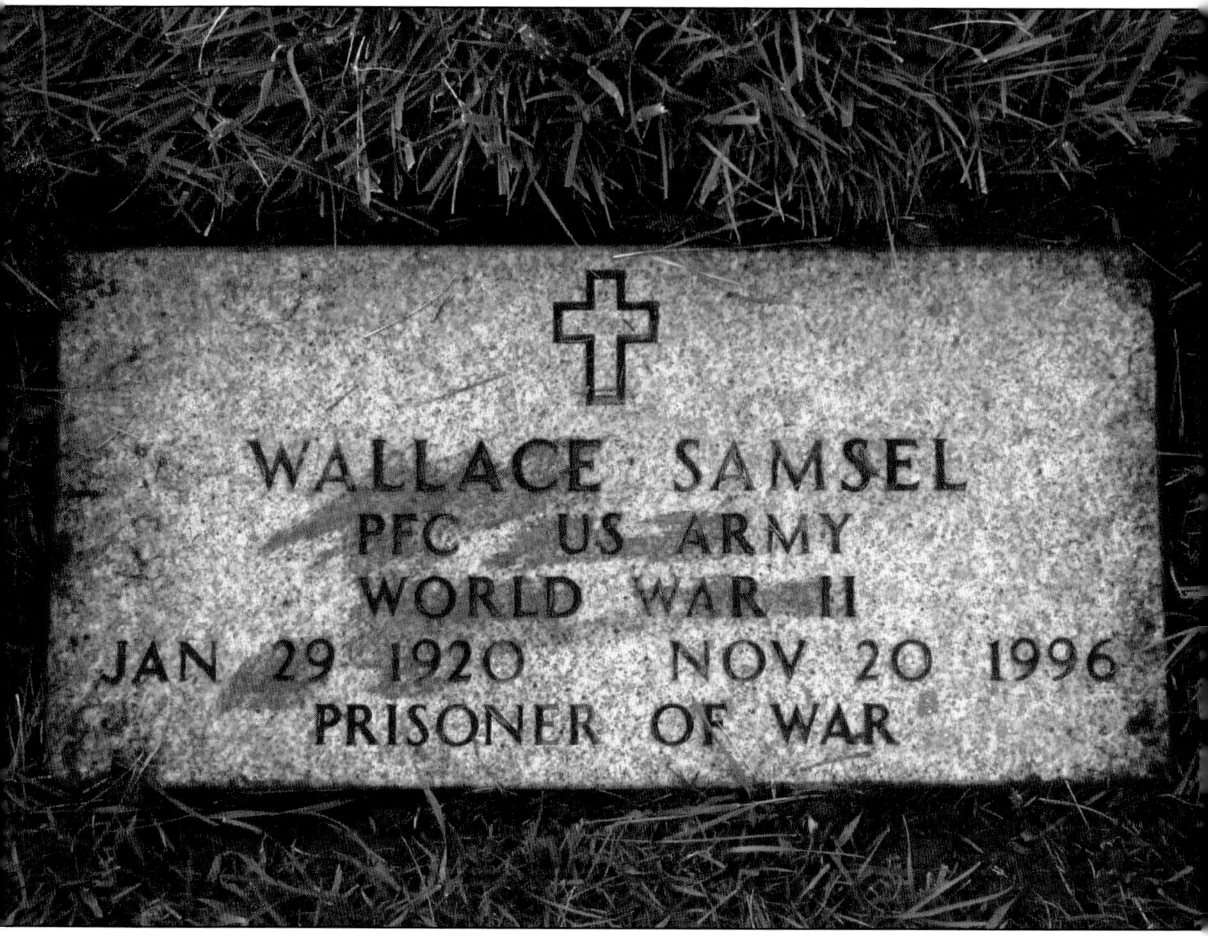

Truly a part of the Greatest Generation, Pvt. Wallace Samsel, United States Calvary, was on patrol with six other men when taken prisoner in 1944 and sent to Stalag 7A at Moosburg, Bavaria. Only three of the seven survived to make the trip to Moosburg, the largest prisoner of war camp in Germany. Built on 85 acres to house 10,000 prisoners, it held approximately 110,000 at the time of liberation in 1945, including 15,000 American, British, and Russian officers and 200 generals. In order to save his life, Samsel set out on day trips to work camps working in factories and on farms or repairing railroads. The winter hit the prisoners hard; their shabby wooden barracks and worn clothes offered no protection from the bitter cold. Samsel suffered severe frostbite, a condition that ailed him the remainder of his life. At the time of his repatriation, Samsel weighed 90 pounds.

After his return home, Samsel spent nearly a year recuperating at the Veterans Hospital in Allen Park and afterward worked for maintenance on the hospital grounds. For the remainder of his life, Samsel suffered from nightmares and cold sweats bound to his ordeal. In the late 1940s, Samsel met and married his wife, Ruth, in Kentucky and had two children. Their daughter Anita (below) was born on December 25, 1955, and died from pneumonia on January 19, 1960. The couple moved to Mesa, Arizona, for their retirement years, and that is where Samsel died, in the veterans hospital. They are buried in section W; Anita is buried in section U. (Daniel Samsel.)

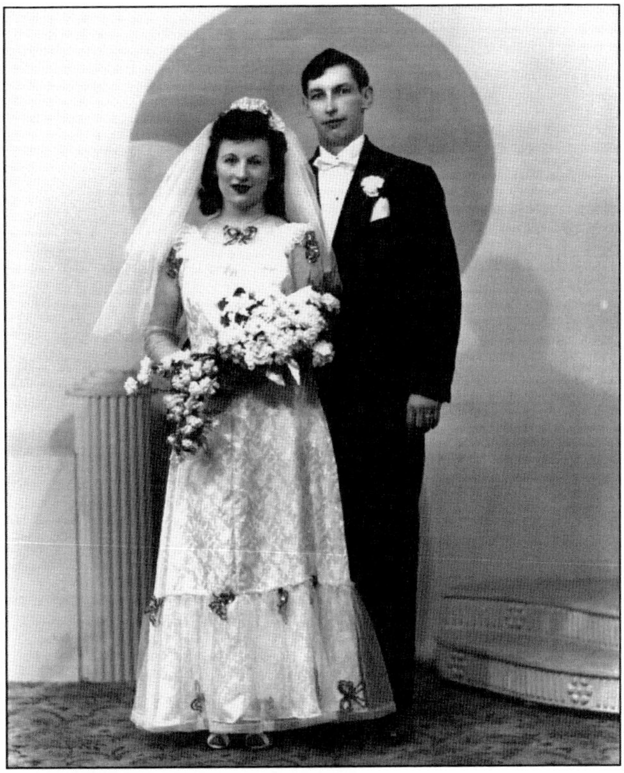

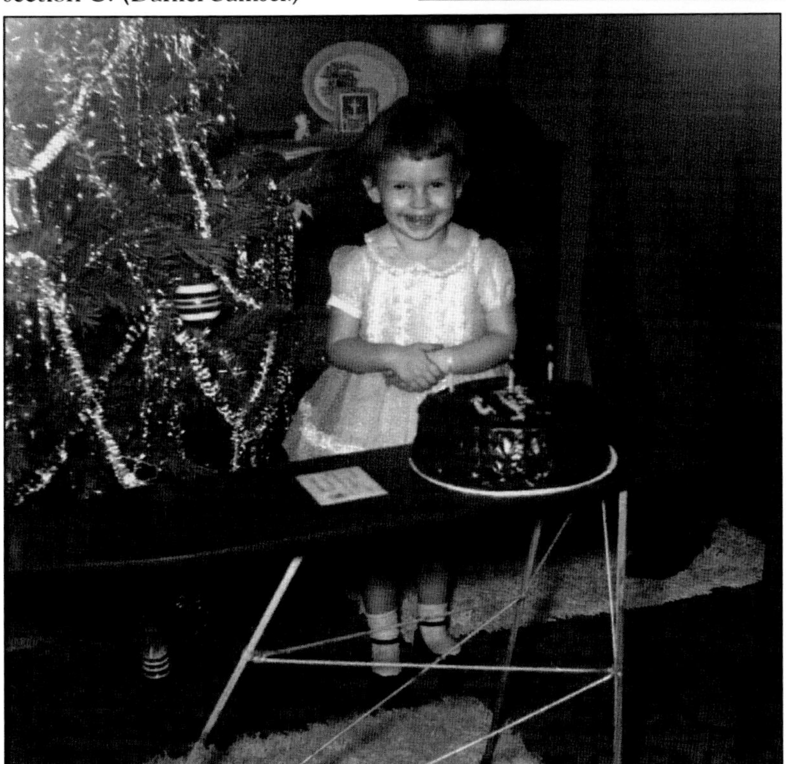

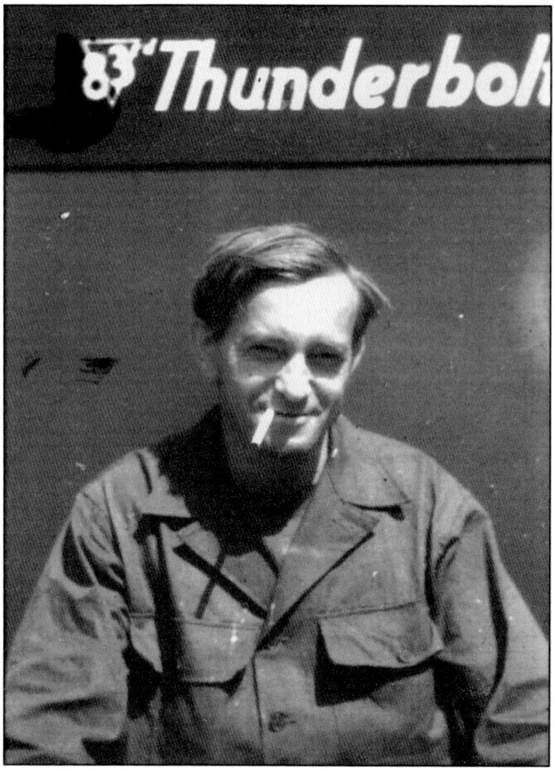

Some 12 days after the Allied invasion at Normandy, Anthony Sitek and the 83rd Infantry Thunderbolt Division passed over Omaha Beach and into the heart of the war. He was part of the incredible dash across northern Germany in 13 days to establish a bridgehead across the Elbe River, the only Allied force to cross into the Eastern European Theater. (Robert Brescoll.)

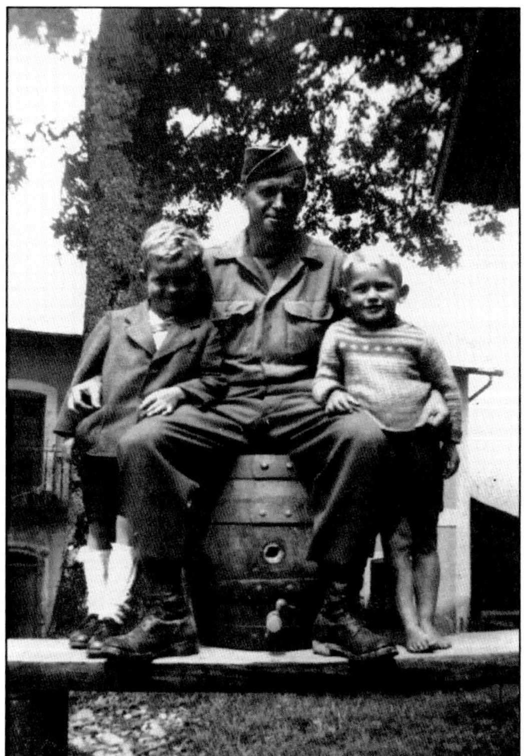

Here Sitek relaxes with two Belgian children after the Battle of the Bulge. Sitek was wounded twice during his three years of service overseas. He returned home in 1946 to his job as a truck driver for the *Detroit Times* newspaper. He died in 1952 at 40 years old and is buried in section U. (Robert Brescoll.)

Cpl. John Barry earned five medals during the New Guinea campaign, Gen. Douglas MacArthur's stepping-stone to the Philippine Islands in the Pacific Theater during World War II. Barry spent nearly two years there as an MP (military policeman) after MacArthur's forces retook the Philippines in 1944. He returned home to Kansas on January 20, 1946. (William Barry.)

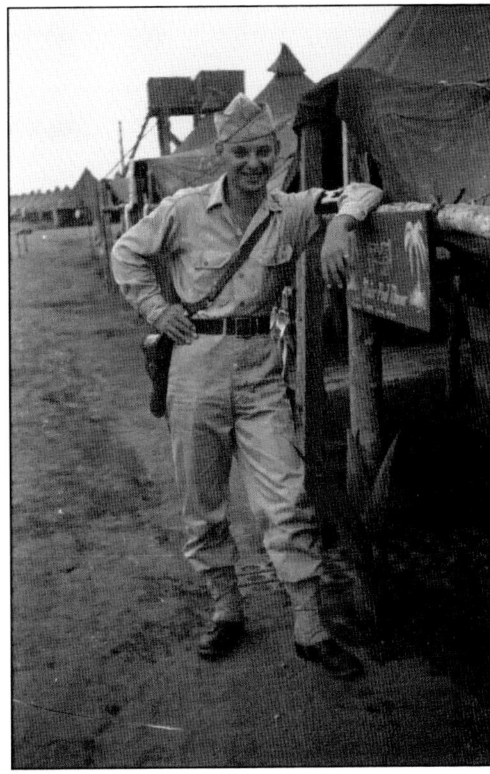

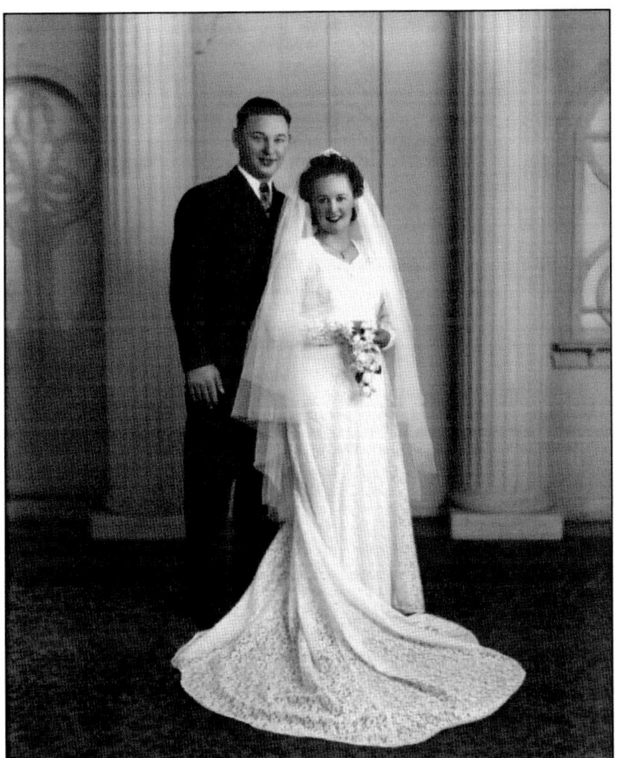

Ruth Morrisson did her nurses training at Borgess Hospital in Kalamazoo. Stationed at Camp Custer and preparing to ship overseas, Barry went to a USO dance where he met Morrisson. Smitten, he walked her home after the dance. They married on April 27, 1946, and celebrated their 60th wedding anniversary in 2006. John and Ruth are buried in section U. (William Barry.)

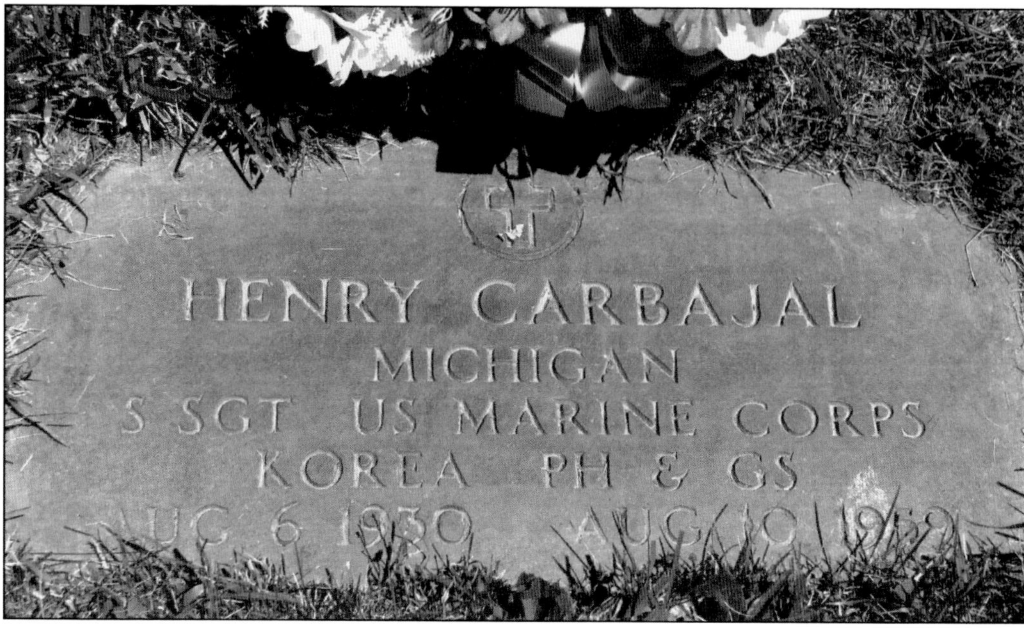

A sergeant in the U.S. Marines, Henry Carbajal left behind a wife and two young children, the youngest just 11 months old, when Henry died at the Camp Geiger firing range at Camp Lejeune, North Carolina, where he was a veteran weapons instructor. The bazooka anti-tank rocket he was handling exploded prematurely, penetrating his chest. Henry earned the Purple Heart and Gold Star. He is buried in section G.

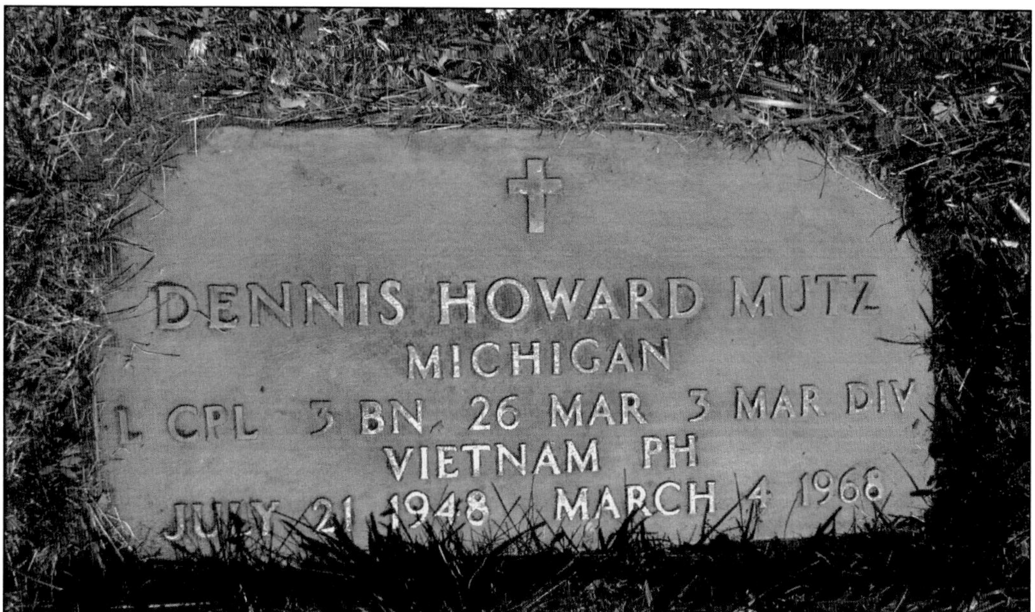

The Vietnam Veterans War Memorial in Washington, D.C., bears the name of Lance Cpl. Dennis Howard Mutz. The young 19-year-old Marine earned the Purple Heart and lost his life in Khe Sanh, South Vietnam, on March 4, 1968. Mutz became a fallen hero when his company, Kilo Company, took heavy enemy artillery fire, estimated more than 1,300 rounds per day. He is buried in section T.

Six

HELP ALONG THE WAY

After a loved one dies, many people step in to help ease the way. From the cemetery's earliest archives, dozens of church names pepper the cemetery records. Other than the 1835 mission, St. Alphonsus is historically the first connected with the cemetery; Most Holy Redeemer, the largest parish; Holy Cross Hungarian, the most stalwart. The list is reflective of the community's history—as settlements amalgamated into sprawling cities parishes formed and as the population dwindled, churches closed. The once-standard practice of a graveside ritual has given way to a short service in the cemetery chapel. The little chapel at Holy Cross Cemetery evolved from a log house to small frame structure to cement block, but its sedulous mission has always been to provide comfort.

The cemetery is the final resting place for several of Detroit's early funeral directors. Some started out as carpenters who naturally fell into the casket-making business and then into the funeral business. Some purchased and built new funeral homes for their expanding businesses or changed their profession during the depression into the more viable funeral business to support their family. Some left their businesses to their children, and some, like the churches, closed.

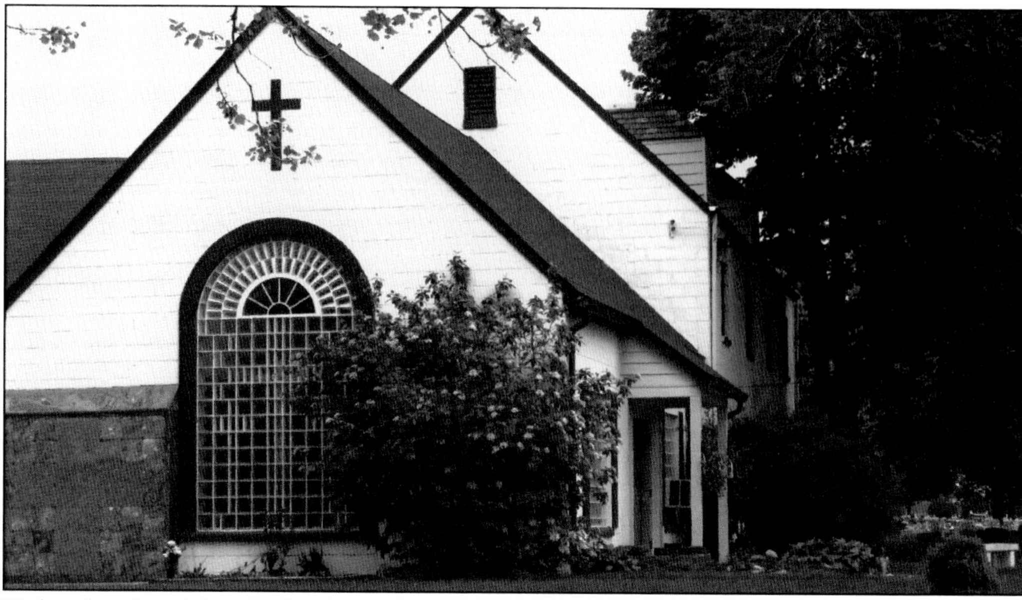

Today the chapel has fresh white paint and charming landscaping. The new pale blue, pink, green, and yellow stained-glass window, installed in 2005, filters a soft glowing light into the chapel. Trees next to the garage have gracefully matured, and the cremation niche butts against the chapel window.

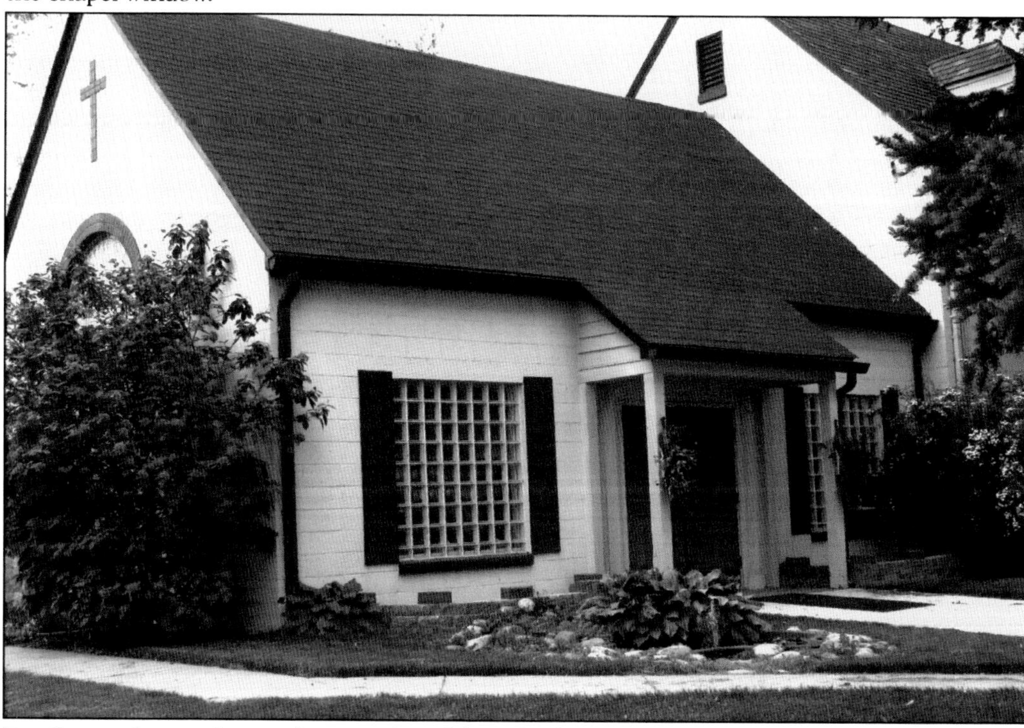

Family members gather in the cozy chapel for a final service prior to burial. For most, this is the last chance they have to say goodbye to their loved ones as most families opt to forego graveside services. From this point, the groundskeepers place the casket in the vault and proceed to the grave site, accompanied by mourners who wish to see the concluding burial.

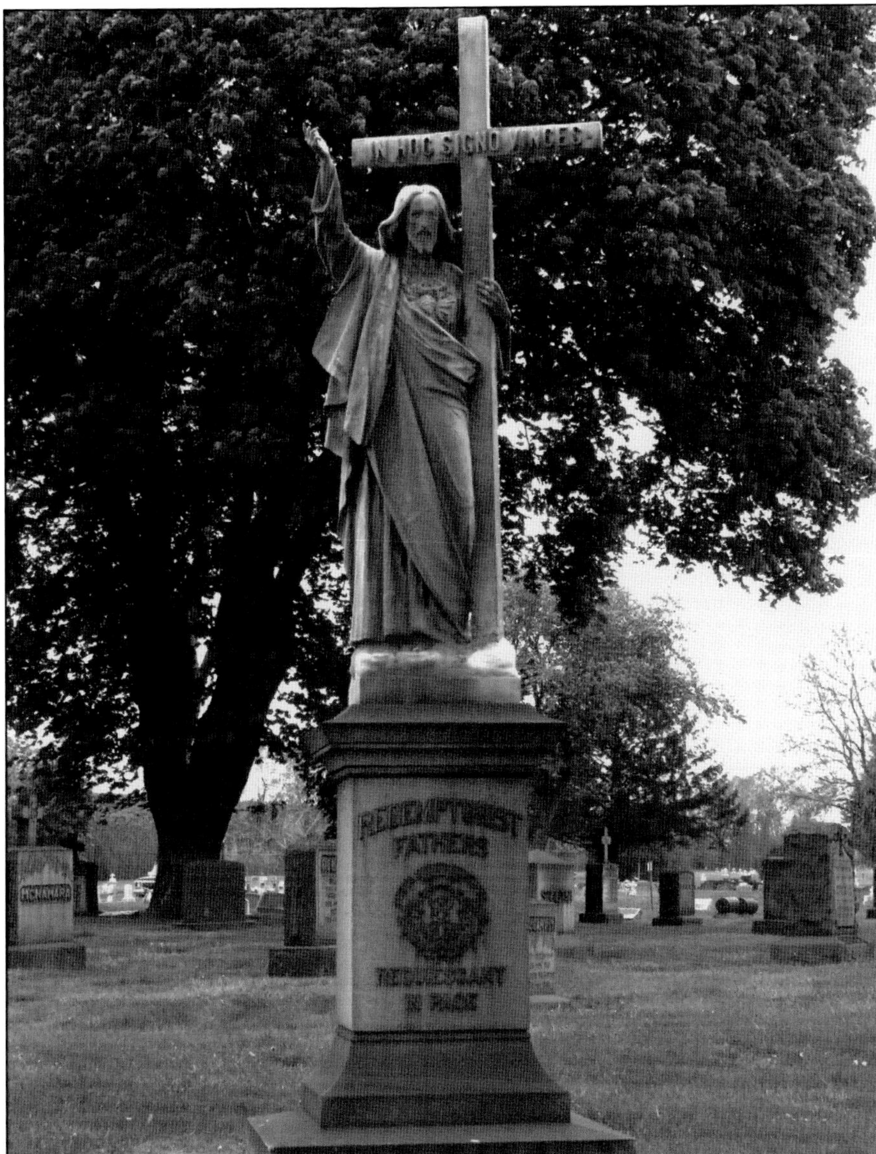

At the end of the 18th century, as the early French settlements spread out from Detroit, Redemptorist missionaries arrived in the United States with the sole purpose to establish missions and schools. Detroit, which at the time was nothing more than an outpost town with fewer than 5,000 residents, did not have the draw or means as larger cities such as Green Bay. But by early 1880, Bishop Caspar Borgess requested Fr. Aegidius Smulders establish a parish at Springwells on Detroit's west side to serve the 300 families located there and to satisfy the growing Irish immigrants unhappy with the long-standing French masses at Ste. Anne Church and the German services at St. Mary Church. Father Smulders, for six weeks, held mass at the chapel at Holy Cross Cemetery until he found a suitable building to rent for the church and priest residence. In 1881, the Church of the Most Holy Redeemer held its first service. The church became a cornerstone for the Redemptorists, boasting to be the largest parish in North America by post World War II. To serve its 15,000 parishioners, the priests held 14 Sunday masses. There are 138 Redemptorist fathers buried at Holy Cross Cemetery.

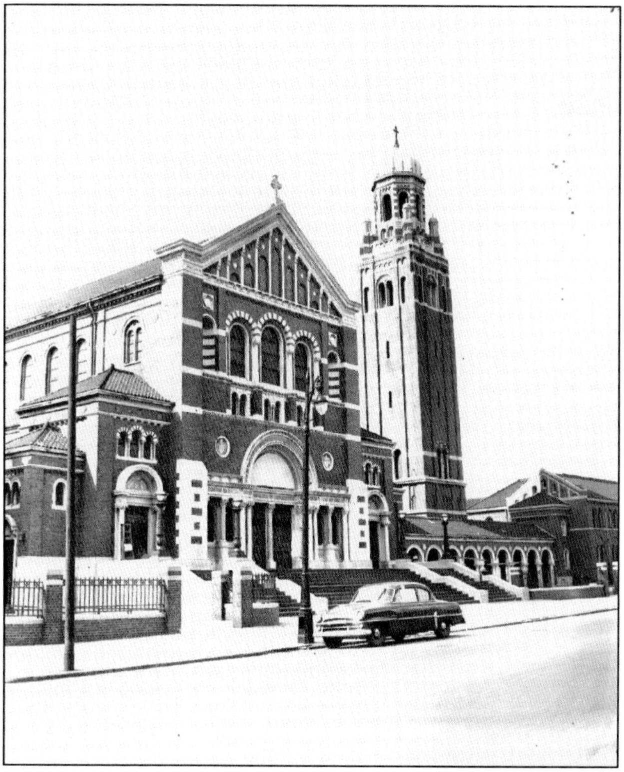

Located just two miles from the cemetery at the corner of West Vernor and Junction Streets, Holy Redeemer Church sits on four acres. The current church, built in 1923 and designed by prominent architects Donaldson and Meier in the Romanesque style, resembles the Church of St. Paul in Rome. (Walter P. Reuther Library.)

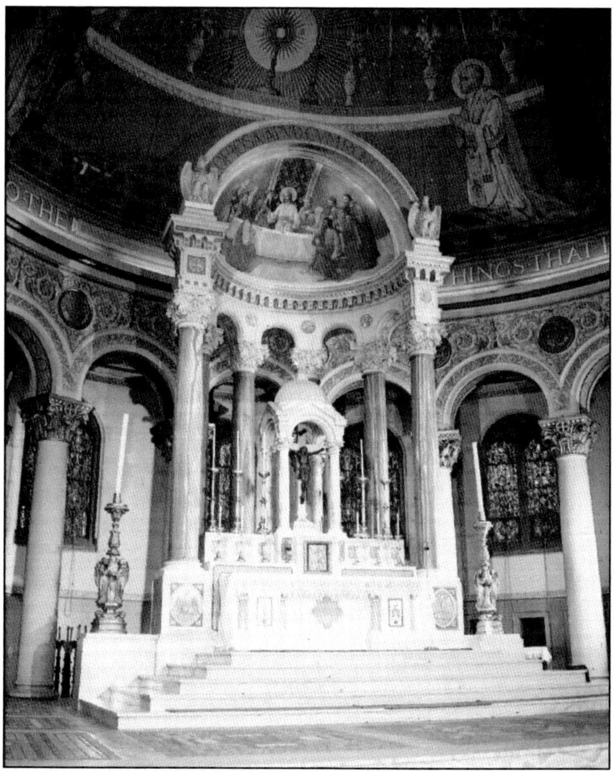

The church is 210 feet long, 68 feet wide with transepts 120 feet high and seats close to 1,000 people. The massive baldachin marble altar, adorned with symbolic designs in Venetian glass mosaic, is inspiring with its stately beauty. (Walter P. Reuther Library.)

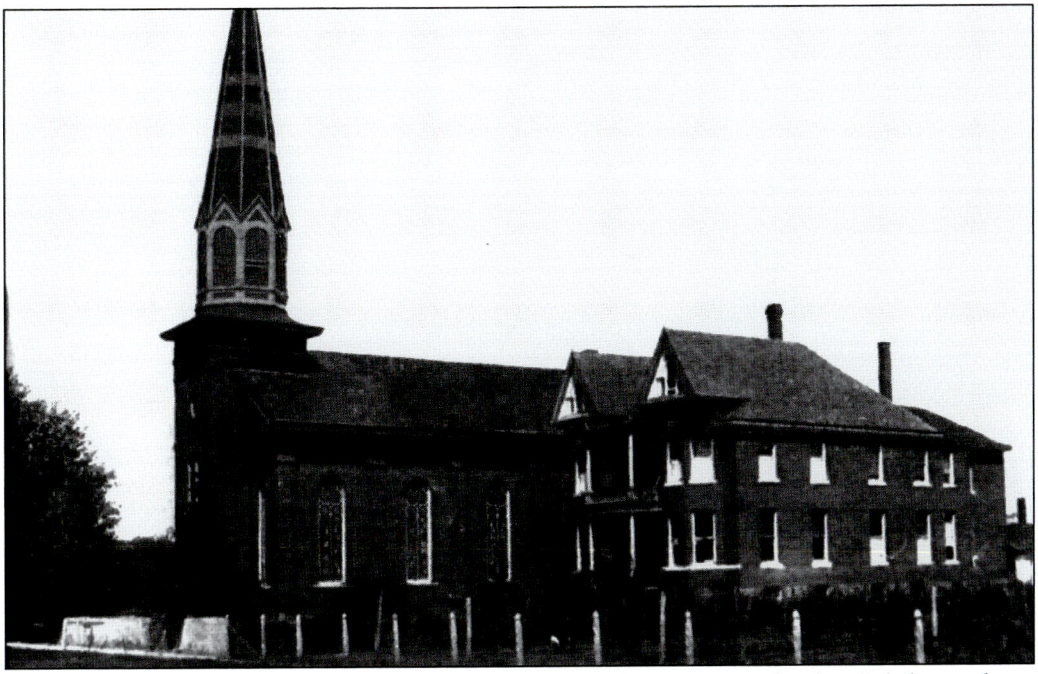

St. Casimir Church, located on Twenty-third Street in Detroit, was the first Polish parish on Detroit's west side. An influx of Polish immigrants necessitated the addition of a Polish parish to serve the ever-increasing west side population working in the industrial and automobile factories. The temporary church, built in 1883, gave way to the permanent structure pictured here, built in 1889. (Walter P. Reuther Library.)

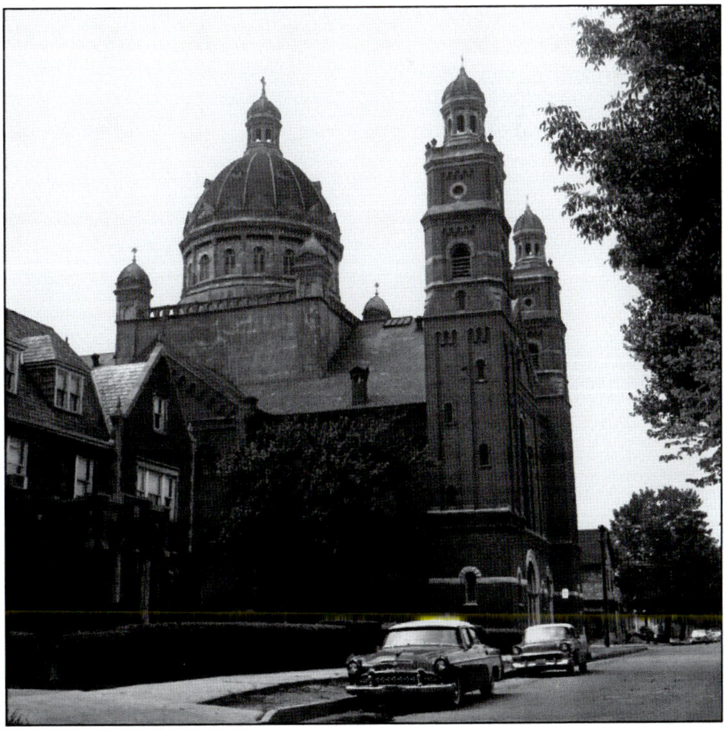

Because the Holy Cross Cemetery chapel built in 1835 was a mission, no permanent priest was located there, so priests from Detroit and surrounding parishes saw to services and burials. One such priest was from St. Alphonsus Church (right) who reported the good condition of the mission and cemetery in an 1869 report to the Detroit Chancery Office. Early German settlers to Dearborn's northeast side realized the need for an area church, resulting in the construction of St. Alphonsus Church, founded in 1852. (Lori Katona.)

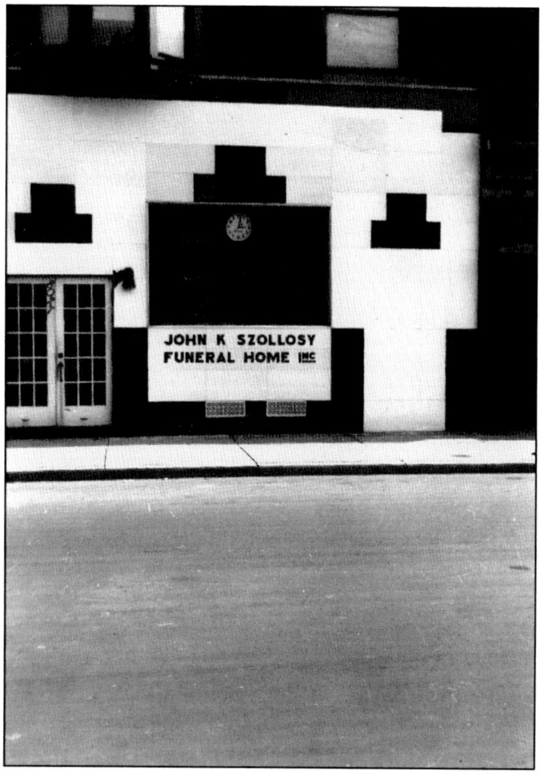

Kalman Solosy owned a bar and worked in real estate when the depression hit. As a means of supporting his family, he purchased this home on Jefferson Avenue in Delray, without any knowledge of the funeral business and began the John K. Solosy Funeral Home that he named after his son. In 1956, the funeral home moved to Lincoln Park, where it is today. (John Solosy.)

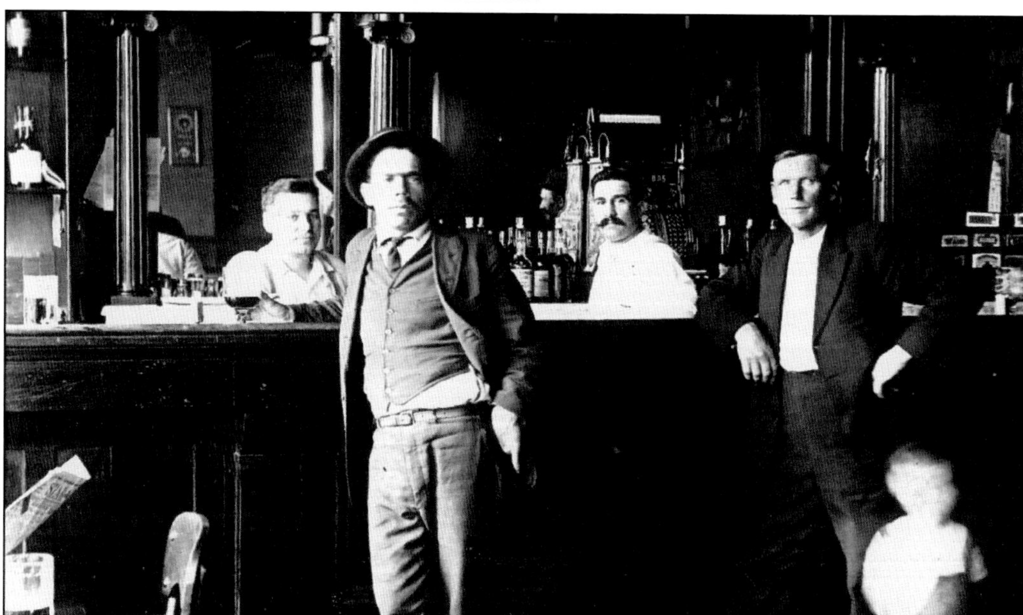

Standing in his saloon on Crossley Street in Delray, Kalman Solosy (third from left) realized that the saloon business would not thrive in a depression, but nothing would stop people from dying. His son John had wishes of becoming a dentist; however, dental school tuition was expensive. Selling the saloon and entering the prosperous funeral business allowed Kalman to send his son to mortuary school. (John Solosy.)

After willingly foregoing dental school, John graduated from Worsham College of Mortuary Science at Chicago and stepped into his father's funeral home business that he then passed down to his son. This is his graduation photograph. (John Solosy.)

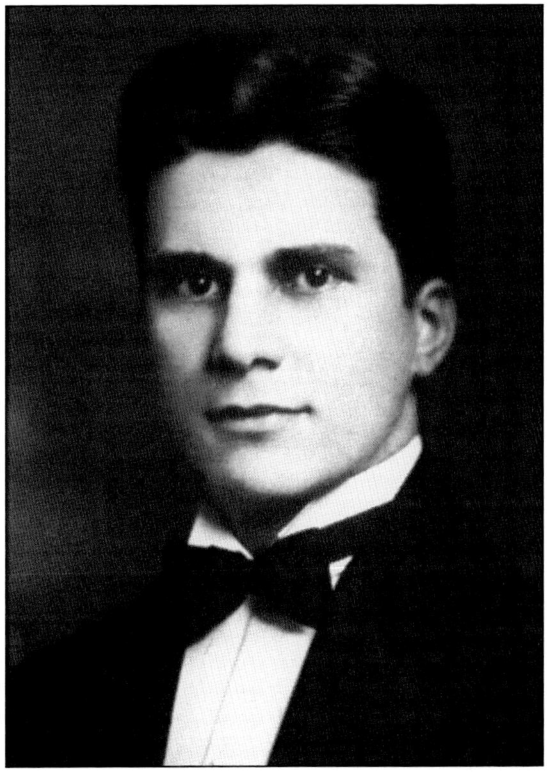

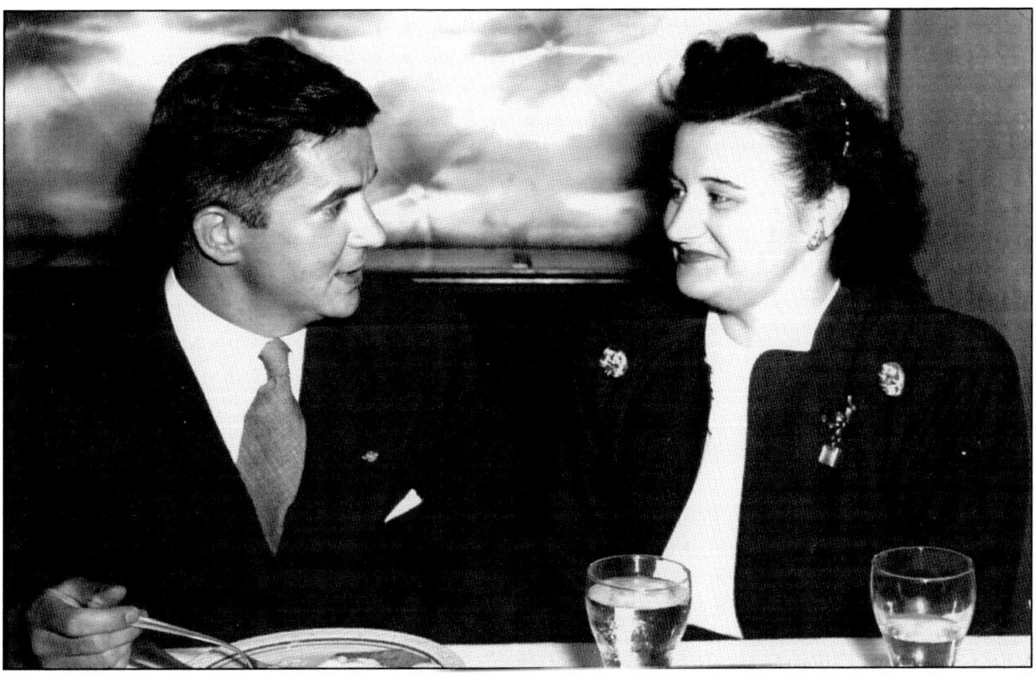

John met his wife, Clara Malicki, at the bar she owned, the Bridge Café in Delray, where he would stop for lunch. Clara's mother was Martha Nykiel, sister to bootlegger August Nykiel and Joseph Nykiel, founder of Joey's Stables. Both John and Clara are buried in section F. (John Solosy.)

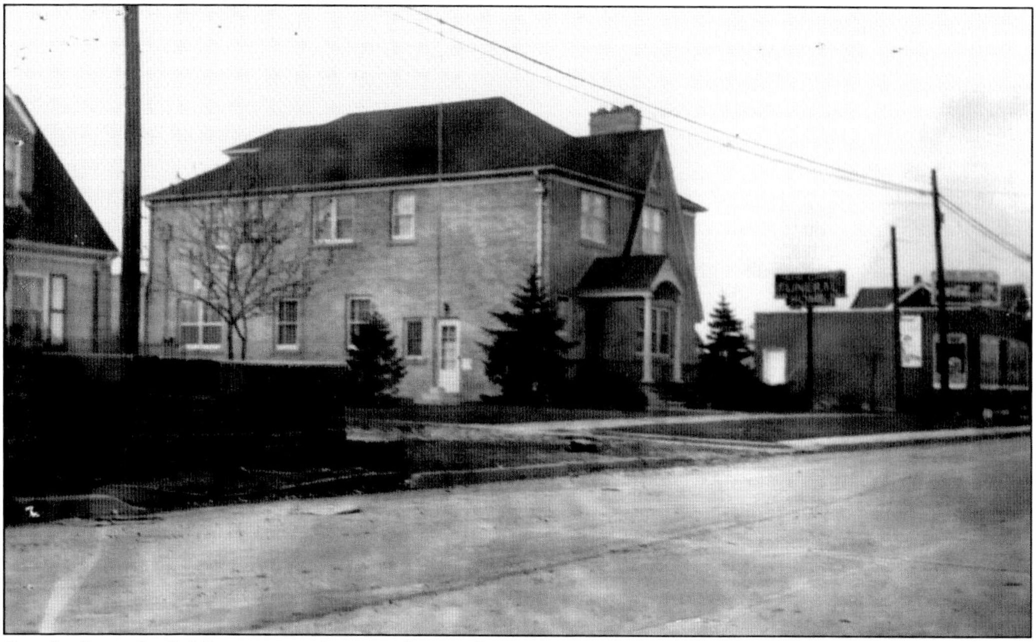

Frank Czopek did his internship at the Pinkos-Szwapa Funeral Home, eventually opening his own funeral home in 1935 at the corner of Ninth and Oak Streets in Wyandotte. In 1939, he moved the business into a newly built funeral home (shown here right after completion) at the corner of Oak and Twenty-second Streets, just 10 blocks away. Czopek was so dedicated to his profession that he felt it absurd for his employees not to recall the name, date, and time of each funeral for weeks after and he sent one employee to a psychiatrist to determine why. Czopek is buried in section W. (Czopek Funeral Home.)

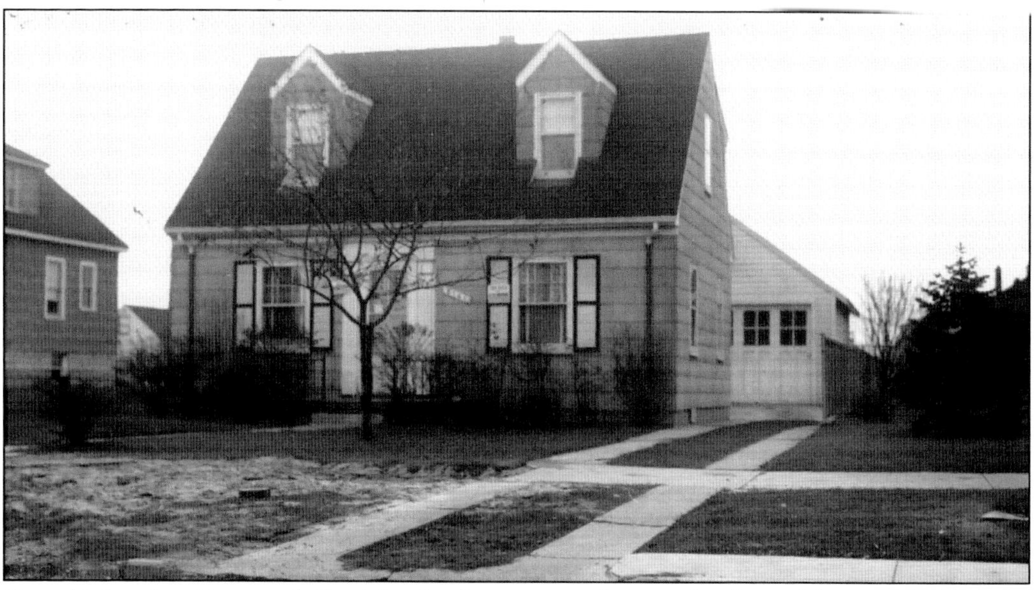

Czopek's brother, Raymond, lived in this house next door to the funeral home. Needing the land for funeral home expansion, Raymond moved his house to Twenty-Second Street where it now stands. A portion of this house is visible in the previous photograph. Raymond is buried in section W. (Czopek Funeral Home.)

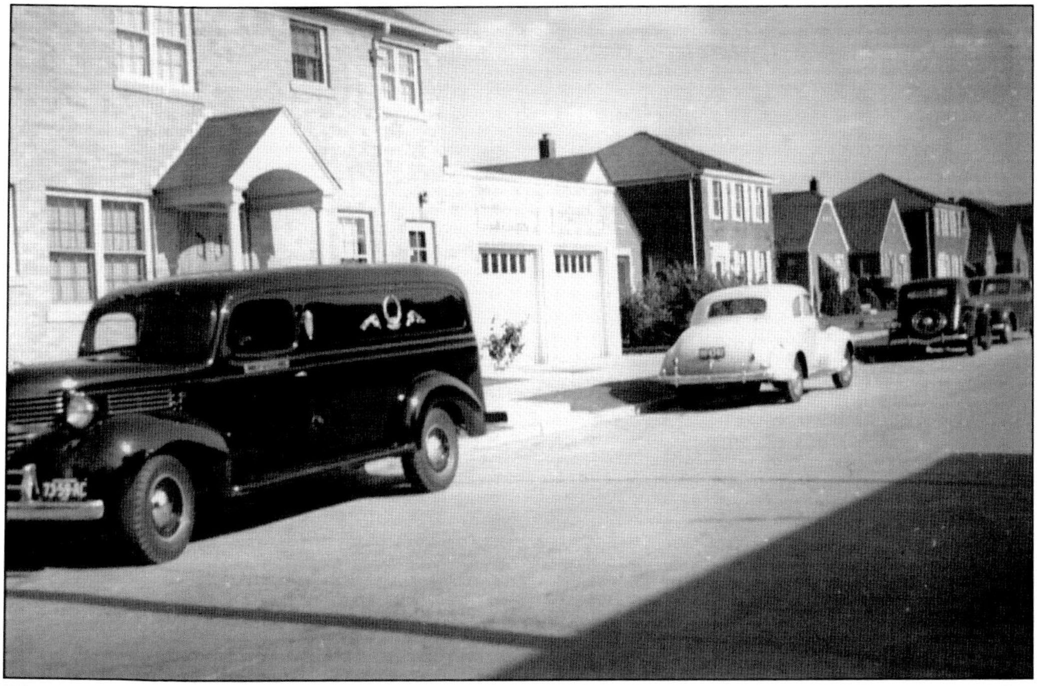

The Czopek Funeral Home underwent several expansions until it reached its current size. This photograph from the 1940s shows two garage bays, one less than today's home. Sitting at the curb is a removal vehicle used to transport bodies from the morgue or hospital to the funeral home. Removal vehicles, although nicely adorned, were far less ornate than hearses of the same era. (Czopek Funeral Home.)

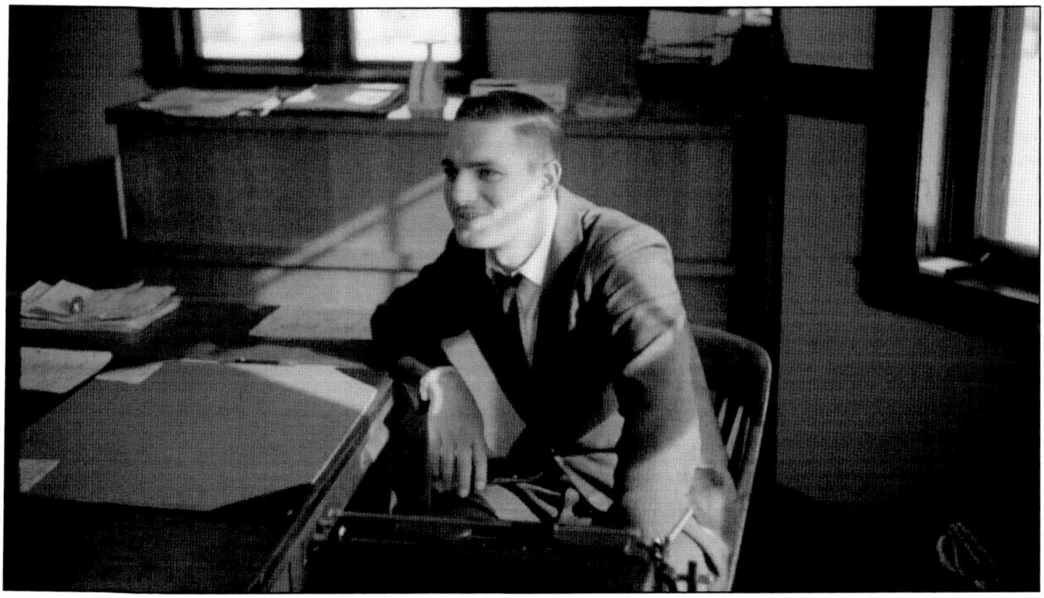

Dapper young Gene Swiantek is sitting in the office in 1962, ready to conduct cemetery business. Pipe and cigar smoke permeated the office air back then. The old roll-top desk behind Swiantek is long gone, replaced by a more modern one, and no longer necessary is the oak typing table where he works. (Harry Schueren.)

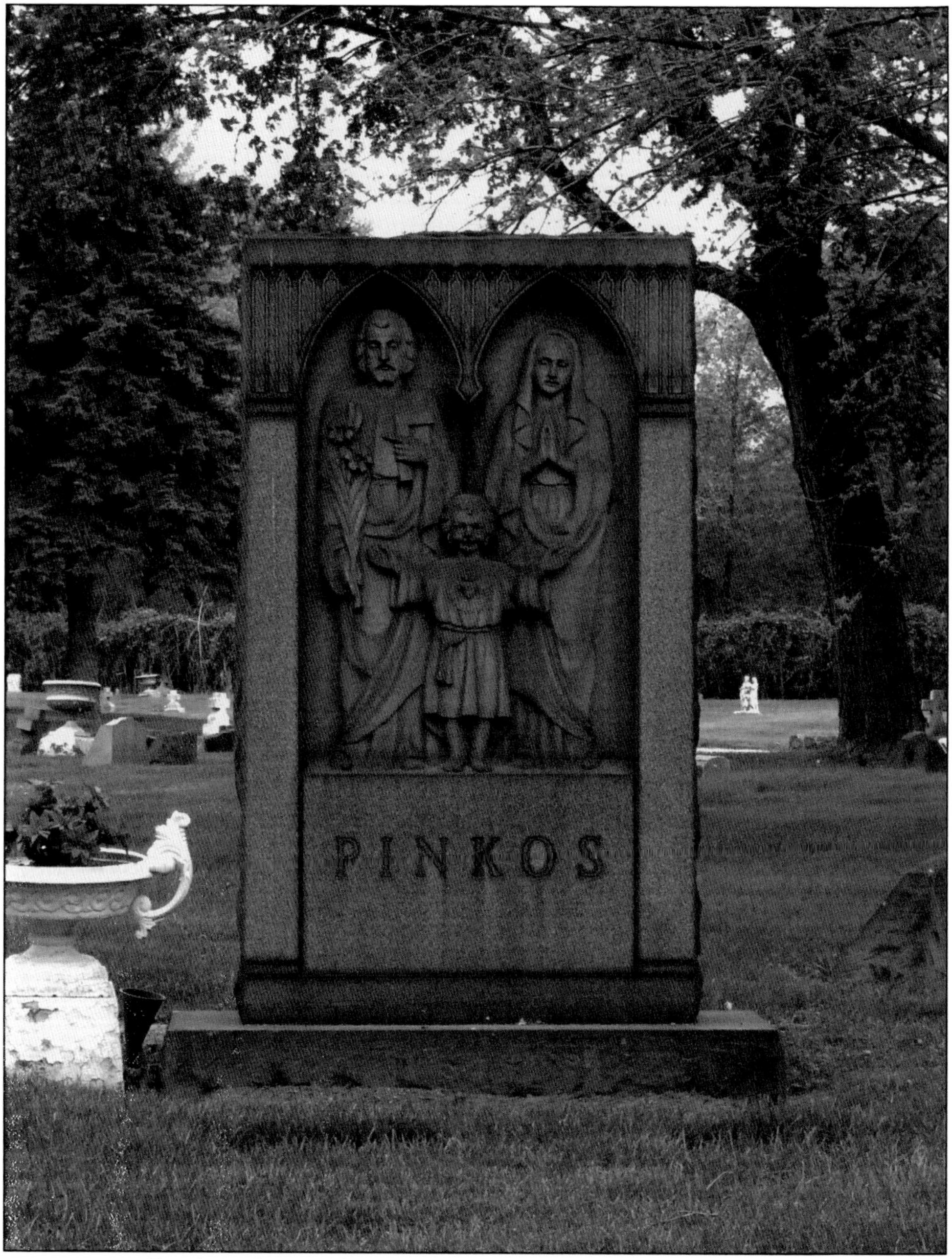

For many years, Frank Pinkos and his son-in-law John Szwapa ran the Pinkos-Szwapa Funeral Home, the second building from the corner of Junction Avenue and St. Hedwig Street, across from St. Hedwig Church. Pinkos opened the business first at a home across Junction Avenue from its current location. Pinkos purchased the newer home and corner building in 1935 from a woman in the neighborhood known as the "black widow" for always wearing black and driving around town in an electric car. A speakeasy occupied the corner building's basement, and a tunnel ran from it to the Pinkos house. With no one to carry on the family business, the Szwapa family sold both buildings in the late 1980s. The current owner rents the corner building to the St. Hedwig Flower Shop. Pinkos is buried in section H.

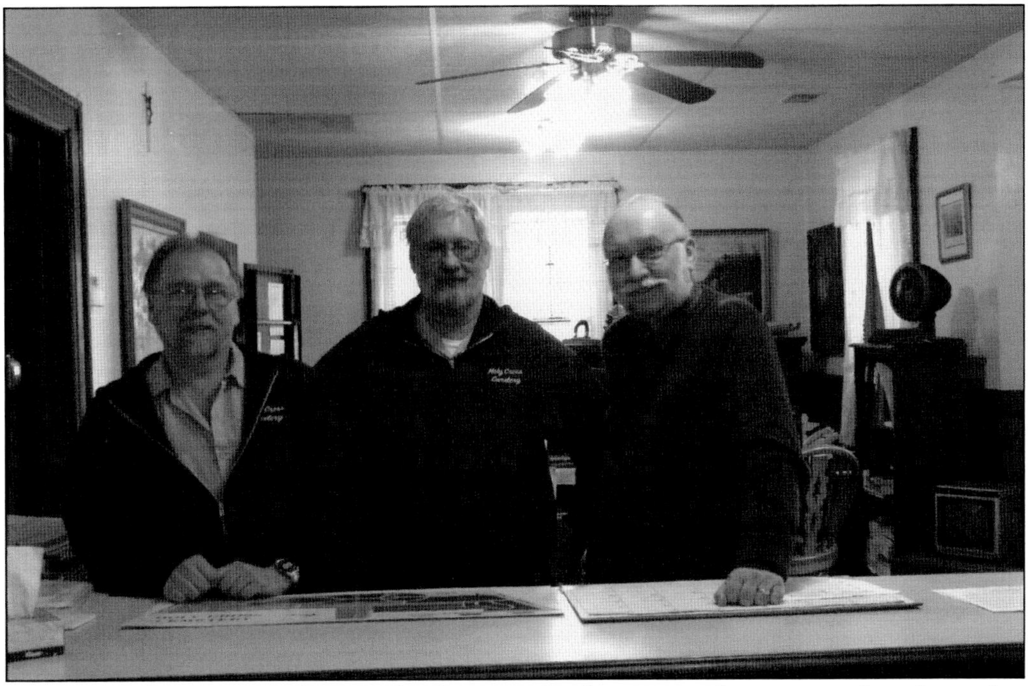

Standing in the cemetery office are the three people who manage the cemetery from day to day. They are, from left to right, Timothy Daniels, groundskeeper; William Barry, groundskeeper; and Gregory Kolasa, manager. Both Daniels and Barry began working for the cemetery in 1999, while Kolasa started as office manager, a part-time position at the cemetery, in 2001.

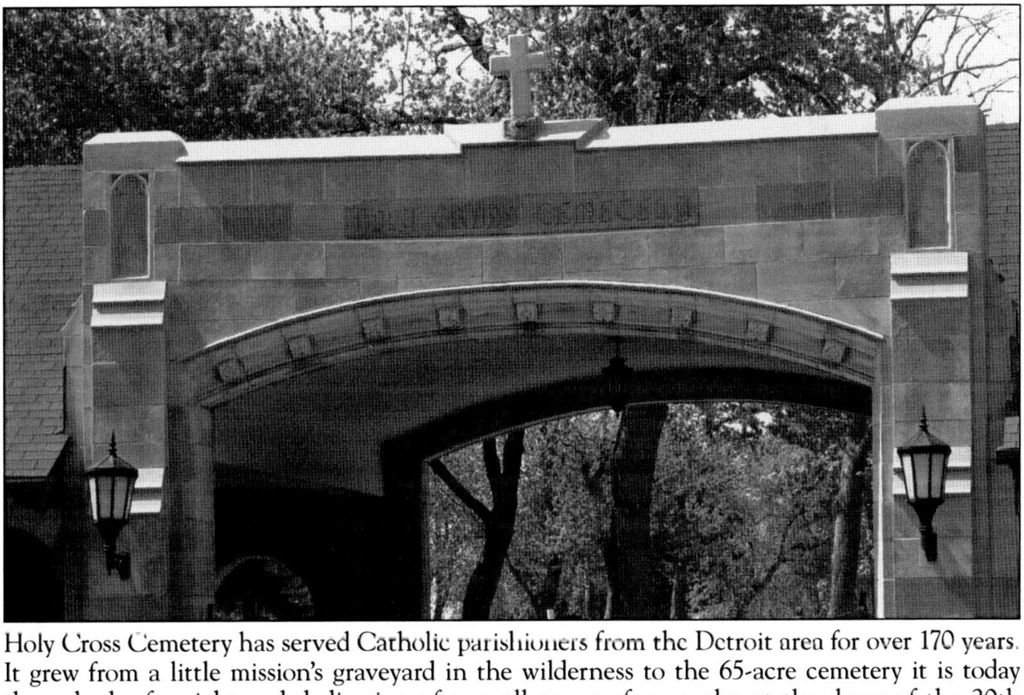

Holy Cross Cemetery has served Catholic parishioners from the Detroit area for over 170 years. It grew from a little mission's graveyard in the wilderness to the 65-acre cemetery it is today through the foresight and dedication of a small group of men who at the dawn of the 20th century recognized the need for a Catholic cemetery on the west side of Detroit.

www.arcadiapublishing.com

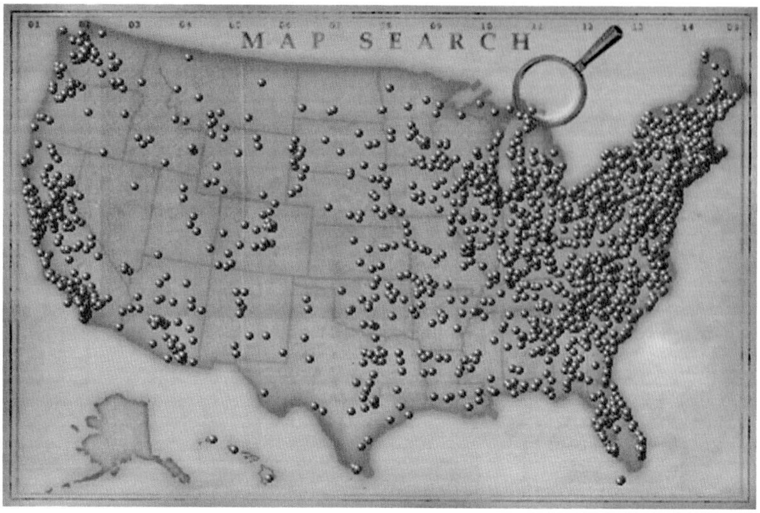

Discover books about the town where you grew up, the cities where your friends and families live, the town where your parents met, or even that retirement spot you've been dreaming about. Our Web site provides history lovers with exclusive deals, advanced notification about new titles, e-mail alerts of author events, and much more.

MADE IN THE USA

Arcadia Publishing, the leading local history publisher in the United States, is committed to making history accessible and meaningful through publishing books that celebrate and preserve the heritage of America's people and places. Consistent with our mission to preserve history on a local level, this book was printed in South Carolina on American-made paper and manufactured entirely in the United States.

This book carries the accredited Forest Stewardship Council (FSC) label and is printed on 100 percent FSC-certified paper. Products carrying the FSC label are independently certified to assure consumers that they come from forests that are managed to meet the social, economic, and ecological needs of present and future generations.

FSC
Mixed Sources
Product group from well-managed forests and other controlled sources

Cert no. SW-COC-001530
www.fsc.org

Find Your Place in History.